D1017294

Hunting
Trophy Black Bear

Hunting Trophy Black Bear

Hunter's Information Series™
North American Hunting Club
Minneapolis, Minnesota

Hunting Trophy Black Bear

Copyright © 1990, North American Hunting Club

All rights reserved.

Library of Congress Catalog Card Number 90-62104
ISBN 0-914697-33-1

Printed in U.S.A.
     5 6 7 8 9

The North American Hunting Club
offers a line of hats for hunters.
For information write:
    North American Hunting Club
    P.O. Box 3401
    Minneapolis, MN 55343

Contents

Acknowledgments

I've got a lot of people to thank for their help, indirectly or directly, in gathering material for this book by sharing their experiences, knowledge and hunts with me, plus assisting with photos. It won't be possible to list them all, and please forgive me if I forget some that I should mention.

Thanks to Wisconsin's Art LaHa for passing information along about baiting black bear, whose help led to bagging my first bruin on my own. The list of houndsmen who let me tag along and helped me better understand dogging bear includes the crew from Munising: Dan Flynn, El Harger, Jim Corriveau, Bill St. Martin, Paul Anderson, Kip, Bo, Larry, all of their families and more; Andy Tingstad, Ed Vander Zanden (who gave me my first bear hound), Rodger Gorham, Lawrence Edwards, Russ Nelson, John and Donna Saxton and D. DeMoss. Two more dogmen and guides who provided helpful interviews are Leo Dollins and Wayne Bosowicz.

Colorado guide Jim Jarvis put me onto my first brown black bear and provided helpful information, along with his wife Pat. Other guides and outfitters who have been helpful on various hunts across North America are Len Rich and Jim Hefford from Newfoundland; Mike and Claire Aftanas, John Bardahl, Paul Marek and Dave Kelbert from Saskatchewan. Hunter and trapper Jerry Weigold took time out from a busy schedule for an interview. Thanks also to Bill Niemi, Dave Pietro, Phin Walsh, Melvin Myllyla, Rene Meyskens and Chuck Godfrey for their bear stories and help with photos. Wildlife biologists across North America and other fish and game employees were tremendously helpful in providing biological information. Many of them are mentioned somewhere in the pages that follow. A special thanks is due Pennsylvania bear biologist Gary Alt for the time he spent with me and the information he provided. The same goes for his assistants—Pat Carr and Janice Gruttadauria. I would also like to thank Shane Mahoney in Newfoundland and Randy Sequin in Saskatchewan for their generous help.

Last, but not least, are friends and family members who are always ready to help out in any way they can. At the top of the list are my mother and father, wife Lucy and sisters Kathy and Linda. Brother Bruce has always been a part of my bear hunts and brother-in-law Bruce Dupras and Uncle George have willingly helped trail or drag bear. George's son Craig has also been a tremendous help hauling bait to remote locations and with photos. Beryl Jensen helped me drag one of my first bruins. Thanks also to friends Dave Raikko, Jim Haveman, Terry DeBruy, Gene Ballew, Mike Hogan, Gary Lohman, Mike Holmes, Mike Pollard, Duaine Wenzel, Richard Robinson, Ray Juetten, Buck LeVasseur, George Gardner, Bob Eastman, Ted Nugent, Linda Judson, Phil Grable, Dave Richey and Tom Huggler who have played a part in my black bear experiences in some way.

Richard P. Smith

Art & Photo Credits

Additional photos in this book were generously provided by Leonard Lee Rue, Judd Cooney, Bill Vaznis, Tom Edwards, JoAnn Speelman and the Michigan Department of Natural Resources.

Illustration for this book was provided by David Rottinghaus.

Special thanks to NAHC Publisher Mark LaBarbera, Hunter's Information Series Managing Editor Jay Strangis, NAHC Editor Bill Miller, Associate Editor Dan Dietrich, Editorial Assistants Jane Boers and Debra Morem, Layout Artist Dean Peters, Vice President of Products Marketing Mike Vail, Marketing Manager Linda Kalinowski and Project Coordinator Laura Resnik.

Steven F. Burke, President
North American Hunting Club

The Author

Some ten years ago I rounded the bend of a remote trail in Ontario at a dead run, anxious to get back to the lake where my canoe was waiting. I had been retrieving some gear from my pickup, parked at a trailhead a mile through the bush. Suddenly, we were face to face.

The black bear hit the brakes at the same time I did, except that my speed caused the heels of my boots to skid on the soft soil. If we were friends, we would have been close enough to shake hands. For an instant, two very different creatures stared into each other's eyes. Then the big black bruin wheeled and broke for the bush.

My heart was in my thoat, and the exertion of running and shock of meeting a wild bear twice my size made my pulse pound through my head. With knees wobbling, I lowered myself onto a patch of moss and began to ponder this and other experiences I had had with bear.

Working with Richard P. Smith on this landmark book reminds me of all the things I did not know about black bear at that time, and have yet to learn.

Richard has dedicated himself to finding answers to many of the mysteries of black bear, and he is uniquely qualified to do so. As hunter, biologist and naturalist, his studies of the life histories of these beasts have taken a wide-ranging approach.

Besides a Bachelors of Science in biology, Richard has also participated in post-graduate studies at Northern Michigan University, Marquette, and his association with Gary Alt, one of the country's leading

Richard P. Smith

black bear biologists, has helped him gain an even greater understanding of these animals.

When not working at home as a full-time freelance outdoor writer with his wife and administrative assistant, Lucy, Richard spends as much time as possible observing, photographing and hunting. As you can see from the photographs in this book, most of which are the author's, Richard is as talented with the camera as he is with the pen. He is an award-winning writer who has authored two editions of *Michigan Big Game Records*, and such titles as *Deer Hunting*, *Animal Tracks And Signs Of North America*, *Tracking Wounded Deer* and *Hunting Rabbits And Hares*. He has contributed innumerable articles to magazines dealing with outdoor subjects.

Richard has traveled extensively, including all parts of the U.S. and much of Canada, in addition to South Africa and Zimbabwe. He describes himself as "a naturalist who is interested in the outdoors, and especially all types of wildlife. The black bear and white-tailed deer are two of my favorite species."

It has been almost 30 years since Richard first became interested in black bear, and he has followed them in every season and in every kind of habitat to be found. When we set about to select the one author who could provide NAHC members with the most in-depth black bear book ever written, there was little question—Richard P. Smith was the man.

Jay Michael Strangis
Managing Editor,
Hunter's Information Series

Dedication

To black bear and the people whose efforts and experience have led to a better understanding of these animals.

Foreword

Black bear hunting is pure, unadulterated excitement. It's the kind of excitement that makes the little hairs on the back of your neck stand on end and electric chills course your spinal cord. It's the kind that makes you suddenly realize you've been holding your breath so long that you're about to pass out. It's the kind that makes your heart pound so violently you would swear it is bruising your ribs.

That is the kind of exhilaration known well by all black bear hunters. It is what transforms a mere pastime into a passion.

Just what triggers that overwhelming excitement depends on the hunting technique you choose.

Over bait, the announcement of furred company betrayed by the unexpected snapping of a twig will get your adrenaline flowing. Even more nerve shattering is the ability of a trophy bruin to suddenly materialize at close range.

When hunting with hounds, locating the fresh tracks of a huge boar is the moment of hyperventilation which intensifies as the bawling dogs line out on the hot scent. For hunters who love hounds, the chase is everything. It's happiness, sadness, defeat and victory all rolled into a few hours of euphoria. When the bear is brought to bay, the excitement can take on sudden, brief intensity that leaves the hunter haggard, but happy.

Simply looking through a spotting scope at a black blob in the distance affords an entirely new kind of bear hunting excitement for the glass and stalk hunter. It provides the charge of excitement that comes from pitting yourself one-on-one against the far superior senses and instincts of a true trophy animal.

For the hunter who plays on the hunger of a bear with a predator call, there is the unequalled thrill of making one's self the object of a meateater's hunt. The bear is looking for you!

Without a doubt, all bear hunting is exciting—exciting like no other kind of hunting. But not *all* of bear hunting is exciting. To reach those moments of thrill takes some research, some study and some plain hard work. In the pages that follow, we'll certainly share some exciting bear hunting moments with you, but, more importantly, we'll also share what it will take for you to experience the excitement for yourself.

There's an added bonus, too! This book is far more than just a text on hunting black bear. It offers the excitement to be experienced in learning more about the life history, biology, behavior and present day management of this truly magnificent North American game animal. The facts and figures contained in these pages will prove valuable, and I believe exciting, to all North American Hunting Club members who want to learn more about black bear and increase their chances of seeing them in the wild.

On a personal note, almost 30 years have passed since I became interested in black bears, first and always as a hunter, but also as a photographer, biologist and naturalist. I've learned a lot about the animals over those years through personal experience and from other hunters. I've also had the privilege of meeting and working with many of this country's foremost wildlife biologists who have established incredibly intimate relationships with North America's black bear.

Along with learning more about the animals themselves, discovered that there was a dearth of good, readily available information on black bear in general and hunting them specifically. For North American Hunting Club members, this book answers a need for a place to compile *true* information about black bear and the sport of hunting them. We've gone to great extremes to make sure all of the information is as accurate as possible. There is already too much inaccurate, if not downright false, material about these animals in print.

Black bear are clearly misunderstood and misrepresented far too often. We've tried to set the record straight.

Readers who are looking for information about grizzly, brown or polar bear will have to look elsewhere in the NAHC Hunter's Information Series. Although reference is made to grizzly bear in a few places in this book, it is only to mention the differences between black bear and grizzlies. This book is devoted to black bear in its entirety. Whenever the word bear is used, it is in reference to black bear, not all bear in general.

Too many people have a tendency to lump black bear with grizzly and brown bear, and sometimes even polar bear.

This is inappropriate in most cases. The fact that black bear are so different than other bear is the reason they are as common and wide-spread as they are today. Their numbers are on the rapid increase in some areas while grizzlies continue to lose ground or, at best, hold their own.

With proper management, black bear will continue to provide hunters and nonhunters alike with the adrenaline rush that comes from simply seeing a bear. After enjoying this book, I'm certain you'll know what I mean.

Richard P. Smith

1

Black Bear Basics

Black bear are perhaps the most misunderstood big game animal in North America. It's easy to understand why. There is simply a lot of misinformation circulating about these animals.

It's a simple fact of human nature that animals without antlers or horns do not generate as much interest as those with massive headgear. Consequently, the reality that black bear are very different from most other big game in terms of habits and life cycle is often overlooked. And it has, at times, been fashionable to categorize a black bear as a dangerous beast that must be feared, or a perpetual pest that is worthless to have around.

Fortunately, people's attitudes toward black bear and their knowledge about how to hunt them is beginning to change. There has always been a fraternity of hunters who pursued this big game trophy. Although small at first, our ranks have grown to a significant level. This increasing interest in North America's most abundant member of the bear family has led to more scientific studies about them. These studies by dedicated black bear biologists have uncovered amazing new information about the animal that will help hunters better understand the habits and behavior of black bear. There's still a lot to be learned about black bear, but enough valuable information has already been gathered to uncover many of their secrets and to discount myths and outright falsehoods that have persisted for too long.

Appearance

Most black bear are easy to identify. As their name implies, many of them are predominantly black in color, with brown muzzles. The amount of brown on snouts varies, as does the shade of brown. I've seen some bruins with very little brown on their muzzles, being almost totally black, and others with brown being more prominent than normal.

Contrary to one school of thought, the amount of brown on the muzzle of a black bear is not an indication of the animal's sex. A boar's muzzle is not always darker than a sow's. I've seen both males and females with little brown on snouts in the same general area and males with just as much brown, if not more, than females in other areas. Tips on differentiating between the sexes will be mentioned later in this book.

In addition to brown muzzles, some black bear have white markings on their chests. These markings are little more than spots on some animals and are prominent, V-shaped designs on others. Friend Jimmy Dean shot a black bear in Montana one fall on which almost the entire chest was white. I've seen both males and females with white on their chests. Most of the bear I've seen lack chest markings, but this feature may be common in some regions.

Color Phases

Not all black bear are black in color. Some are described as blue and others white, while the most common coat colorations other than black are various shades of brown. They can be blonde or cinnamon, dark brown, reddish brown or any shade in between.

In the eastern U.S. and Canada more than 99 percent of black bear are black, with color variations rare. Brown phase bear occur more often in western Ontario and Minnesota, with an estimated six percent of the bear population in Minnesota being brown. On one occasion I saw a black sow with three brown cubs in Minnesota. Brown black bear become even more common in parts of the western U.S. and Canada.

In southwestern Colorado, for example, over 80 percent of the population is dark brown or chocolate, with another five to eight percent the lighter blonde color phase. Black–coated bruins are obviously in the minority there. Other western states such as Wyoming and Montana have more of an even split between black and brown color phases, but there may be local variations.

The regional distribution of color phases in Washington is an example of how much variability there can be in one state. Studies indicate that all bear on the Olympic Peninsula and the northeast Willapa Hills are black in color. Bear inhabiting the southeast Willapa Hills were found to be 78 percent black and 22 percent brown. The black phase ac-

Most black bear are black, with brown muzzles. Brown phases occur most frequently in the West. It is impossible to determine sex by color alone.

Some black bear have white markings on their chests, like the animal in this photo displaying a V-shaped mark. Other animals display a white chest spot.

counted for 88 percent of the population along the Skookumchuck and Newaukum Rivers and 82 percent along the Toutle, Green and Coweeman Rivers. Up to 30 percent of the bear along the Kalama and Lewis Rivers were brown and 50 percent along the upper Cowlitz River. One particular bruin reported in Washington, which must have been an unusual sight, was both black and brown. The upper half of its body was brown and the lower half black.

Brown-coated black bear are better adapted than the black color phase for living in open country like that which is found in parts of the west, where more exposure to direct sunlight results. One test showed that black-coated animals in direct sunlight increase in temperature by a degree every 15 minutes while there was little change in body temperature of bear with brown hair. The test was halted to prevent overheating of the black animal. A study of the distribution of brown and black color phases on a mountain range in southern Arizona showed that light brown bear were most common on arid south slopes and darker animals were dominant on north slopes where it was more shaded, cooler and wetter.

Not all black bear remain the same color all of their lives. Some animals that are brown as cubs become black. Older bear can change coat color, too. One biologist in Colorado reported that a radio-collared bear that was found to be black in its den had been a chocolate color earlier in the year. He said bear that are dark brown during spring may be blonde through bleaching from the sun by fall. The blonde bear I've seen in Colorado actually exhibited two shades of brown. Their bodies were blonde and their legs dark brown.

True albino black bear are rare, but a few of them have been reported. One was captured and photographed in Clearfield County, Pennsylvania, during 1969 by District Game protectors Lynn Keller and Gerald Zeidler. Another more recent albino black bear was bagged by bowhunter Brad Borden from Kalispell, Montana, during May of 1983. It was a two-year-old female estimated to weigh between 110 and 130 pounds. A couple of off-white to yellowish-coated bear have been tagged by hunters in Michigan, but they didn't have the pink eyes, nose and skin of a true albino. White-coated black bear in British Columbia, referred to as Kermode bear, are not true albinos either.

Kermode bear, which are primarily found along the coast of British Columbia in the center of the province, have been considered a separate race or subspecies of black bear. However, biologists are currently labeling the Kermode a different color phase of the black bear. A photograph from British Columbia of a Kermode sow with two black cubs is evidence of this. Nonetheless, they are protected in the province. They were legal to hunt for about a year during the fall of 1964 and spring of 1965, but then were protected again because of concern for their welfare. Little is known about the animals, and they are considered to be rare.

Michigan hunter Art Hutchings bagged a male Kermode, estimated to weigh 400 pounds, on Princess Royal Island during the brief period these animals could be hunted. The bear was described as white on its sides and rump, with face, shoulders and feet being a bright yellowish-orange color. The nose and tongue were gray, unlike most other black bear.

Some people have also described Kermode bear as having a very light brown coloration. One representative with this coloration was at the Stanley Park Zoo in Vancouver, British Columbia. Arthur Popham obtained a special permit to collect a Kermode bear before Hutchings shot his, and a mount of the animal he eventually bagged is in the Kansas City Museum in Missouri.

Glacier bear, or the blue color phase of the black bear, have also been classified as a separate subspecies. Their distribution is limited to southeast Alaska into northern British Columbia, and they are thought to be more common than Kermodes, but still not easy to find. Glacier bear can be hunted in Alaska, but are protected in British Columbia. The only Glacier bear known to be in captivity is in the San Diego Zoo in California.

There are 26 recognized subspecies of black bear besides the Kermode and Glacier varieties, although veteran bear biologist Charles Jonkel said there isn't total agreement on exactly how many subspecies of the animal exists. Besides coat color, minor features such as characteristics of the skull and teeth are used to separate black bear into subspecies. Differences in coat color are the only features that would be readily apparent to anyone seeing a bear in the wild.

There is agreement that the most common and widespread subspecies of black bear is *Ursus americanus americanus*. This scientific classification of black bear refers to genus, species and subspecies, in that order. They are in the same Class as other mammals (Mammalia), the same Order with other (Carnivora) and in the same Family (Ursidae) with other bear. Distribution of most black bear subspecies includes most of Canada and Alaska, plus much of the U.S.

One commonly held belief is that black bear are related to pigs. This is not true. As carnivores, they are more closely related to wolves, dogs and raccoons.

Despite the lack of relationship of black bear to swine, male bear are usually referred to as boars and females as sows, and these names will

Brad Borden from Kalispell, Montana, with the albino black bear he bagged. Albinism is rare in black bear, though blonde or light brown coats occur with some frequency.

probably stick until someone comes up with something better.

Distinguishing Black Bear From Grizzlies

In areas where the range of brown black bear and grizzly bear overlap, it is usually possible to distinguish one from the other. A grizzly normally has a distinct hump on its back above the shoulders, while the back of a black bear offers a straight line profile. When viewed from the side, the head of a black bear, from forehead to nose, slopes downward in a straight line. Faces of grizzlies are indented or dished.

There's an old joke about another means of determining whether a bear is a black bear or grizzly, although it's not a foolproof method. Simply sneak up to the animal in question, kick it in the rear, then run to the nearest tree and climb it. If the bear follows and climbs after you, it's a black bear. Bear that can't climb are grizzlies. If you are caught and killed before reaching a tree, it's probably a grizzly, too.

Black Bear Anatomy

Black bear have five short, curved claws on each paw, well designed for climbing trees. The animals also use their claws for ripping stumps and logs apart, plus digging for roots and insects. Claws on front feet are longer than those on rear feet, being better adapted for digging, and for securing prey.

The eyes of the black bear are brown, not black. They are small in

Black bear and grizzly bear can usually be identified by distinctive features. A black bear has a flat back, and a round, sloping face.

proportion to head size and in comparison with other big game animals, making eyesight one of the black bear's weakest senses. However, bruins see movement very well and it has been determined that they can distinguish colors.

This animal's rounded ears, which range between $4^1/_2$ and $5^1/_2$ inches in length, enable them to hear well. However, their sense of smell is probably the best developed.

Black bear do have tails, but they are easy to overlook. The animals keep them clamped down against their rumps most of the time. Tails are roughly three to five inches in length.

Most black bear are between four and six feet, nose to tail, although a few big males will be longer. When on all four feet these animals don't stand very high off the ground, averaging between two and three feet at the shoulders. Ferns and other vegetation sometimes make it difficult for black bear to see any distance. To overcome this handicap they will stand on their hind legs or climb stumps and fallen tree trunks.

*A grizzly bear has a distinct hump on its back and a dished face. Its fur may have a some-
what grizzled appearance—hence the name.*

Speed

Despite their short legs, black bear can run fast when they need to, at
least for short distances. One bruin in Wisconsin, estimated to weigh
200 pounds, was clocked at 33 miles an hour. Other bear reached speeds
of 30 miles per hour, which is faster than any human can run. Black bear
are also good swimmers and they enjoy spending time in water, especially during hot weather.

Travel And Home Range

These animals seldom run if they don't have to, but they do a lot of
walking, often traveling many miles during the course of a year. Boars
usually do more traveling than sows. Consequently, they have a larger
home range or territory. In Pennsylvania, boars have home ranges that
vary from 60 to 75 square miles, with their territory measuring 5 to 15
miles across at the widest point, according to veteran bear biologist Gary

You rarely see the tail of a black bear extended, but they do have tails. The tail is held snugly against the rump where it is not evident to most observers.

Alt. He said that sows in Pennsylvania have home ranges three to five miles across and encompass 12 to 15 square miles.

The home range of black bear in Pennsylvania is a good representation of the upper limits of home range size in North America. The smallest home ranges for black bear were found on Long Island, which is part of southwest Washington's Willapa National Wildlife Refuge, and in the Great Smoky Mountains National Park. On Long Island, boars had average home ranges of two square miles and sows had less than one square mile.

In the Smokies, boars covered 4.2 square miles and sows 2.6 square miles. Home ranges of bruins in other geographic regions can be anywhere in between those found in Pennsylvania and the Smokies. Home range is determined by the type, quality and extent of habitat the bear occupies. Bruins obviously have to travel farther to find enough food in poor habitat than in habitat where food is abundant. Bear densities may also have an impact on the size of home ranges.

Boars are most active during the breeding season, which usually begins during late May, peaks during June and July and can continue into August. They cover a lot of ground looking for breeding sows. The home range of an adult boar typically overlaps the home ranges of a number of mature sows.

When on the move, state boundaries and country borders have no meaning to black bear. Boars commonly cross from one state to another

Black bear are strong swimmers and will take to the water for travel, escape or simply to cool off during hot weather.

or from the U.S. into Canada and vice versa. A boar that was ear-tagged in Minnesota, for example, was bagged near Lake Nipigon, Ontario. Karen Noyce with the Minnesota Department of Natural Resources reports that the boar was three years old at the time it was tagged and released on July 7, 1979, about seven miles north of Hovland, Minnesota. It is roughly 100 miles from Hovland to Lake Nipigon and the animal probably did a lot of rambling before reaching the point where it was shot. Ohio bowhunter Randall Collins bagged that bear on May 11, 1982, while hunting with guide Wayne Bosowicz. It weighed 260 pounds then, compared to 122 pounds when tagged.

Activity of breeding sows also peaks during June and July, but they don't cover the territory that boars do. Travel of sows with newborn cubs is restricted during spring and summer months, but increases toward fall, peaking during September as cubs become more mobile.

Biologists know that black bear have the ability to navigate long distances, but they haven't figured out how the animals do it. The homing ability of black bear is amazing. Nuisance bear that have been live-trapped and moved long distances, far enough to be out of their home range, have returned to the point of capture numerous times. A few bruins have found their way home after being moved 140 to 150 miles, but homing trips under 100 miles are more common.

Periods of Activity

The time of day black bear are active depends on the time of year and age of the animal. Mature boars and breeding sows can be on the move at virtually every hour of the day during June and July. During fall months, old boars have a tendency to be more nocturnal than other bear, with most activity concentrated early and late in the day. When actively feeding, however, and especially when food is scarce or scattered, bear can be on the move at any hour.

Weights

Weights of black bear, like home ranges, vary considerably from one part of the continent to another. The heaviest individuals are always boars. Sows are smaller, and once sows start having cubs, the drain of raising a family keeps their weight down. A live weight of approximately 350 pounds is close to the maximum attainable by sows. Some of the largest males have reached weights of 700 to 800 pounds, but the world record black bear was even heavier.

The heaviest black bear on record, according to the third edition of *The Guinness Book of Animal Facts and Feats*, weighed 902 pounds, field dressed! Its live weight could have been 990 to 1,035 pounds! New Brunswick resident Joseph Allan shot the enormous bruin in November, 1976, after it killed his German shepherd in camp.

Although the New Brunswick black bear Allan shot is the heaviest officially recognized, there's an unofficial record of one from Ontario that is still heavier. Outdoor writer Reg Sharkey reports that the late Fred Nesbitt shot a black bear that was as big as an Alaskan brown bear and weighed 1,127 pounds. He killed it as it tried to break into his cabin during the late 1950s. Nesbitt's cabin is on the shore of Wahwashesh Lake, 30 miles north of Perry Sound. Sharkey got the story from fellow Michigan resident Jeff Schauer, who has a cabin in the same area as Nesbitt's.

One method commonly used for estimating the live weight of a black bear is to add 15 percent of the dressed weight (L (live weight) = D (dressed weight) + .15 x D). While this may apply to average size black bear, many argue that it overestimates the live weight of big bear. Ten percent, according to some estimates, is a more accurate representation of weight loss for big bear.

For example, a bruin bagged in Michigan's Upper Peninsula weighed 417 pounds live and 379 pounds dressed, losing 10 percent of its weight. A Pennsylvania bear weighed 632 pounds live and 572 pounds dressed, losing 10.5 percent of its weight. A smaller bear, for comparison, had a live weight of 165 pounds and weighed 137 pounds

Black bear can reach mammoth proportions, though most people tend to overestimate their weight. Males outweigh females of the same age.

when dressed, having lost 20 percent of its weight. Generally, the bigger the bear, the less weight it loses, percentage-wise, when field dressed.

One method of estimating the live and dressed weight of black bear when a scale isn't handy is to measure the animal's chest girth directly behind the front legs. According to Gary Alt, several tables showing chest measurements and the corresponding estimated live and dressed weights have proven reliable. Keep in mind that some of the weights mentioned for boars represent the upper limit attainable by black bear. Most black bear are much lighter, with dressed weights of average animals ranging between 120 and 200 pounds.

Most people have a tendency to overestimate the size of bruins for a number of reasons. Long guard hairs on thick coats during spring and fall months is one reason black bear look bigger than they are.

In addition to variations from one part of the continent to another, there are tremendous seasonal variations in weights of bear. The largest weight gains are usually recorded during late summer and fall months when fruits and nuts are abundant. Information gathered in Pennsylvania shows that cubs averaged a weight gain of one-half pound per day under these circumstances, while sows gained an average of one pound per day and boars put on as much as two pounds per day. One boar gained 128 pounds in 60 days, starting at 348 pounds on July 19 and reaching 476 pounds on September 19. Another boar in Wisconsin put on 130 pounds in two months, from mid-August to mid-October.

Researcher Paul Paquet in Manitoba discovered that bear have an average weight gain of 2.2 pounds per day when they have access to plenty of food. He added that large boars gain more than four pounds per day! One nine-year-old boar weighed 434 pounds when live trapped on June 25. The animal was well on its way to doubling its weight when recaptured on September 9, when it weighed 802 pounds.

In some areas long-legged, lanky bear are referred to as dog bear, and those that appear to have short legs with bellies close to the ground are called hog bear. What most people who use these terms fail to realize is that both designations can apply to the same animal at different times—during mid-summer (when it is at its lightest weight) and during early fall (when it is at its heaviest). Young bear are usually lean and lanky, but fill out as they age.

Weight increases aren't as dramatic during years that food availability is limited. In years when there is a total failure of berry and mast drops, the survival of young black bear may be threatened. West Virginia bear biologist Joe Rieffenberger reported eight incidents of black bear starvation during the fall of 1982 due to mast failure. Lynn Rogers in Minnesota also reported starvation deaths of five yearling bear after

Average Live Weights Of Black Bear
(In Pounds)

State	Males	Females
Arizona	275	150
California	223	138
Florida	305	189
Michigan	287	183
Montana	211	125
New Hampshire	263	183
New York	237	150
North Carolina	368	197
Pennsylvania	402	203
Vermont	238	109
Washington	195	116.5
Province		
Quebec	141 (June & July)	112 (June & July)

Average live weights of adult black bear from across North America show that sows, on the average, are 40 percent smaller than boars.

drought and frost reduced natural food supplies several years in a row. Losses of yearlings to malnutrition have also been recorded in Alaska and Colorado.

Predation can also account for black bear deaths. Young animals account for most of the losses. Adult boars are known to be cannibalistic. Grizzly bear and wolves also prey on black bear when they get the chance. There is one record of a big black bear boar killing a sow and her yearling cubs in a den in Michigan's Upper Peninsula. In Minnesota, a sow and her newborn cubs were killed in their den by a pack of wolves. Bear are also killed by vehicles as they try to cross highways. In Pennsylvania, an average of 130 black bear are killed annually in bear-vehicle accidents.

Records also indicate that three black bear have been electrocuted, one in Texas and two in Michigan. All three climbed poles holding power lines, apparently attracted by the buzzing of electricity through the lines. The bear may have thought bees were responsible for the

Estimating Black Bear Weight

Chest Girth (inches)	Estimated Live Weight (pounds)	Estimated Dressed Weight
25	65	55
26	73	62
27	81	69
28	89	76
29	98	83
30	108	92
31	117	99
32	128	109
33	138	117
34	149	127
35	161	137
36	173	147
37	185	157
38	198	168
39	211	179
40	225	191
41	239	203
42	253	215
43	268	228
44	284	241
45	300	255
46	316	269
47	332	282
48	350	297
49	367	312
50	385	327
51	403	343
52	422	359
53	442	375
54	461	392
55	481	409
56	502	427
57	522	444
58	544	462
59	566	480
60	588	500

To estimate the live weight and dressed weight of black bear, measure the girth of the chest directly behind the front leg, then compare with this table.

noise. The two bear that were electrocuted in Michigan were killed at the same site at different times.

Age

Black bear have the potential to live much longer than most people realize. Studies show that some bear, both in the wild and in captivity, can live for 30 years. However, the all-time record belongs to a male shot in New York during 1974. It was $41^3/4$ years old! Another bruin from the same state was $34^3/4$ years old when harvested. Wild bear over 30 have been aged in other states, too.

An old, gray-muzzled sow that Terry Frint bagged in Ontario was probably in her late 20s, if not early 30s, but we'll never know for sure. Her teeth were well worn from years of use. Terry sent some of the teeth through the mail to have her age determined, but they fell out of the envelope and were lost.

Black bear are aged by looking at a cross section of a tooth under a microscope. Small premolar teeth are used most often for the determination. The inside of teeth have rings or annuli representing each year of a bear's life. Premolars are located directly behind canine teeth on the upper and lower jaw. They can be removed by cutting the gum with a knife in front of and behind the tooth, then extracting them with a pair of pliers.

Diet

Although classified as carnivores, black bear are actually omnivores, meaning they have a varied diet including both plant and animal matter. Their teeth are well suited for this purpose. They do eat meat, but also graze on grass and other vegetation, and dig up roots. They also consume a wide variety of berries, fruits, nuts and insects. The bulk of their diet consists of items other than meat. These animals are absolute geniuses when it comes to filling their stomachs.

Stomach analysis of black bear in Washington found that an average of 86 percent of the contents was composed of vegetation. Similar results have been recorded in other states. Insects comprised another nine percent of the contents, while mammals, birds and fish comprised the final five percent. Specific items that proved to be important foods were wood fiber, skunk cabbage, huckleberry, fungus, salal, cascara, devil's club, grasses, blackberry, apple, evergreen needles, insects and meat.

Wood fiber or sapwood was eaten most frequently during April, May and June. The bark of evergreen trees is peeled by bear to get at the inner sapwood, sometimes resulting in damage to the tree. For years, in hopes of reducing this tree damage, the Washington Forest Protection

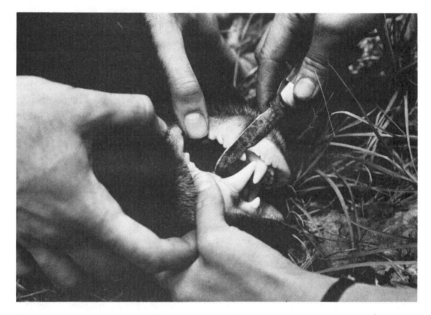

By examining a cross section of a premolar tooth under a microscope, biologists can determine ages of black bear. Premolars rest behind canines.

Association paid professional bear hunters and trappers for dead bear. Now, sport hunting adequately manages the population in problem areas. This type of feeding activity is basically restricted to the northwest United States and adjoining portions of Canada.

Skunk cabbage, huckleberry, fungus, grasses, evergreen needles and meat are consumed in varying amounts practically every month that black bear are active. Although evergreen needles are frequently present in black bear stomachs, they are never present in large quantities. Leaves and blossoms of huckleberry plants are eaten before berries are ripe, with peak use during November. Fungus is most important during August and September. Meat consumption is highest during April.

Salal is eaten from June through October, but is most important during August and September. Cascara use peaks during September and October, with devil's club appearing most frequently during May through July. Blackberries are consumed with regularity during July and August. November is the time when black bear feed on apples most heavily. Insects are eaten from April through September, but are most important in July and August.

In Minnesota, black bear depend on grass and other green plants, buds, catkins, leaves, mushrooms, insects and what meat they can find during spring months. Buds, catkins and leaves of aspen trees are eaten regularly by black bear, but they will feed on the same items from other types of trees, too. Fruits and berries are summer staples, along with insects.

Wild strawberries are usually ripe first, followed by blueberries, raspberries, serviceberries (also called Juneberries or sugarplums) and blackberries. When blueberries are abundant, bruins will concentrate much of their feeding time on them. Important foods eaten during late summer into fall include dogwood berries, hazel nuts and wild cherries. Mountain ash berries and apples are consumed during fall months, too, along with the all-time favorites—acorns, beech nuts and hickory nuts. Black bear will eat acorns and beech nuts during the spring, too, following years of good production when some of the mast crop remains on the ground.

Black bear throughout the eastern half of their range eat foods that are similar to those in Minnesota. Squawroot was also found to be important in the spring and summer diets of bear in Great Smoky Mountains National Park. I've also seen evidence of black bear feeding on these parasitic plants in Michigan.

In areas where fruits and nuts may not be available during the fall or when there has been a mast crop failure, black bear turn to vegetation and meat for sustenance. The major nut—producing trees in the western portion of the black bear's range are white bark pines, which are found in the Rocky and Sierra Nevada Mountains. Red squirrels store quanti-

Morel mushrooms like these are eaten by black bear during the spring.

Wild strawberries are among the first wild fruits to ripen, and bears love them.

ties of these pine nuts in various locations, which black bear frequently seek out and consume. This reduces the amount of effort western bear have to spend to obtain a meal. Pine nuts are eaten during both spring and fall months.

Pinyon pine nuts are also eaten by black bear in Utah, and the seeds of limber pines are utilized as food in Montana. Some other black bear foods unique to the western part of their range are manzanita berries (bearberry), coffeeberry, salmonberry, bitterberry, elderberry, snowberry, buffaloberry, and the fruit of prickly pear cactus in desert areas like those found in Arizona. Pears and apples were reported eaten where these fruit trees were available in California. Cranberries are an important spring and fall black bear food in Alaska, and are eaten in other states where they are found, too.

As far as consumption of animal matter goes, black bear are opportunists. They will catch and eat whatever they can. They eat fish such as suckers, salmon and trout when they are abundant and easily caught during spring and fall spawning runs. Suckers discarded on riverbanks by fishermen are also consumed. Frogs are sometimes eaten, too. A Michigan bear that was hit by a car as it entered a roadway from a streambed disgorged a large quantity of frogs it had apparently just eaten.

Birds and bird eggs are consumed when the opportunity presents itself, as are small–to medium–size mammals. Michigan trapper Greg Ledy told me about finding the carcasses of three beavers that a black bear had caught and killed one spring, then covered with vegetation for a later meal. He said it looked like the bear laid at the base of a beaver dam at night and grabbed the beavers with a forepaw as they swam by, then bit them behind the head.

Black bear will also eat deer fawns, and elk, moose and caribou calves. Most bruins simply stumble across these young animals and take advantage of the opportunity for a meal. At least three yearling black bear got lucky when they gained access to a square mile enclosure used for white-tailed deer research at the Cusino Wildlife Experiment Station in Michigan's Upper Peninsula during different years when fawns were being born. All three bear caught and ate a number of fawns in the enclosure. The bear probably got in the fenced area by climbing the fence, officials say.

Opportunistic predation on fawns and calves by black bear have been recorded in other areas, too. In situations where healthy populations of deer, elk, moose and caribou are involved, losses to bear are not significant in regard to overall population levels.

The loss of moose calves to black bear was studied on the Kenai National Wildlife Refuge in Alaska from 1978 to 1982. During that time black bear were only seen on seven calf kills. Different black bear were

Two berry pickers work a powerline clearing in Michigan as they search for wild strawberries. Captive black bear reveal much about the food habits of their wild brethren.

involved in each case and they represented various age classes. Three of the bear were adult boars, two were adult sows and two were juveniles (one boar and one sow).

Black bear were observed chasing moose calves whenever they were encountered, but the bruins were unsuccessful in all but one attempt. In most cases, a cow and calf either outran the bear, a cow defended her calf or the bear gave up pursuit. The calf kill that was observed involved a cow with two calves. The trio was walking along the shoreline of a lake with one calf in front of the cow and one behind. A sow with two cubs was in mature timber nearby and ran out, catching and killing the trailing calf before its mother had a chance to react. In response to the attack, the cow and remaining calf started swimming across the lake. However, the surviving calf only made it halfway across when it weakened and eventually drowned.

Black bear seldom prey on adult deer and moose, unless the animals are handicapped in some way. There was a white-tailed deer, for instance, that was being watched at night with the aid of a spotlight in Cades Cove of Great Smoky Mountains National Park. The deer's visibility was hampered by the light, of course, and a black bear took advantage of the opportunity to attack and kill the whitetail. Bruins also feed on injured deer and other game. They feed on entrails remaining after hunters field dress a harvested game animal. In the spring, black bear frequently scavenge the carcasses of animals that died as a result of harsh winter weather, and beaver carcasses that are discarded by trappers after pelts are removed.

There appears to be an exception to black bear predation on big game in Newfoundland. Bear biologist Shane Mahoney said these bear prey on adult moose and caribou on the island, in addition to calves. Bear have actually been observed killing adult caribou and have been found on freshly killed adult moose a number of times.

Mahoney said black bear there operate from an ambush situation. Since they take their prey by surprise and are much quicker off the mark, bear stand a good chance of catching what they are after. When an animal is caught, Mahoney says, the bear grabs both of the animal's flanks with its front paws and pulls it down. He added that black bear neatly skin their prey, whether calf or adult, before beginning to eat.

Why are Newfoundland's black bear more active predators than elsewhere? Mahoney said he feels the circumstances there have resulted from a combination of big, strong bear and a limited food supply. Newfoundland has a low density of black bear, but many of those that inhabit the island are large, according to the biologist.

Black bear occasionally prey on livestock and poultry such as cattle,

A bowhunter visits a cornfield that may attract black bear. Feeding signs are obvious in corn because the bruins usually wreak havoc in the crop.

calves, horses, sheep, goats, pigs and chickens. When natural foods are scarce, black bear turn to any alternative food source that is available. Free-roaming livestock in black bear habitat is readily accessible to hungry bear and some losses can be expected. However, as scavengers, bear are sometimes wrongfully accused of killing livestock that may have died of natural causes or been killed by another predator.

When it comes to wrecking bee hives though, black bear usually stand alone in the amount of damage they do. Honey, and the insects that make it, are high on the black bear's list of preferred foods. Owners of bee yards in bear country can best protect their investment by enclosing it with electric fence using three strands of barbed wire 10 inches apart, with the first strand 10 inches off the ground, according to Gary Alt. He said barbless wire is less likely to administer a shock to bear because of the length and density of their hair. Beef suet should be wrapped around wires to attract the attention of any black bear that are interested in honey, according to Alt, so they are sure to get a shock when trying to secure the suet.

An alternative to protecting bee hives with an electric fence is elevating them on a platform that is about 10 feet high. Metal poles that can't be climbed by bruins should be used to hold up platforms.

Some of man's crops, such as corn and oats, are also appealing to black bear, and they do their share of damage in fields that are readily accessible to them, along with raccoons and deer. Like livestock placed in black bear habitat, there's bound to be some damage to crops grown in bear country, especially where fields extend to the edge of prime bear habitat. Due to the size of most corn and oat fields, they can't be protected from bear as effectively as bee yards can be.

Not all food black bear obtain directly or indirectly from man is given up unwillingly. Where hunting black bear over bait is legal, the animals' natural food supply is supplemented by handouts during a portion of the year that may range from a few weeks to a number of months. Some non-hunting individuals also feed bear, along with other wildlife, at or near their homes on a regular basis because they like to see the animals. In areas where black bear have access to open pit dumps, or dumpsites where bear proof containers aren't in use, the animals feed and grow fat on discarded people food.

Available evidence shows that bruins that supplement their diet with food from man, whether provided directly at feeders or indirectly at dumps, are generally healthier and more productive of young than bear subsisting solely on a natural diet. Information gathered about black bear while they've been observed at these feeding sites is also valuable.

However, there are circumstances under which black bear shouldn't

Male black bear are easier to distinguish than females during spring and summer months. A long tuft of hair at the back of the belly marks the penis.

be fed for the benefit of both people and bear. This rule applies to national parks and other public areas where black bear and people frequently come in close contact.

Identifying Sexes

Black bear can be difficult to sex when viewed in the wild, especially during the fall. An animal with cubs, whether during spring or fall, is obviously a sow. However, immature sows and those that have either lost or been separated from their cubs, are harder to sex.

The sex organs of sows are only visible from the rear and you have to be close or use binoculars to see the vulva. Urine soaked hair usually extends downward from the vulva.

Males are easiest to distinguish from lone females during spring and summer months. Their testicles are usually prominent and visible between the hind legs. A long tuft of pointed hair that hangs down from the belly in front of the hind legs marks the location of the penis.

By late fall testicles are no longer visible, having been drawn up into the abdomen, and scrotums are obscured by hair. Bear seen at this time of year without cubs, and in a position where a penis or vulva aren't visible, could be either a male or female. However, body size may be a clue. Boars are generally bigger than sows, with larger heads and longer bodies. However, this isn't foolproof because an adult sow may be larger than a young boar.

The front feet of young boars usually appear large in proportion to their body. Front feet of adult sows, on the other hand, might look small in proportion to the size of their body. Bear that appear short and squat are often sows, while boars tend to look long and lanky. Few sows will have bodies that exceed $5^{1}/_{2}$ feet in length.

If two adult black bear are seen together during June and July, the larger of the two will often be the boar, especially if it is following the other. Boars will grunt when following a sow in heat.

2

Black Bear Biology

The life cycle of black bear is a world apart from other popular big game animals. Many bruins spend three to seven months each year in a dormant state. They seek shelter from the cold winter weather and slumber so they don't have to worry about feeding themselves during the leanest months of the year. Yet, this is when black bear cubs are born in a weak and helpless state after developing for a mere six weeks in the sow's womb, even though she was bred seven months earlier.

This may sound strange, but that's the way a black bear's life is. Honest. Bear with me as I explain.

Breeding

The breeding season for black bear begins during late May and extends into August, with most matings taking place during June or July. Although mature boars generally participate in reproductive activities on an annual basis, few sows do. In the best of habitat, some sows successfully mate when they are $2^1/2$ years old. Most of them are bred successfully when they are $3^1/2$ or $4^1/2$ years old. Sows in poor habitat may not conceive for their first time until they are $6^1/2$ or $7^1/2$ years old.

If mature sows are nursing young cubs during the breeding season they do not breed. The production of milk normally prevents them from becoming fertile (going into estrus). There are, however, two cases on record, one in North Carolina and one in Pennsylvania, where nursing sows have been bred. Roger Powell with North Carolina State University suggested that estrus may not be blocked in sows of good physical condition in food-rich areas. This enables them to raise cubs every year rather than every other year. There is also the possibility that those sows may have been separated from their cubs for a short time. An interruption of lactation for as short a time as two days can initiate estrus. Sows breeding in consecutive years typically have lost their cubs prior to or during the summer breeding season, which halts lactation. Since large boars are known to prey on cubs, that raises an interesting question. Is cannibalism among boars directed toward producing another estrus cycle in sows as well as securing a source of protein to nourish their bodies? An answer has yet to be uncovered, but it's something to speculate about.

Although most mature sows produce cubs every other year, some may skip two or more years between litters, especially during years when natural food production is poor. Lynn Rogers has conducted research in Minnesota that indicates there is a minimum weight denning sows must attain to initiate the final stage of cub development. Mature sows weighing less than 150 to 160 pounds when they entered dens did not produce cubs.

Once mature sows go into estrus, they remain in a breeding condition until bred, according to Gary Alt. Although one boar will stay with a breeding female for two or three days, some sows will mate with more than one boar. At a location where black bear are fed and observed in Pennsylvania, three different boars mated with the same sow one evening. Where more than one boar is involved in breeding, not all cubs in the same litter will necessarily be sired by the same boar.

Black bear boars are more polygamous than sows. They reach sexual maturity when $2^{1}/_{2}$ years old, in some cases, but maturation is delayed in many areas until $3^{1}/_{2}$ to $5^{1}/_{2}$ years old. Boars that cross the path of a sow in estrus will trail her much the same way a white-tailed buck will follow a doe in heat. Two boars competing for the same sow sometimes fight.

One June in Montana's Glacier National Park, my wife and I encountered a boar and sow together. The smaller sow departed first, then was followed by the boar. We remained where we were for a few minutes and saw another larger boar come along, following the same sow. The second boar was obviously irritated. As he walked through the timber he swatted a number of dead trees, knocking them to the ground with loud crashes.

We hung around a while longer, listening for sounds of a fight, but didn't hear anything. When there is an obvious difference in size between boars, the smaller animal usually retreats. Fights are most com-

Boars will often square–up against each other during the breeding season, especially if they are of about the same size. They may meet while trailing sows in heat.

mon between boars similar in size.

Most mature boars still have plenty of fat reserves when they leave dens during the spring. They continue using these energy reserves through the breeding season, losing weight in the process. For this reason, breeding boars usually reach their lightest weight of the year during July, but quickly start regaining what they've lost once the breeding season ends.

Once a sow is bred and eggs are fertilized, development of the eggs begins, but they only reach what is called the blastocyst stage before development stops. Round blastocysts are so small they are difficult to see without a microscope. Rather than becoming connected to the wall of the uterus like developing eggs of most mammals, blastocysts remain suspended in fluid within the uterus. Blastocysts eventually implant on the uterus wall about the time a female enters a den for the winter, and they develop rapidly during six to eight weeks. Cubs are born at the end of that time while in the den. Gary Alt said that in Pennsylvania the final stage of development of black bear cubs begins around December 1.

This reproductive process is called delayed implantation. Although female black bear are actually pregnant for seven months, cubs develop in a fraction of that time. Due to the fact that cub development doesn't usually begin until denning, it can be difficult to determine if sows bagged during fall hunting seasons are pregnant.

Cubs

Cubs weigh 12 ounces at birth, on the average, according to Gary Alt. Thirty-three newborn cubs he weighed ranged between 10.2 and 16 ounces. By the time they leave the den, cubs from small litters will average larger sizes than cubs from large litters. There's obviously less milk to go around when four or five cubs must be fed versus one or two. In Pennsylvania, single cubs averaged 9.5 pounds by late March compared to 6.8 pounds for twins and 5.3 pounds for three- and four-cub litters. Cubs that weigh at least five pounds when they leave dens have a good chance of survival.

Black bear cubs have little, if any, hair at birth and their eyes are closed. However, hair grows quickly and covers the small animals' bodies. Their eyes generally open when six weeks old.

Litter size varies from one through five. Average litter size in the western portion of the black bear's range is between one and two. In the east, it's between two and three. Pennsylvania bear are among the most productive in North America, records indicate. Alt said over half of the sows there give birth to three cubs, and litters of five are as common as single cubs. Sows with four cubs have been reported in Maine, Michi-

Black bear cubs average from 5 to 10 pounds in weight by the time they leave the den. Litters range from one to five in size.

gan and Minnesota.

Sows giving birth for the first time generally have one or two cubs. The largest litters are produced by experienced mothers that are in good physical condition. The record for the most cub production by a wild black bear is probably held by a radio–collared female Alt monitored from 1974 through 1984. She raised 26 cubs during that time, giving birth to a minimum of four cubs at a time.

The sex ratio of cubs usually favors males slightly. Alt said he found an average of 57 males and 43 females for every 100 cubs. In most black bear populations, there is normally a higher mortality rate among the male segment than females, which might account for more males than females produced.

Most cubs are born during January and February, but some are born during late December and some during early March. Melvin Myllyla discovered a sow with cubs in upper Michigan on December 27. Jerry Weigold reported he and his brother found a sow with cubs that were

Even tiny black bear cubs can climb trees, like this one climbing a rough–barked jack pine. They use trees throughout their lives as escape cover.

pink and appeared hairless, indicating they weren't born long before, on March 1. The average birth date of 20 litters in Pennsylvania was January 14, with a range from January 1-25.

Denning

Black bear dens are probably not as large as most people think. Based on measurements of 400 dens, Alt says the average den entrance is 17 inches wide and 18 inches high. They average $5^1/_2$ feet from front to back and are 32 inches wide by 23 inches high. As far as volume, dens average 19 cubic feet, according to Alt.

Bruins use a variety of sites for dens. Sows usually select more sheltered locations than boars, but not always. Black bear may den in rock caves, hollow trees or logs, old beaver houses or culverts; under uprooted trees, stumps, brushpiles or man-made structures; and some simply build a nest on top of the snow or curl up in a convenient location such as on the top of a new muskrat house. Basically, anything that suits a bear can be used for a den. Their thick coats usually protect them from the cold when curled up.

In some areas, such as the Great Smoky Mountains, sows show a preference for denning in tree cavities off the ground. Most of the sows in the park are thought to den in trees, with cavities being as much as 80 feet above ground. Reports of black bear using elevated dens have also come from Georgia, Arkansas and Michigan. Disturbance of animals in these locations is minimal, which is a major reason that they use them.

When using a nest, black bear simply curl up in a thick patch of cover and break off branches or twigs to use as a base, then add grass, leaves and tree bark as bedding. Boars make nests more often, but sows with cubs also use nests. Bear that den in more protected locations will also rake bedding into them.

The time when denning begins among black bear varies from year to year in the same region, with greater variations from one region to another. Sows den earlier than boars in most cases. Length of time spent in dens gradually decreases from north to south, as would be expected. Bruins in the southern part of their range, such as in Florida and Virginia, may not den at all.

There's even a case of a young boar in Michigan's Upper Peninsula, where winters are typically long and cold, that did not go into a normal winter sleep. There was human interference in this situation, though. The animal showed up at a rural residence sometime during December and human disturbance forced it up a tree. Concerned about the animal's welfare because of cold weather, Frank Pollard put an empty barrel filled with straw at the base of the tree. The bruin accepted the man-

Average Denning Dates

State or Province	Entry	Emergence
Alaska	early to mid-Oct	late Apr/early May
Alberta	early Nov	late Mar
Arizona	late Nov	late Mar/early Apr
California	mid-Dec	mid-Mar
Colorado	late Oct/early Nov	late Mar/early Apr
Idaho	late Oct/early Nov	mid-Apr
Maine	late Nov/early Dec	early Apr
Michigan	mid-Nov	mid-Apr
Minnesota	early Nov	early Apr
Montana	early Nov	mid-May
New York	late Nov/early Dec	early Apr
North Carolina	late Dec	late Mar
Ontario	late Oct/Nov	late Apr/May
Virginia	late Dec/early Jan	late Mar
Coastal Washington	early Dec	early Mar

Average black bear denning dates show the longest denning period where winters are most severe, but food availability will influence dates also.

made shelter as its home, but left it daily to eat food the Pollard family put outside the "den."

Food availability plays a role in when black bear enter dens for the winter. They are generally active longer when food is available and will den earlier when quality food is scarce. Photoperiods, or the length of daylight, decrease in the fall; this also plays a role in when bear enter dens, probably more so than prevailing weather conditions. In early November Richard Robinson stumbled across a sow and a cub sleeping soundly under a fallen tree when temperatures were in the 70s.

I returned to the den with Robinson, and as we approached the location the cub left the den and climbed a nearby tree. The sow remained under the fallen tree. We stood within a matter of feet of her and talked in normal tones. She struggled to raise her head a couple of times in recognition of the fact we were there, but could never keep it up for long, which was an indication of how drowsy she was.

Those bear didn't remain there for the winter, though. I checked on

A black bear hollowed the base of this stump to form a den. Dens take many forms. Some are simple lined nests on open ground.

This black bear Buck LeVasseur decided to film was denned under the logs in the lower left of this photo. Closed hunting seasons are designed to protect denning bears.

them about a week later and they were gone. A heavy rain had fallen in the meantime, and I'm sure they got wet because the location offered little protection from precipitation. Ken Lowe reported another bear in Upper Michigan that was temporarily denned on October 1 when temperatures were in the 80s, then moved following thundershowers.

The transition from normal activity to total dormancy is probably a gradual process in most cases. Bruins may sleep for days at a time in temporary dens like those used in the two examples above before occupying a permanent winter location. Black bear in permanent winter quarters may even change locations, if sufficiently disturbed by dogs or people. If chased from dens, sows with cubs sometimes abandon their cubs.

The ease with which bear awaken from winter sleep varies considerably. Some animals may leave dens at the mere approach of people, while others can actually be touched and moved without waking. The sow and newborn cubs that Jerry and Terry Weigold found on March 1 were located while the pair were hunting snowshoe hares. Fresh tracks of a hare led into a hollow log occupied by the bear. Unaware that the bear were there, and without looking, Terry jabbed a long stick into the log in an effort to chase the snowshoe out. In the process, he poked the sleeping sow. The animal barely moved in response to the disturbance.

Jerry said they couldn't see the hare, and he's convinced it hopped over the bear and was hiding behind her.

On another winter outing Jerry jumped on top of a brush pile and fell through, dumping snow and other debris on a sleeping black bear. He said the animal rolled around, groaning and growling while he struggled to get out of there. He eventually got out of the brushpile, making a lot of noise in the process, but the bear stayed put. Jerry and Terry watched that bear throughout the winter and they were able to tell it was an old one. When the bear yawned, its teeth were noted and they were badly worn.

Winter or spring thaws sometimes flood dens or cause them to collapse, usually resulting in departure of residents. Some cubs are lost under these circumstances, according to Alt.

Sows with newborn cubs probably get less sleep than other bear during the winter. Cubs are often noisy, making contented purring sounds while nursing, similar to a running motor, and squalling or bawling when upset or hungry. When sows with cubs are discovered in dens, it's sometimes the noises that cubs make that lead people to them. I've attempted to photograph a number of sows with cubs in dens and most of the sows were very much awake.

Denned black bear can be observed and photographed. However, disturbance should be kept to a minimum, especially when sows with cubs are involved. Too much noise or continued disturbance may force a sow to abandon her cubs. If a sow with cubs appears upset or runs off, leave the area immediately. The location of cubs that are abandoned for good should be reported to appropriate state or provincial wildlife officials such as biologists and conservation officers.

The black bear's normal body temperature is between 100 and 101 degrees Fahrenheit. When in dens, this temperature may drop to as low as 88 degrees, but can be as high as 98. Heart rate may slow to about 10 beats per minute when asleep, and breathing slows to one breath every 45 seconds in some animals.

Due to slowed body functions and the lack of food intake, black bear don't have to eliminate waste from their bodies like they normally would. Although these animals may not urinate while denned, they do occasionally defecate, especially bear that are in dens for six to seven months. I've seen droppings deposited by denned bear between my visits to den sites on a number of occasions.

Black bear do not form fecal plugs before denning or while denned. Feces form in the lower digestive tract from dead cells and may contain hair from a bear licking itself, plus debris from the den that may be ingested. Although denned black bear don't eat, sows with cubs will consume waste from their cubs. Bear commonly eliminate large quantities of waste products from their bodies after they leave dens.

Hardened layers of foot pads are shed by black bear while in dens. Consequently, bruins may lick the bottoms of their feet after pads are shed, and their feet may be tender for this reason when they leave dens. Black bear slowly become active again during spring, sometimes remaining near dens for a while after they leave them. Sows with cubs are usually the last to leave dens, and when they do, they commonly remain nearby for weeks. Boars generally emerge from dens before sows, whether or not sows have cubs.

The timing of den emergence varies from north to south, with the weather having an impact on when this happens.

Sows that are nursing cubs will normally lose 30 to 35 percent of body weight while in dens, sometimes more. Other black bear lose an average of 20 percent of their peak fall weight during the denning period. A pregnant sow that weighs 300 pounds when she enters her den, for example, will lose an average of 90 to 105 pound by the time she leaves the den with her cubs. A boar weighing 300 pounds in the fall may only lose 60 to 75 pounds. Both sexes keep losing weight until their caloric intake substantially increases, which is usually sometime during the summer.

Yearlings that weigh less than 20 pounds when they leave the den have a 50/50 chance of survival, according to Lynn Rogers. Yearlings that exceed that weight when they emerge from dens have a much better chance of reaching adulthood.

Cubs will continue nursing until August, but will start eating solids before then. Sows and cubs remain together throughout the year. Cubs that lose their sows will instinctively seek out a den on their own, provided they are weaned when orphaned. A study conducted in Michigan by Al Erickson showed that orphaned cubs as young as five months old and weighing as little as 18 pounds can survive on their own. However, the mortality of orphaned cubs is probably higher than those that remain under the sow's care.

Sows with youngsters that are almost a year old seldom enter the same dens they occupied the previous winter. In fact, den reuse by black bear is very low in areas where an abundance of den sites is available. The opposite may be true in locations where suitable den sites are limited. In Pennsylvania, Gary Alt has documented that a black bear will reuse a den site only 4.8 percent of the time. Of those dens that are reused, half of the bears were sows or one of a sow's female cubs.

Cubs as young as five months old and weighing as little as 18 pounds can survive on their own. But life is tough for these little fellows.

Black bear cubs stay with the sow until after their second winter. Yearling males disperse at this age and sometimes wander as far as 100 miles.

Family Break Up

When black bear are about a year old, canine teeth will replace the milk teeth that formerly occupied those positions. After their second winter, young black bear are referred to as yearlings. Families split up at this time, with yearling males dispersing as far as 80 to 100 miles and females often settling down in a portion of the sow's home range. Long distance dispersal of young boars prevents inbreeding. However, yearling dispersal takes place whether or not the cub's sow is alive. Alt said that when males disperse, they usually head out in a particular direction and keep going at that heading until they settle into a new home range. These bear are often the ones that show up in towns and cities as they travel cross-country.

Once yearlings are on their own, sows go into another estrus cycle. Mature sows normally have cubs only every other year because of the long time they spend with their young. Other than the association of sows with cubs, and sow and boars during the breeding season, black bear are basically solitary animals. Concentrations of food, however, whether natural or provided by man, will bring the animals together, and their social interactions can be interesting to watch.

Interaction

A hierarchy of dominant and subordinate animals usually develops at most feeding sites that attract a number of black bear. The biggest boars, plus sows with cubs, generally command the most respect, and yearlings are at the bottom of the pecking order. Subordinate animals usually move out of the way of dominant bear, but if they don't they may be chased away. Young bear are usually tolerant of one another.

Threat displays are occasionally exhibited between two bruins when choice feeding sites are being contested or one animal gets too close to another. A sound frequently heard from one bear warning another is referred to as "huffing" by biologist Steve Herrero from Alberta. When making this noise, bruins inhale and exhale loudly a number of times in quick succession. This warning sound is also called "woofing". Black bear also snort by loudly expelling air through their nose and mouth once.

Young black bear frequently play and wrestle with each other. A female (left) and male look like they are hugging in this playful bout.

When two bear are close together facing each other in a challenging position with heads down and backs arched, they sometimes make a "gurgling" sound. This is an odd rumbling sound that goes up and down in volume and is hard to describe. A person who heard it for the first time said it sounded like a bear crying.

"Jawing" is a rapid opening and closing of the mouth with distinct clicking sounds resulting from teeth coming together. Some people refer to this warning as bear "popping their teeth," and that's exactly what it sounds like. A "paw swat" or "false charge" sometimes accompanies a vocal warning. When using the paw swat, a bear usually strikes the ground or a tree. During a false charge, bear will move quickly toward the bear being warned, but stop after going a short distance, which is often only a step or two.

Black bear will use the same threat and warning signals toward people who get in their way as they do with other bear.

As far as submissive behavior goes, one hunter in Michigan said he watched a subordinate animal, in the presence of a dominant boar, roll on its back with its legs in the air, a submissive posture often exhibited by dogs, allowing the boar to thoroughly sniff its body. He didn't say if the subordinate animal was male or female, and perhaps wasn't able to tell. The same hunter said he saw a dominant boar urinate on subordinates.

Yearling and subadult black bear frequently wrestle and play with each other, and this behavior is sometimes observed. I've seen pairs of young males, as well as males and females, engage in wrestling matches. When females are involved in bouts, they often playfully run off for short distances periodically, then pounce on males that follow. Gary Alt's father, Floyd, once observed from his airplane a group of seven young males playing in a field. He said six of the animals were paired off like they were dancing.

3

Reading Sign

Regardless of what technique is used to hunt black bear, it is important for hunters to know they are in an area frequented by at least one animal. Actually seeing a bear is the most reliable way to determine whether animals are in an area, but this is not always possible due to their secretive nature, coupled with the heavy cover and rugged terrain they often occupy. So, in many cases, hunters have to rely on reading sign.

Hunters who want to avoid areas occupied by black bear should also be familiar with sign left by these animals, so they are better able to steer clear of locations with the most bear activity.

There are three basic types of sign left by black bear—tracks, droppings and feeding activity. Other indications bear are or have been in an area are "bear trees." The full significance of bear trees is not yet fully understood, but they appear to be territorial markers or signposts primarily used by adult boars.

Bear Trees

Boars reportedly stand on hind legs with their backs against marker trees, rubbing and scratching themselves on the trunk while reaching around with their mouth and biting the bark or treetop. In some cases, claws may also be used to mark tree trunks. Various sizes and types of trees are marked by black bear in this fashion. Oak and hemlock trees marked by bruins were seen in Pennsylvania. A variety of hardwoods and softwoods were marked by bear in Great Smoky Mountains Na-

A bear tree that is marked year after year in Pennsylvania. The height of bites and scratches reveals the size of the bear that made the marks.

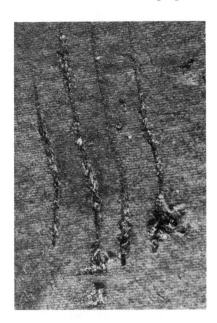

Claw marks on the wallboard of a hunting shack reveal the distinctive scratches of a black bear.

tional Park. In the Midwest, trees from five to twelve feet high were marked.

Some trees have been marked by bear for years. On large trees, pieces of bark are chewed or clawed away revealing the inner wood. Large scars develop on trees used over a long period of time. Young evergreen trees marked by black bear characteristically exhibit broken tops that may or may not remain attached to the tree trunk. Clumps of bear hair are usually visible on broken limbs where a bear has rubbed.

The height of bite marks generally corresponds to the height of the bear that made them. The bear's scent is also left on the tree as a result of rubbing. There appears to be a connection between tree marking behavior among mature boars and the breeding season, because most marking occurs before and during peak mating activity—May through July. Tree marking by boars may serve the same function as scrapes made by white-tailed bucks—calling cards advertising their availability to receptive females. Sows also rub against marker trees to leave their scent.

In addition to living trees, bear mark signs, poles and buildings. Most markers are along bear trails and are readily visible.

Tree tops or limbs that have been broken recently will exhibit light colored wood at the break. Syrup-like sap that hasn't yet hardened should also be in evidence. Inner wood or damaged limbs darken and become dry over a period of time after exposure to the air.

Another place to look for black bear hair is on the underside of fallen trees suspended between two and three feet above the ground. When traveling through heavy cover, bruins often go under these windfalls and hair rubs off in the process, especially on stubs of limbs that project downward. Hairs may also be left on low-hanging tree branches.

Feeding Activity

Signs of black bear feeding activity can be found on trees, too. Bruins are often destructive of trees they feed on and the evidence of their presence is easy to distinguish. As an example, the bark of coniferous trees such as Douglas fir, spruce and redwoods is stripped by hungry bear that are after the inner sapwood. Sometimes bark is removed in a band all the way around the trunk of a tree, which is called girdling and results in the death of the tree. Loss of trees to girdling by black bear is a well-known problem in the state of Washington. I saw my first evidence of black bear stripping the bark off white cedar trees in the northern part of Michigan's Lower Peninsula. Black bear feed like this in the spring when there is a scarcity of other types of food.

Foraging bruins can be just as destructive of fruit trees such as wild cherry, serviceberry and apple. I've seen numerous cherry and berry trees completely broken down by feeding bear. Some trees that have sturdy enough trunks to resist breakage end up with many of their limbs broken after a bear feeding spree, which limits the trees' chances of survival. Future fruit producing potential is limited on trees that survive this damage.

Feeding activity on trees does not always result in long-lasting damage. The only evidence that a bruin has visited some fruit trees are the claw marks in the bark and the breakage of a few small limbs. Some limbs are broken by feeding black bear in nut-bearing trees such as oak and beech, but the most frequent sign of their visits to these trees are claw marks. The same sign can be seen on the trunks of aspen trees, which black bear climb in the spring for buds and catkins.

Fall is the time of year to check fruit and nut trees for signs of feeding activity. Recently-broken limbs should have fresh green leaves still attached. Leaves will die and turn brown after limbs have been broken a while. Wood visible inside fresh claw marks will not yet have darkened. Count on black bear to return to a tree that still offers a good food supply. If signs of feeding activity are a year or more old and the tree has a supply of fruit or nuts again, a bruin will probably stop by for his share once they ripen.   '

Some black bear spend most of their time foraging for nuts on the ground rather than climbing trees to get them. For this reason, the absence of claw marks on the trunks of mast producing trees does not mean

There is no question a black bear has been feeding here. Ripping down branches of trees like this wild cherry bring the fruit within reach.

there are no bear in the area. Other sign such as tracks and droppings should be sought to determine if bear are using groves of nut trees.

Before discussing tracks and droppings, there are additional signs of feeding activity to cover. Black bear are fond of insects in addition to fruits and nuts. To get at ants, hornets and bees, bear often roll rocks and logs, rip apart stumps and logs, and dig holes in the ground. Claw marks can usually be found on logs and stumps that a black bear has manhandled. Scratches from claws are sometimes visible on displaced rocks, too. Remnants of a hornet or bee's nest at the bottom of a hole in the ground or in a ripped stump or tree is a sure sign a black bear was responsible. Large areas of soil may also be excavated by bear in search of plant tubers and bulbs.

Droppings

Black bear droppings are distinctive and are not likely to be mistaken for those left by another game animal in North America, except possibly in locations where the range of black and grizzly bear overlap. Dung is usually deposited in large piles. Numerous piles of droppings will be evident in favored feeding areas. Bear dung is normally white, brown or black, depending upon what the animals are feeding on. Evi-

This hunter has located a torn log where a black bear searched for insects. Rocks, rotten stumps, ground with insect nests or growths of tender tubers may also be excavated.

Quantity and size of black bear droppings can be an indication of the bear's size. Blades of spring grass visible in this dung shows the animal was grazing.

dence of the type of food bruins have been dining on most recently can be determined by examining droppings.

Black bear scats seldom appear fresh for more than a few days, unless the weather is cold. Piles of dung usually dry out and start to break down quickly.

The size of droppings may indicate, to some extent, the size of the animal that deposited them. Presence of bear scat of average size in the same area with small, raccoon-size dung may indicate the presence of a sow with one or more cubs, for example. As a general rule, the larger the droppings the larger the bear. Black bear scat averages $1\frac{1}{4}$ to $1\frac{1}{2}$ inches in diameter, but may measure as much as two inches. After looking at black bear droppings over a period of time, hunters will get a feel for what larger-than-average droppings look like without measuring them. The same holds true for tracks.

Tracks

Tracks left by black bear can be a lot harder to find than many novice hunters realize. Despite the black bear's bulk, the animal has to walk over soft ground such as sand or mud to leave distinct impressions. The best places to look for bear tracks are along sand or gravel roads, muddy roads, in patches of sand or mud near feeding areas, and along the banks of rivers and streams. Many gravel roads in bear country are too hard to show much, if any, sign of a bear's passing. It takes an experienced eye to pick out the shallow imprints or scuff marks left by a bruin's large, flat paws on these roads.

The most efficient way to check gravel or sand roads for track is on foot. If gravel roads are checked from a vehicle, they should be driven at a snail's pace, preferably with a spotter on a front fender. Rain usually washes out tracks on roads, so if a track is located shortly after a rain, it is bound to be fresh. Some bear hunters who use hounds "drag" roads on a daily basis by pulling a tree branch, log or old bedspring behind vehicles to ensure that any tracks seen the next morning are less than 24 hours old. A bear that walks across a road that has been dragged is more likely to leave tracks that are easier to see.

Bear tracks usually consist of imprints of foot pads and toes, with five toes per foot. A track left by a black bear's hind foot is similar in appearance to a print left by a person who is barefoot. The pad is longer than it is wide. Rear pads are widest just behind the toes and taper down to a narrow, rounded heel. Front pads are at least twice as wide as they are long.

Black bear have short claws compared to grizzlies, and impressions from claws don't usually show in front of toe marks, unless the prints are made in soft sand or mud, or if the animal was running. When claw marks are present in black bear tracks the small indentations they leave are often close to the toes. Claw marks are more prominent in tracks made by grizzly bear.

It is usually possible to get a general idea of how big a bear is by the size of its tracks. The front pad of an average black bear will measure from $3^1/_2$ to $4^1/_2$ inches across. Rear pads on an average black bear will be from five to six inches in length. This measurement only takes the pad into account, not the toes.

My definition of an average black bear is one that has a dressed weight of 120 to 200 pounds. Heavier bruins are better-than-average, in my book, and will generally, but not always, have larger pad measurements than those listed above. Boars have larger feet than sows.

Hunters who find tracks with front pad marks that measure five to six inches across and rear pad marks that span about eight inches, are

It takes soft soil to record a bear track. Bear have five toes on each foot. Average–size bear have a front pad $3^1/_2$ to $4^1/_2$ inches across.

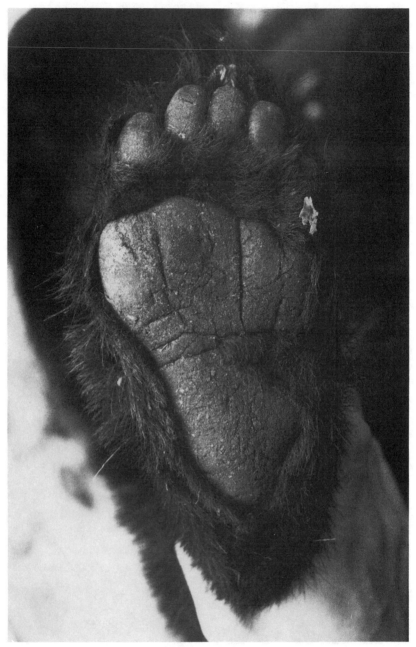

The hind foot of a black bear has a humanlike form. The large pad should measure more than six inches in length on a big black bear.

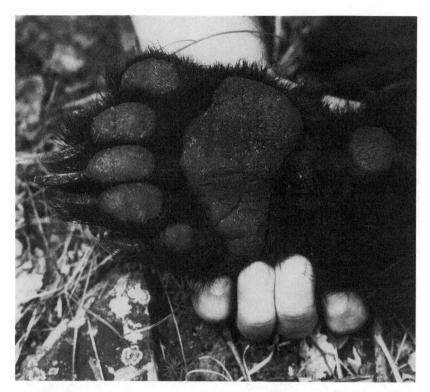

Although black bear have formidable claws, they seldom are as obvious as a grizzly bear's claws when each are seen in imprints.

looking at the prints of a trophy class black bear. I measured the pads on a Michigan bear with a dressed weight of 520 pounds. The front pad was six inches in width and the pad on the hind foot measured $8^{1}/_{2}$ inches from front to back.

Front foot measurements of boars and sows in New York state illustrates the difference in track size made by each. The average width of front feet of sows from yearlings ($1^{1}/_{2}$ years old) on up to animals $10^{1}/_{2}$ years old was 3.12 to 3.76 inches. Average measurements for boars in the same age classes were 3.79 to 5.00 inches. Boars $7^{1}/_{2}$ years of age and older seldom had front foot measurements less than 4.50 inches. Most significant, however, is the fact that yearling boars had wider front feet than all of the sows measured, meaning there is very little, if any, overlap in front foot size between the sexes. Any print of a front foot that is over four inches across should have been made by a boar.

Measurements of hind feet of black bear in Washington state came up with similar results. The length and width of pads on hind feet were

When you find good tracks, take the time to study them. You will learn something about the bear that made them, and about tracks you might find in the future.

Successful black bear hunters spend more time scouting than actually hunting. Pinpointing the favored haunts of your quarry is essential to bagging the bruin. The bark of this live tree has been ripped by a black bear's claws.

combined. Those measurements for adult sows were between 8.4 inches and 10 inches. Width and length of rear pads of the majority of adult males were at least 10 inches.

Trails

Regular trails will be packed down in areas frequented by black bear. All vegetation is usually flattened along these trails and may even be worn down to bare soil from heavy use, such as at a bait site or garbage dump. Bear trails sometimes tunnel through thickets at a height of about three feet. Trails used by a heavy bear will develop depressions every place the animal puts its feet because black bear have a tendency to step in the same spots each time they walk the same route.

Bed

Black bear beds are similar in size to those made by deer, but are more rounded, appearing circular. Deer beds tend to be made in more of an oblong or oval shape. Bruins may bed down in grass, but often lay at the base of large trees. It isn't unusual to see bear beds at or near bait sites. The animals frequently lie down to feed.

Wallows

Wallows are commonly used by black bear to keep cool during hot summer months. Pennsylvania bear biologist Gary Alt showed me several wallows in a swamp. They consist of circular pools of spring water. A well-worn bear trail was evident to the wallows. Bear leaving wallows sometimes shake mud and water on nearby trees and vegetation.

Smart black bear hunters will spend as much time as possible scouting for bear sign before hunting season begins so they can make the best use of valuable hunting time. Preseason or prehunt scouting is especially important for hunters who intend to use bait or hunt natural feeding areas, but will also work to the advantage of houndsmen. Black bear range farther, and are simply not as abundant as other big game animals like deer. Consequently, it often takes a lot of time and effort to locate a black bear's favored haunt.

Once prime bear country has been pinpointed, hunters are well on their way to success. It has been my experience that hunters should devote 60 to 70 percent of their hunting time scouting and 30 to 40 percent hunting. Sometimes looking for a place to hunt requires an even greater share of the total hunting time.

When I'm scouting an area for bear activity, I usually look for prime sources of food first. If any bruins are around, signs of their presence should be in the vicinity. Black bear usually do a good job of looking after their stomachs.

4

The Best Time To Hunt

Bear stand alone as the only major big game species that can be hunted during both spring and fall seasons, with black bear the most numerous and widespread. However, only states and provinces with the highest black bear populations have hunts during both times of year. Spring bear hunts are common across Canada, Alaska and in many western states. Fall hunts are the norm in the Midwest, South and Eastern U.S.

Bear hunting can be excellent during either time of year, provided a hunt is properly timed in accordance with the weather, which has a direct effect on bear activity. This is sometimes difficult to do, but becomes easier once the general activity patterns of bruins are known. In the spring, for example, most bear don't leave dens and become active until April or May, although there can be local variations. Big boars are usually the first to leave dens, some of them probably vacating winter quarters during April, with younger, smaller animals joining them later. By late May into June, breeding activity begins and boars become very active in their search for breeding sows.

Spring Hunts

An early spring will speed up bear emergence from dens. A late spring, or a cold snap will slow it down by as much as two weeks. Generally the later a spring bear hunt is planned, the more bear will be out of dens and the better a hunter's chances of seeing the animal will be. One spring, I had a hunt scheduled with Wayne Bosowicz in northern Ontario for mid-May. The hunt was canceled, however, because there was still a foot or more of snow on the ground at the time, and bear activity was minimal.

In Colorado, Jim Jarvis says his best hunting is always during June, the last month of the season. Most of his baiting is done at around 9,000 feet above sea level. He said that for every drop of 1,000 feet in elevation, bear activity generally picks up a week earlier. Good hunting can then be expected to begin sometime during May at lower elevations. Hunters interested in big bear probably have just as good a chance of encountering them late in the season.

Two other factors play a role in planning a spring bear hunt. One is the quality of hides and the other is emergence of biting insects.

Quality Of Hides

Bear hides are at their best soon after the animals leave dens, when hairs have grown long and thick to protect them against the cold winter months. As the weather warms, heavy winter coats are shed. The animals sometimes accelerate the process by rubbing against trees and other objects, creating patches of short hair on an otherwise long coat. I've see a few scruffy-looking black bear on spring hunts, but the vast majority of mature bruins have respectable hides throughout spring seasons. Hunters who are concerned about the quality of bear hides can plan a hunt accordingly, or should be prepared to pass up bear with rubbed pelts if hunting late in the season.

Biting Insects

Unfortunately, biting insects begin emerging about the time black bear hunting gets good during spring seasons. Mosquitoes and black flies can be annoying or downright disruptive pests, but they are generally tolerable when hunters come prepared with headnets, gloves and plenty of insect repellent. Mosquitoes aren't usually as much of a problem in western mountains as they are in much of Canada and Alaska.

In Colorado during the last week of June, for instance, mosquitoes were worse than normal, according to Jarvis, but I got by without using a headnet and bug juice. Hunters who hope to avoid biting insects altogether should plan on spring bear hunts during May, with the first two weeks of the month usually the safest, or late April, if there's any sign of bear activity.

Scheduling Conflicts

Regardless of the other considerations, spring may be the best time

Prime bear hides can be had in spring soon after the bruins leave their dens. Their heavy winter coats will be shed by summer.

of year for some hunters to plan black bear hunts if they are too busy with work or other hunting opportunities to find the time for a fall bear hunt. With most hunting seasons held during fall months, hunters who have limited time must carefully choose which species to hunt.

The choices are much simpler in the spring. Black bear hunts are the best thing going as far as big game, besides limited opportunities for grizzly bear and wild pigs. Turkey hunting is also big during the spring, but that shouldn't pose much of a problem for hunters interested in black bear, even if they want to hunt both. I usually manage to hunt both bear and turkey during the spring, and know other hunters who do the same. Hunters who can only go on one hunt will have to make their choice, but choosing black bear over turkey has got to be a lot easier than selecting between bear, deer, antelope, elk, moose, caribou, sheep and goats.

Quality Of Meat

There's absolutely no truth to an old myth that black bear are not fit to eat during the spring. They may scavenge some carcasses, but most of their diet is composed of grass and other vegetation. If anything, bear harvested in the spring may be better eating than those harvested in the fall because there is less fat, making the meat leaner. Some people contend that bear meat collected during the fall isn't good to eat, either. This can be chalked up to pure and simple ignorance or improper handling of carcasses.

Fall Hunts

Mosquitoes and other insect pests aren't usually a problem during fall bear hunts, although some may be present early in the season on days when temperatures are high. Black bear hides are normally in good shape in September, but hairs aren't as long then as they will be in October or November. Bear activity is generally at a peak during early fall as the animals finish layering their bodies with fat in preparation for denning, and tapers off during late fall until the animals enter dens. Black bear in the northern U.S. and Canada are most active in September and October, and some continue feeding into November. In southern states, bruins may remain active through December and into January.

Denning

The timing of denning sometimes depends on the availability of food. When food is scarce, bear may den early rather than expend energy to obtain little nourishment. Denning may also be delayed to enable the animals to take advantage of abundant sources of food such as acorns or beech nuts available late in the year. In years when food supplies have been abundant, enabling bear to build up sufficient fat reserves earlier than normal, they may retire to dens early. Boars usually remain active longer than sows.

More specific information on when black bear enter dens during the fall in different parts of North America and when they leave them during the spring is included in the first chapter of this book. Unlike fall deer hunting in some areas, fall black bear hunting isn't always best the first week of the season. Unless, of course, the season lasts a week or less. Don't get me wrong, opening week is usually good, but better hunting is sometimes possible later on. Fall black bear hunts start during early September in a number of states and provinces. The weather then can be cool, hot or rainy.

Weather Conditions

Cool conditions are great for bear hunting. Hot weather and heavy rain aren't. I've seen as many opening weeks with unfavorable weather

With a shiny, jet black coat, few animals are as handsome as a bear in the prime of its life. A big black bear is a trophy no matter when you choose to hunt.

conditions as favorable. Unfavorable weather reduces bear activity along with a hunter's chances of seeing the animal. Poor weather can strike at any time, but I often find conditions during the last week of September and the first two weeks of October more favorable than early September. There are other advantages of hunting then, too.

Temperatures, generally, are consistently cooler, resulting in optimum bear activity. Also, when a bruin is bagged, immediately butchering the carcass isn't usually necessary to salvage it. There are also fewer competing bear hunters with which to contend. This can be doubly good news in areas where baiting is legal. Once other hunters discontinue baiting, bear that were feeding at those bait sites start roaming in search of a food supply and may end up visiting baits still being maintained. As a result, late season baits that may have had only one bruin on them earlier, suddenly have two or three, and the chances of scoring go up as well. Even where baiting isn't legal, there is normally a "fall shuffle" of bruins seeking supplies of natural food.

Weather conditions that are both good and bad for black bear hunting are generally the same during fall and spring, regardless of which hunting technique is used. Heavy rain, strong wind and sudden changes in temperatures, whether up or down, are all bad news. It's been my experience that black bear just don't move much during downpours, and bear hunters will be better off staying where it's dry. If there is an extended period of heavy ran, try to hunt when it lets up because bear should be active then.

Black bear may move when it's windy, but the chances of seeing them are reduced. Wind direction frequently changes from one minute to the next as the velocity increases. Bear frequently smell hunters who are stand-hunting under these conditions, unless hunters are far enough away from baits that it is impossible for the animal to wind them. Hearing hounds is next to impossible when it's windy, too, and the sound of a predator call would also be drowned out. When tracking a bear in the snow though, wind may work in the tracker's favor by covering up the sound of his approach.

Stand hunters may do more harm than good if hunting when it's windy close to where they expect to see a bear. A bear that winds them may not return for days. If the animal does return the following day, it will be more cautious than before or simply approach after dark. For these reasons, it is better not to hunt when windy.

Hot and cold spells frequently reduce bear activity. Cold snaps during early spring and late fall may put a temporary halt to bear movements until the weather changes. A normal, gradual cooling trend that occurs from early to late fall can increase bear activity. The same is true

Use bug repellents with a high percent-age of the active ingredient Deet. Several brands are available in scentless form.

for normal warming trends during spring months. Temperatures that are uncomfortably warm for humans may also be uncomfortable for heavy-coated black bear, and their movements are often restricted to the cool-est hours under these conditions.

Hunting In The Rain

Stable weather conditions with normal temperatures and a light breeze are great for black bear hunting. The only circumstances that are better, and which I rate as the absolute best for bagging a bruin from a stand, is a light rain or drizzle with a calm wind. Black bear are more active than normal under these conditions, according to my experi-ence—even the older, larger animals.

To illustrate what I mean, consider the success of a father and son, Carl Klemencic Sr. and Jr., who hunted with me a number of year ago. It was the third week of bear season when they arrived and there was a steady drizzle falling. Conditions were ideal. I placed the two baits sev-eral miles apart late in the afternoon, knowing there was a good boar vis-iting both sites.

The location where the boy was positioned hadn't been hunted pre-viously, but the bait his father watched had been hunted on five different days during the first week of the season. A sow and cub had been seen there, and another bear that was approaching as shooting light faded was spooked as the hunter left. I had seen tracks of a decent boar at that loca-

Spring or fall, one of the best times to hunt is during a light drizzle or rain with no wind. Be sure to dress properly to avoid hypothermia.

tion, but he had never showed himself during shooting hours.

That changed at least an hour before the end of shooting time on that drizzly day. The father got a shot at 25 yards and he dropped it with at .30-30 Win. The bruin weighed 200 pounds dressed.

At about the same time, his son saw an even bigger bear. Since it was the boy's first bear hunt, I stayed with him. He was sitting with his back against a tree facing the bait and the direction I expected a bear to come from. I was seated directly behind him. The bait was situated in a small opening in a thick cedar swamp.

We heard the bear before we saw it. The animal was approaching at a fast walk, with branches and limbs cracking and popping under his weight. Instead of coming from the heart of the swamp, however, he came along the edge bordering a stand of hardwoods behind us. At first it looked as though the bruin was going to pass us on our left and continue on to the bait, which would give the boy a good shot.

When the bear was even with me, however, it turned abruptly and came directly at me. The animal was close enough at that point, and I wanted to be ready in case he ended up in my lap, so I started to raise my .30-06. The boar saw the movement and stopped no more than 30 feet away.

It would have been a simple matter for me to nail that bear, but it was the boy's hunt. I know he could see the animal, but it would have been awkward for him to turn and shoot. Before he could get off a shot, the movement would certainly spook the bear .

After pausing briefly, the bruin started to circle us. We heard him breaking brush minutes later, but he never showed himself again. If the boy had been where I was, he would have connected like his father did. I estimated that bear's live weight at more than 300 pounds. Later that week the boy connected on a sow that was about half the size of the boar we saw in the rain. The rain was probably not the only factor that resulted in such success for the father and son on their first day of hunting, but I'm convinced it was a deciding factor. I've seen it happen too many other times.

Another hunter who has hunted black bear with me a number of times, for example, connected on boars in the rain two years in a row. It was the second week of the season before Chris Schimik started hunting the first year. He was watching a bait that had been hunted the previous week. Several small bear had been sighted, but not the adult I was sure was in the area. He hunted for two days without seeing anything, then it started raining on the third day. It rained on and off, but never hard, and there was no wind.

We got wet in the morning without seeing our quarry, so we changed into dry clothes and returned in the evening. About 45 minutes after we got in position, a nice boar stepped out by the bait and Chris dropped it with a single shot from his .308 Win. That bruin dressed out between 180 and 200 pounds.

The following year, Chris hunted the first week of the season. He drew a blank on opening day. It was raining hard the morning of the second day, so we didn't hunt. It tapered off to a drizzle by afternoon, so we took up stands for the remainder of the day.

Chris didn't have long to wait before a bear appeared. However, it grabbed a mouthful of food and disappeared before he could take a shot. Twenty minutes later a larger bruin stepped into view and Chris claimed an average size boar.

The first day of my spring hunt in Colorado was cloudy with intermittent rain and no wind. I was on a bait that my partner knew was being used by a blonde bear. He said to expect activity any time after 8:00 p.m. Activity on that bait was far better than expected and I think the weather was responsible.

A red-coated bruin showed first at 7:00 p.m., an hour earlier than activity was normally noted. From that point on I saw bear on and off until it was too dark to see. I saw at least three different bear and possibly a fourth. There were at least two different blonde bear.

Why is bear hunting in the rain so good? I suspect part of the reason bear hunting during a rainy, windless day can be so productive is that the animals know from experience that they are less likely to encounter hunters under those conditions. Let's face it, hunting in the rain certainly isn't as pleasant or comfortable as on clear, dry days. As a result, there are fewer hunters afield on rainy days than on dry ones. I won't pretend to understand a black bear's power of reasoning, but I suspect that over a period of years, older bear become aware of this pattern and adjust their movements accordingly.

Black bear might also be more comfortable moving during periods of light rain, especially when the weather is warm, because the water keeps them cool when temperatures reach the 70s or 80s. Their heavy coats shed water, so getting wet doesn't concern them.

Water-soaked ground makes walking quieter for bear, too. Maybe this helps make them feel more at ease. Barometric pressure might have something to do with bear movements as well, but I haven't checked that while bear hunting under various weather conditions.

Whatever the reason or reasons, black bear are active, as a rule, on rainy, windless days. One advantage to hunters under these conditions is that their scent is usually confined to their immediate area. Rainfall tends to keep scent close to the ground. This is a big aid to hunters be-

This hunter wore chest waders in addition to his rain jacket to ward off wet weather long enough to bag this fine black bear.

cause the black bear's nose is one of its most important lines of defense. Many bear approaching feeding sites smell waiting hunters and disappear without hunters realizing it. This is less likely to happen during a light rain.

If there were a reason for not hunting black bear in the rain, it would be that the chances of losing a bear are increased because rain might wash out the blood trail of an animal that has been hit. However, this consideration should be of little concern if hunters pick their shots properly. When using a bow in the rain, a gametracking device is highly recommended.

If you plan to hunt in the rain, be prepared. During spring and fall, a rainy day can represent some of the most miserable, coldest-feeling weather imaginable. Good wool clothing will withstand a light drizzle, keeping you warm all the while. If more moisture is expected, wear quality rain gear. A poncho or parka and pants will keep you dry, but unless it is of a woven-type fabric, the noise, or rustle, it creates during movement may create a handicap and spook the bruin before you get a shot.

Always use common sense when hunting during cool, wet weather. Sitting for long hours on a stand can lead to hypothermia. If you feel seriously chilled, don't take chances. There will always be another day.

5

Hiring A Guide

Hiring a black bear guide is a lot like preparing for a hunt on your own. You have to do your homework to end up with what you want. However, in this case, hunters must select an experienced person who can help put them in position for a shot at a black bear. Hunters who don't take the time to choose guides carefully can end up dissatisfied, disappointed and worse, unless they happen to be lucky.

It is an unfortunate fact of life that all persons claiming the title of black bear guide are not deserving of the title, although I know many of them who are. Some who aren't are simply in it for the money, knowing little or nothing about black bear and how to hunt them. Others may try hard, but lack the experience or area to produce consistently, and still more rely on illegal hunting methods to fill their clients' tags.

So-called guides that fit in the above categories can generally be weeded out in the selection process, if done properly. One of the first steps in this process is deciding how you want to hunt and what services you desire from a guide. A corresponding consideration is how much money you are willing to spend for a guide's services. The services of quality guides don't generally come cheap, but there are some bargain black bear hunts available for hunters who require little assistance during a hunt.

Services
There are bear guides available who specialize in hunting with

hounds, baiting, spotting, and stalking and calling. Some use a combination of techniques in an effort to bring client and bear together. Lawrence Edwards and Wayne Bosowicz, for example, employ both bait and hounds in their hunting. Lawrence primarily relies on his hounds, but during days when there has been no success with dogs during the morning, he puts hunters on stands overlooking baits in the evening. Most of Wayne's Maine hunts are over bait, but he also maintains hounds for hunters who prefer to hunt in that fashion.

Rodger Gorham from Veneta, Oregon, is one of the guides who specializes in hunts with hounds. He sometimes starts his dogs from baits, but his hounds normally strike bear scent where animals have crossed roads; chases are started at those points. Rodger has one of the best-trained and effective packs of bear dogs I've hunted with.

Some guides provide transportation, while others expect hunters to use their own vehicles. Meals and lodging may be included as part of the package available from guides, which is the case with the hunts Jim Hefford offers in Newfoundland. I enjoyed an excellent hunt over bait out of Jim's camp one June. Other guides may simply provide lodging or expect hunters to make arrangements for their own meals and lodging, only taking care of details dealing with the actual hunt.

One of the simplest and cheapest guide services offered deals with baiting, where a guide baits a location until the hunter arrives. Once the hunter is taken to the bait, he's on his own. The potential for problems is greatest on a hunt of this type, although no guided hunt is exempt from misunderstandings and less-than-expected services. For this reason, hunters who hire bear guides should select the person they plan to hunt with carefully, and clarify in advance what they will be getting for their money.

Make A List

Once you know what type of black bear hunt you want and how much you can spend, start compiling a list of guides that may offer what you are looking for. Many guides advertise in magazines that publish hunting material, and some names can be obtained from the pages of these periodicals. State and provincial agencies that manage black bear maintain names and addresses of guides in some cases, so check with them in an effort to obtain possible additions to your list. Taxidermists can also be good contacts to get names of guides.

The North American Hunting Club maintains a list of guides for its members, along with reports, both good and bad, on hunter experiences with guides. Final additions to a list of potential black bear guides can be obtained from friends and acquaintances who have hunted with guides.

Studying a listing of approved guides is the first step in planning a successful bear hunt. The NAHC offers members a complete reference brochure.

Recommendations of reputable guides from friends are often the most valuable, because acquaintances can provide a firsthand account of a guide's performance and services, giving hunters an accurate account of what can be expected. The reason I selected Caribou Trail Outfitters based in Leoville, Saskatchewan, for a hunt in that province was due to recommendations from friend Mike Aftanas who knew outfitter Paul Marek. The referral proved to be accurate because I saw 10 different bear on a 6-day hunt. Recent experiences of friends are the most valuable, of course. A guide's services, as well as the quality of hunts offered, can change over a period of years, either for the better or worse.

Never assume guides with ads in national magazines are reputable. Anyone with enough money can place such an ad regardless of their credentials. The advertising departments of most magazines don't investigate guides who purchase space, nor should they be expected to. It is the responsibility of hunters who wish to employ guides to check them out.

Narrow your list of possible guides as much as possible, based on available information, then make an initial contact by mail or telephone. The guide selection process, by the way, is something that should be done as far in advance of hunting season as possible. Starting preparations for a guided hunt a year or more in advance is not unusual. This may be necessary in situations where licenses are limited and have to be applied for well in advance. Popular guides often book all of the hunters they can handle early.

Initial Contact

Don't ask guides for their life story on the initial contact. The services they provide, their average success, what they charge and if they have any openings are the primary bits of information that will be most helpful in determining which guide best fits your needs.

The best letters are brief and to the point. Guides don't like to read long letters any more than they like to write them. In fact, some guides may reply by telephone rather than writing, so be sure to include your telephone number and your address in your letter. Give guides at least a month to reply by mail, and longer if you write during hunting season when they are busiest. You may want to phone guides who are slow to respond, or eliminate them from consideration if a suitable guide has already been located.

Cost

Keep in mind when gathering this type of information that quality black bear hunts cost from $600 to $1,500 and sometimes more. Guides who charge less are probably providing fewer services, although some

MARCH 15TH

DEAR BEAR GUIDE:

I'M IN THE PROCESS OF PLANNING A
SPRING (OR FALL) BLACK BEAR HUNT WITH
BOW AND ARROW (OR RIFLE, MUSKET,
HANDGUN) AND AM INTERESTED IN THE
HUNTS YOU OFFER. COULD YOU PLEASE
SEND ME INFORMATION ABOUT THE SERVICES
YOU PROVIDE AND HOW MUCH THEY COST?

I AM ALSO INTERESTED IN THE RATE
OF SUCCESS YOUR HUNTERS HAVE ENJOYED
DURING RECENT YEARS AND WHAT PART
OF THE SEASON USUALLY OFFERS THE BEST
HUNTING. PLEASE INCLUDE THIS INFORMATION
WITH YOUR REPLY.

SINCERELY,

Joe Bear Hunter

When writing to a guide for information, be specific about the season and type of hunting you prefer. Don't hesitate to ask the guide to provide details about success rates.

A good guide should offer you a hunting plan covering every eventuality. Small details in planning, like transportation for your trophy, can avoid wastes of time in the field.

good part-time guides may charge less. Most guides require a deposit of up to 50 percent of the hunt cost to confirm dates for a hunt. Some charge hunters who don't connect less than those who do. When corresponding with guides in Canada, find out if their rates are in Canadian or U.S. funds.

Rates Of Success

As far as rate of success, any guide who averages 50 percent or better is doing terrific. In all fairness to guides, the success ratio need not only include bear that were actually tagged. Bear that are wounded and not recovered should have been dead bear in most cases and are the individual hunter's responsibility, and therefore shouldn't be held against the guide, unless he was negligent in attempts to find the animals. Missed shots are generally not the guide's fault, either.

So guides who put at least half of their clients in position for shots at bear, are doing good. Guides who report lower rates of success, only including actual kills in their percentages, are still doing a good job, and are being honest. Not all guides are honest, with some inflating their success ratios to attract more clients.

Follow-up

If there are questions remaining in your mind about services, fees or success of guides after they've responded to your initial letter, give them a call or write again to clarify the points in question. More information can usually be gathered over the phone much faster than by mail. If you do call guides with specific questions, write them down before placing the call, leaving room to write answers, so they won't be forgotten.

There are a number of important questions to ask of guides who will simply be baiting a spot for hunters until their arrival, then turning it over to them. One is, "Will the bait be active," meaning will the site be visited regularly by at least one legal black bear? Hunters should also determine if additional bait will be provided once the existing supply is gone, if alternate sites will be available if the bait becomes inactive or is only being visited after shooting hours, and if assistance will be provided to trail wounded animals, plus getting bagged bruins out of the woods.

References

Once you've narrowed your list of possible guides to candidates who are seriously being considered, ask them for references, hunters who have hunted with them during recent years. Ask for names, addresses and telephone numbers of unsuccessful as well as successful hunters. Try to obtain references that live as close to you as possible, then contact them by letter or telephone for their comments about the guide. Also ask them for names of other hunters you can contact. I recommend using the phone to check out references. If you do so by mail, be sure to include stamped, self-addressed envelopes for replies.

By the time references are checked you should know who you want to book a hunt with. Send in your deposit for the desired dates, requesting a receipt, and ask any last minute questions you might have such as what distance to sight your gun or bow in for and what type of clothing or footwear to bring. You should already know what your license is going to cost, plus where and when one can be obtained. Don't forget to ask if there are any special regulations or provisions you should know about. In Colorado, for instance, anyone born after January 1, 1949, must have a hunter safety card to obtain a hunting license.

If you are only interested in a trophy bear, this should have been mentioned in your initial contact. You should also spell out what you mean by a trophy. The word means something different to many hunters. It may be a bruin that weighs at least 300 pounds, one that measures six feet in length or an animal with a skull that scores at least 19 inches by Pope & Young and Boone & Crockett standards.

If you book a hunt with hounds, plan on doing some prehunt conditioning to prepare for the strenuous exercise that often comes with such a hunt. Hunters who are in poor physical shape are doing both themselves and the guide a disservice by booking a hunt with hounds. Hunters who have any handicaps, physical problems or special requirements should inform the guide of these when booking a hunt, not after arrival.

Booking Agents

An alternative to going through the process of selecting a black bear guide yourself is using a booking agent. You tell them what type of hunt you want and they arrange a hunt for you with a reputable guide. Booking agents usually receive commissions from guides, so their services shouldn't cost hunters anything extra, but check to be sure. North American Outdoor Adventures, a service to NAHC members, can be reached at 12301 Whitewater Drive, Suite 220, Minnetonka, MN 55343.

Trust Chosen Guide

After a black bear hunt is booked with a guide you are satisfied with, and you arrive on your hunt, trust your guide's judgment. He's obviously highly recommended for a reason. The guy should know how, where and when to hunt black bear in his area better than you do, so

Recommendations from friends can also be valuable in deciding on a black bear guide, as was the case when the author (right) hunted with Jim Jarvis in Colorado.

don't try something he recommends against. The biggest mistake some hunters make on guided hunts is not having confidence in their guides or not following a guide's instructions.

Some guides who use bait only hunt evenings, reserving mornings for trailing wounded bear or checking baits. Unless special arrangements have been made to hunt at other times, hunt when the guide says it's best. On days when conditions are adverse for hunting, a guide may recommend not hunting at all, with good reason. Trust your guide's judgment. I've been a guide and have hunted with guides, so I speak from experience. Some hunters simply don't give their guides enough credit once they've hired them.

And although most good guides try their hardest to get every hunter a shot at a black bear, it can't always be done. He has no control over the weather and, in many cases, other hunting pressure. And even though your guide may be knowledgeable about black bear, the animals aren't always predictable.

Guides can make mistakes or choices that turn out to be the wrong ones at a later date. However, they are human like everyone else and hunters have no right to expect super-human results from them.

To increase the chances of success, hunters should plan on booking five- to seven-day hunts with guides. It isn't unusual to lose a day or two to weather during some weeks. Even if the weather is favorable, it may take that long to get a look at a bear. Hunters who book two- and three-day hunts limit their chances of success from the start.

Hunters who don't see action on the first day or two of their hunt shouldn't become discouraged. It often takes patience and persistence to get a chance at a bear, whether hunting with a guide or on your own. Hunters who become discouraged simply don't hunt properly and reduce their chances of success regardless of their guide's performance. A bowhunter who hunted with me one year blew a chance at a bear because of a poor attitude or, perhaps, unrealistic expectations.

He was bowhunting over bait, and left his stand an hour before dark, which was prime hunting time, on the first evening of his hunt. When a nice bear finally showed on the third evening, he was totally unprepared, sitting in his treestand with his legs dangling in the air. When the hunter tried to bring his bow into play he bumped it on the stand, alerting the bear. He still got a shot as the bear walked off, but missed. If that hunter had been on his feet prepared to shoot, as he should have been, I'm sure he could have bagged that bruin.

Proper selection of a black bear guide can be a simple matter, if going on the recommendation of a friend or using the services of a booking agent. However, when doing it yourself, the process can take a lot of time and effort, as much as planning a do-it-yourself hunt. You're sure to reap the benefits of doing your homework though, when it comes time to take part in the guided black bear hunt you've chosen. That is, if you have confidence in your guide and are persistent.

6

Setting Up Baits

T here has probably been more written about black bear hunting over bait than any other technique. The reason is that it's an effective, proven method for bringing bear within range. This approach is perhaps the most effective way for a lone hunter to connect on a black bear.

Baiting is so effective it's controversial, and is not legal in all states and provinces that permit black bear hunting. The technique would result in too high a harvest in some states with limited black bear populations and/or large numbers of bear hunters. In some cases in the western U.S. and Canada, baiting is prohibited or restricted due to the fact grizzly bear would also be attracted to baits, which is an undesirable situation.

Another reason there has been a lot written about hunting black bear over bait is that there are many different ways to do it. Bait can be put on the ground, hung from trees in a variety of ways, put in barrels or placed in holes in the ground. Some states, such as Wisconsin, require that bait be placed in a hole in the ground no larger than two feet square, while others have no restrictions on the placement of bait. Be sure to understand the regulations pertaining to baiting in the state or province where you intend to hunt.

Bait Site Selection

Bait site selection is the most important aspect of this hunting method. A poorly-placed bait or a poorly-placed stand for the hunter will not produce the same results as one in a good location.

A good bait location is one placed in the vicinity of a natural food supply near security cover. Such a spot should also have a suitable place for a ground blind or treestand in position where incoming bear aren't likely to detect a hunter. Bait stations should be selected in areas where there will be little or no competition from other hunters. If several people are baiting in the same vicinity, a hunter's chances of success are lower than they would be without competition, because bear become less active as human activity increases, and with an abundance of food, bruins are more likely to feed after dark than during hours of daylight. The same bear feeding at your bait might be visiting a competitor's bait, too, and if they see and shoot the animal before you do, you're out of luck.

If baiting where hunting with hounds is also permitted, try to place baits as far as possible from roads so bear can't be winded by dogs on roads. The farther baits are from roads, the less likely bruins are to cross them to reach the food, reducing the chance of bruins leaving scent and tracks for dog hunters to find. Better yet, select bait sites in areas that aren't appealing to hunters using dogs.

Generally speaking, houndsmen prefer to hunt locations with a network of woodland trails or logging roads to increase their chances of keeping contact with their dogs and intercepting a bear ahead of the hounds. Locations with few roads are normally avoided by dog hunters because it can be easy to lose track of hounds. Locations with a number of paved roads that receive a lot of vehicular traffic are usually avoided, too, because dogs could be killed by cars if they chase a bear across a heavily traveled road.

Hunters who will be hunting on private land won't have to be as concerned about competition as those on public property, but locating a spot that meets the other criteria is just as important.

Look for bear sign to determine where the animals are or have been. It is sometimes easier to first locate a good source of natural food, then make a concerted search for bear sign in that area. In the spring, black bear do a lot of grazing on greens such as grass and clover. They also feed on roots, insects, spawning fish and carcasses of deer, elk, moose, cows and horses.

Water is important to black bear in the spring. Their systems need water after leaving dens and they drink it from creeks, rivers and lakes. The heavy cover often associated with water is also used for daytime resting areas. River valleys or drainages are natural travel routes for bear, especially during the spring.

Fruits and berries are staples for black bear during summer and fall

Fruit crops, whether wild or domestic, can be a hunter's best friend when trying to select a bait site. Fruits and berries become staples for bear during summer and early fall.

This ear–tagged blackie was spotted feeding in a picked corn field. Black bear also love crops such as oats and their signs of grazing are easy to spot.

months, although they continue feeding on insects and grass. Other favored fall foods for black bear are nuts from oak, beech and pine trees.

Once you find a food source that is being used or has been used by black bear, locate the largest chunk of heavy cover nearby where bear are likely to rest during most of the day. Select a spot to put a bait along the edge of heavy cover or in an opening somewhere inside the cover. Baits situated along the edge of heavy cover are sometimes best because visibility is usually better than in a swamp or heavy timber, both in terms of how far you can see and how long shooting light lasts. Black bear will almost always approach from a known direction from within heavy cover when baits are on the edge, whereas they may approach from any direction when a bait is in security cover.

However, bear may show up earlier at baits surrounded by thick stuff than they will on edges. In addition, there is less chance of other hunters stumbling across a bait in heavy cover versus one on the edge of it. Hunters have to weigh the pros and cons to determine what type of bait site is best. If one option doesn't work, the bait can be moved. In mountainous or hilly terrain with a scarcity of evergreen trees, bear often bed down on ridgetops, hilltops and mountain slopes.

Locations where there is a good supply of heavy cover near a lake or river are ideal for baits. There doesn't have to be food available at the

Coons and other small critters can some-times make it difficult to determine if a bear has visited the site. Place heavy ob-jects over a bait to determine if bear are visiting.

time a bait is placed in an area for it to produce results, as long as there is something that is expected to eventually bring bear into the area such as apples, wild cherries or acorns that are not yet ripe, but have been util-ized by bear in the past.

A good way to locate potential bait sites is to drive wood roads and walk overgrown trails or railroad grades while watching for bear sign and possible food sources. Once a potential spot is identified, check it out as thoroughly as possible. You may find a location with bear sign, but no food supply readily apparent. These could be bear crossings, ar-eas through which one or more bear frequently travel within their home range. Bear crossings can be good bait sites, but bait should be placed as far from roads as possible where the animals are likely to find it and other hunters aren't.

Topographical maps can be used to help locate potential bait sites, too. Look for large tracts of roadless country plus larger–than–normal swamps or patches of timber. Areas that have been logged off are worth checking out because fruit trees and berry bushes frequently grow in the openings created by logging, and the remaining stumps and logs often contain insects that attract hungry black bear.

Wildlife biologists, game wardens and conservation officers can be helpful sources of information. They spend a lot of time in the field and can sometimes direct hunters to areas where they've seen black bear or black bear sign. Loggers fit in the same category, along with other people who spend a lot of time in the outdoors, such as commercial fishermen and trappers.

Test Baits

Hunters who find spots that look as though they should be good bait sites, but can find no bear sign, can place a bait there anyway to test it. If black bear are in the area or pass through, they will find it eventually, although it may be weeks before they do. Baits in ideal bait sites should be hit in a week or less, but it can take longer if placed in areas where the natural food supply isn't presently being used. Always check state game regulations before placing test baits.

Although most baiting of black bear is done on foot, some hunters use canoes or boats to run baits along rivers or around lakes. This is a very effective approach. The only drawback is that they become inaccessible during periods of rough weather. However, hunting over bait isn't usually the best under those conditions, anyway.

Distance Off Roads

Baits should be a minimum of 100 yards from a road or trail to reduce the chances of disturbance. Most of my best baits are at least one-quarter of a mile from roads. This ends up being a lot of work hauling bait in and getting bear out, but it's worth it. The farther from roads baits are, the more comfortable bear are going to feel about feeding there before shooting light fades.

The above advice applies to public land, of course, not necessarily to private land or areas with no competition. A black bear I shot in Colorado, for example, while hunting with guide Jim Jarvis from Montrose, was taken on leased land. Consequently, we didn't have to worry about being disturbed. We were able to drive close to the bait I hunted, which was situated along a little–used tote road. I saw four or five different bear on that bait in two days before arrowing a dark brown adult male.

Placing Baits

In Wisconsin, baiters have no choice about how to place bear bait in the field. It has to go in a hole in the ground. The hole can be covered with logs to prevent smaller animals such as skunks and raccoons from getting at the bait. Hunters using this method will know a bear has been there when the logs are moved.

Where baiting restrictions such as this don't exist, hunters can choose how to leave bait at sites. The practice in Wisconsin is certainly one alternative. However, more popular procedures are to put bait in bags or containers to hang from trees. Fifty–five gallon drums are popu-

Don't underestimate a black bear's nose. It can tell him where hunters are, but it can also lead him on his first visit to your baitpile.

Place starter baits in many likely areas when you begin baiting. Once one is hit, concentrate your baiting efforts in that area. Be sure to clean up afterwards.

lar bait containers because they are big and sturdy. Some outfitters use ATVs or snowmobiles to transport bait barrels to remote locations. Smaller, lighter, metal garbage cans are also used with good success. Garbage cans are easier to carry than the larger drums. Even smaller, plastic five-gallon buckets are used by some baiters, who cover them with logs and other debris that bear have to remove to get at the bait.

Personally, I prefer to hang bait, where legal, from tree limbs. Bait is placed in plastic garbage bags, then tied to suitable limbs that are from chest to head high. I choose dead or damaged trees to hang bait in whenever possible, although any tree with sturdy limbs at the desired level is satisfactory. Small limbs that may be strong enough to hold up a bag of bait are sometimes broken off by feeding bruins. Alternatives to garbage bags for hanging bait from trees include gunny or onion sacks suspended by a piece of rope. These choices are more porous, allowing plenty of scent to escape from the bait. To make sure scent dissipates from garbage bags I put holes in the bags once they are hung. I often take pieces of food from bags and place them on limbs or in tree crotches to give off scent when starting a bait.

Attractor Scents

Bear find bait by its smell most often, so the presence of plenty of scent is important. When starting a bait I frequently use fish or meat, where legal, which becomes more odiferous the longer it ages. Although not necessary, it's also a good idea to use a strong, long-lasting liquid scent in conjunction with bait when starting out. Anise or anise extract is good, but both are expensive for small quantities. Other liquids like maple syrup work as well and are cheaper.

Don Brockman from Vesper, Wisconsin, makes an inexpensive bear potion that works. His scent includes vanilla concentrate, cinnamon and anise. Other scents he is experimenting with have, as bases, fruit-flavored syrups such as cherry, strawberry and orange. All of these scents have sweet aromas.

Guide Wayne Bosowicz swears by scents for attracting black bear to baits. He uses sweet-smelling scent for fall, and liquid that has a more "rank and rancid" odor during spring. For fall baiting, Wayne uses a beaver castor base and a "sweetener." He also uses a lot of anise, buying it in gallon containers.

Hunters can make their own scents or try those available on the market. Liquid scent can simply be applied to a tree or stump at the bait site or put on a scent pad made of cloth or cotton to hang in a tree. Film containers, like those for 35mm film, are great scent dispensers. Simply poke small holes in the container, fill it with cotton balls that are soaked

Use a drag of fat or a towel saturated with grease to help lead bear to your bait site. If a black bear comes in contact with the trail, he'll follow it.

with the scent mixture, and hang it from a nearby limb.

Scent Trails

Another technique that can increase the chances of bear finding a bait is a scent trail. This can be done by dragging fish heads or fat on a rope away from the bait, then back to it along the same course. To make sure plenty of scent is left, smear fish or fat on logs and rocks. You can also put fat or grease on the bottom of your boots to leave a scent trail.

Scent trails can be as long as you want, but one mile is generally the longest, with one–quarter to one–half mile about average. Scent trails can be left in as many directions as desired. Black bear that come in contact with scent trails usually follow them right to the bait.

Discouraging Wolves

Animals other than bear have easy access to bait on the ground. Small critters don't often eat enough to make a difference, but larger ones like wolves or coyotes can. Wolves may be attracted to baits in Canada and northern Minnesota, and coyotes are found in many of the areas occupied by black bear. One technique to discourage wolves and coyotes is to leave an item at the bait that retains a lot of human odor such as a shoe. Other items such as socks or tee shirts might work equally well. The presence of these items doesn't seem to bother black bear.

Positioning Animals

Hunters who plan to bowhunt over bait can increase the chances of getting angling-away shots by controlling the position in which animals stand to get at the food. If using barrels, they can be tied to trees leaning in one direction so bear have to stand where you want them to reach in the barrel. If putting food on the ground, it can be placed in a position where the animal can only get at it from one direction. When natural obstructions aren't available, a V–shaped structure can be constructed of logs and baited at the inside point of the structure. Cribs and anchored bait barrels work well for bowhunters who want to increase their chances of getting the best shot possible. The sides of cribs don't have to be real high or sturdy. Pieces of wood and logs can simply be piled on top of one another to make the sides.

Bait Activity

It's generally easy to determine what animals are using bear baits by the sign they leave. Black bear generally leave plenty of sign such as droppings and claw marks on trees. If bait is covered with big logs or rocks, bear are probably the only animals that will move them. Coyote and wolf scats taper to points at the end, while bear scat is more uniformly rounded or may appear as variably shaped piles of loose dung.

Raccoons, pine martens and fishers will leave claw marks on bait trees too, but their claws generally leave light scratches that usually don't penetrate through tree bark. Claw marks from bear, on the other hand, leave deep scars in the bark and lighter colored inner wood is normally visible. Ravens will also feed at bear baits, leaving white droppings on vegetation and the ground.

Ravens can be used to the hunter's advantage on baits in areas where these scavenging birds are common. Whenever ravens find a source of food, they call to each other, making a lot of noise. Bear that hear feeding calls of ravens often come to investigate. When starting bear bait, it may be to a hunter's advantage to leave some food on the ground in the open for ravens to see, while covering or hanging the rest of the bait for bear.

Where legal, it is a good idea to start baiting about a month before you plan on hunting, but a week or two of preseason baiting is often enough time. States such as Michigan and Minnesota limit the amount of time bear can be baited before the season opens. In other states such as Wisconsin, baiting is legal anytime. Some of the most successful spring baits are those that are put out during late winter when snow still covers the ground.

Caribou Trail Outfitters in Leoville, Saskatchewan, has had excellent results with this practice. Outfitter Paul Marek said he and his

Standard Bait Set-Up

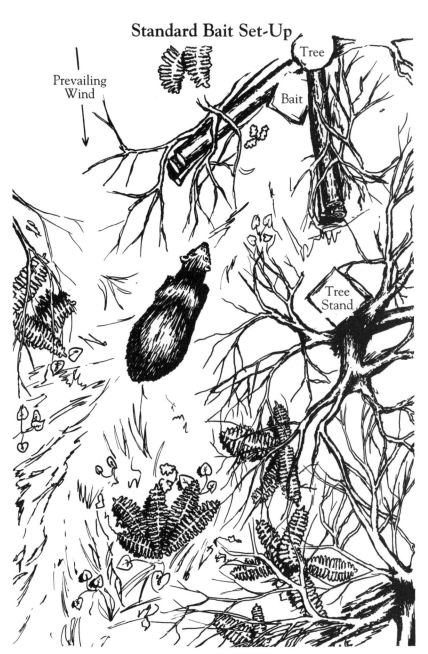

Situate your bait so that a bear must approach from one direction, presenting the best possible shot. Use prevailing winds to your favor when choosing your stand.

Digital timers, designed for monitoring trails, can be an enormous help when trying to pin down a bear's visiting hours. Once you pattern the bear, it's time to hunt.

guides use snowmobiles to haul 50-gallon drums of bait to remote locations. He added that it's easier to get baits in place in roadless country on snow, and then the food is there when bear start emerging from dens. In a six-day hunt with Paul I saw 10 different bear, three of which were brown. Bear number 10 was the biggest and was the one I shot.

When a black bear has been at a bait, the vegetation in the vicinity of the food in often trampled from the animal walking and laying on it. If there is any food remaining when the animal is full, the bear will sometimes cover it with leaves, ferns or other vegetation that is handy. Bear tracks may also be visible.

If there isn't soft sand or mud near a bait, hunters can dig a quantity of soil and leave it around the bait. This is good for saving impressions of bear tracks. Bags of flour can also be dumped on the ground at bait sites to record tracks.

Hair is another clue to look for at bait sites to determine what is visiting there. Bear hairs are long and uniform in color and either black or brown. Raccoon hairs are brown and tipped with black.

Types Of Bait

I've already mentioned a few items that can be used for bait such as fish, fat from cattle or pigs, meat scraps and bread. Here again, check local regulations to determine what baits can and cannot be used. Meat and honey can't be used in Wisconsin, for example. Bear have a sweet tooth, so any items that have sugar, such as donuts, cakes, pies and candy, are great for bait. They will also eat cheeses, fruits, vegetables and grains.

Basically, meats and sweets are the staples of bear baits any time of the year. Fat and meat scraps can be obtained from butcher shops, grocery stores and slaughterhouses. If you know a farmer who has livestock, there may be a possibility of getting the carcasses of dead animals. Beaver carcasses make great bait during spring seasons, although be sure this is legal before using them. Most states prohibit the use of carcasses of game animals such as deer.

Bakeries and donut shops are good sources for bread and sweets no longer suitable for human consumption. Some bakeries sell bags of stale bread as animal food. Plain bread can be spiced up by adding grease, gravy or molasses to it. Molasses and oats can also be used for bear bait.

Restaurants can be another good source of bait. These establishments throw away quantities of old food of all types, including meat, potatoes, gravies, soups, bread — which black bear absolutely love. As far as fish, use the heads and viscera from game fish caught on hook and line. Sometimes larger quantities from commercial fishing operations are available. It is possible to start a bait with fish, but use this type of bait as little as possible once a bait is active, because many black bear prefer other foods to raw fish. They will sometimes abandon a bait that contains only fish, or leave fish to rot, when they have a choice of other foods as a bait. Bear will eat cooked fish more readily than raw.

If possible, use a variety of items at baits. Bear will occasionally get tired of one type of food and look for something else. Bread and sweet goods are often preferred because they are light and easier to carry than other items. Jim Jarvis uses a lot of candy at his baits, but he's fortunate enough to live near a candy factory and can get quantities that are unsalable and would normally be thrown away. Otherwise, the cost to obtain candy for bear bait would be prohibitive.

Fruits such as apples sometimes make good additions to baits. These can usually be gathered from trees in abandoned orchards and other locations. Spots with one or more apple trees can be good bait sites if they are far enough from roads and don't receive much human traffic.

A black bear looks from a bait pile to check out a sound. Bear on bait will be on the lookout not only for you, but for other, larger bear as well.

When using any type of bait, but especially meat and fish, the fresher it is the better. Black bear will eat ripe and rotted meat and fish when they are hungry, perhaps as much for the insect larvae and insects on it as anything else. When they have a choice, though, such as when plenty of food is available, they prefer fresh food. If bait gets too ripe in barrels, empty it and replace it with fresh food. Holes should be put in the bottom of bait barrels to permit water and other liquids to drain out.

When using meat and fish for bait during hot weather, freeze them first and carry them in the woods frozen. They thaw quickly and will be fresher when bear find them. Meat and fish are often easier to handle when frozen.

Carrying Bait

Large canvas backpacks work well to carry food to bait sites. If you have several bear on a bait or won't be returning for about a week, carry as much bait as possible. Large quantities of bait aren't necessary though, if only feeding one bear or if the bait will be replenished every one or two days. Generally, one five-gallon pail full of bait should be plenty, unless several bear are present. Bear normally eat less during the spring than fall.

As a general rule, replenish bait at active sites every day or two as

Black bear are cautious around baits. That's what makes them so difficult to hunt. Even if they are comfortable with the site, they may only visit after dark.

Have a partner help carry bait when you go to the site. His departure may be just what a hungry black bear is waiting for, and it might result in an early visit.

hunting season approaches. Follow the same guidelines for active sites, baiting at least every other day during hunting season.

Approaching Baits

Whenever I go into a bait site I make plenty of noise and don't try to keep my approach a secret. If alone, I whistle or sing. If with someone, I talk freely. This gives any bear at the bait a warning that I'm coming and they can walk off without becoming surprised or alarmed. Before I started my whistling routine, I surprised a number of bear at baits, scaring them. In some cases they didn't return for days.

Bear know full well that people are providing the food they are eating. Hunters who try to sneak into baits to keep their presence a secret in an effort not to spook bear may do just the opposite and aren't giving the animals enough credit. Many black bear visiting baits monitor hunter movements more closely than the hunter realizes.

Some hunters believe that you can even pattern bear to a bait by letting bear know when they are coming. It's like ringing the dinner bell. If you regularly replenish a bait and make a good bit of noise while you're doing it, bear in the area will come to realize that whenever noise has subsided, the bait holds fresh food. Come hunting season you can use that Pavlovian response to your advantage.

Have a partner come to your stand with you. Make the usual ruckus while touching up the bait and have your hunting partner exit the scene making your usual amount of noise. As things quiet down with you in your stand, the bear may not make you wait too long!

Keeping Sites Clean

It is the bait hunter's responsibility to keep all baits clean of debris. This is required by law in most areas where baiting is allowed. All papers, plastic, bottles, cans and boxes should be cleaned up at bait sites during each visit.

When using barrels or buckets, put only edible food items in them. The same applies to bags and sacks hung in trees. Torn bags and pieces of them should be picked up and removed and replaced with fresh ones on each visit. If there are bones too large for bear to eat, these should also be removed.

Baiters in Wisconsin and Michigan, to name just two examples, have no choice. The law prohibits the use of any paper, plastic, cardboard, glass or metal at bait sites. One of the major reasons the law was established was to keep the woods clean. Hunters can keep bait sites clean without a lot of effort.

7

Hunting Over Bait

Consider a hunt on which my brother was trying to fill a black bear tag by hunting over bait. We were using an old, roofless shack as a blind in a small clearing on the edge of thick cover. Several bear were visiting the bait regularly. While Bruce peered out of a glassless window frame at the bait, I sat on the top of the opposite wall where the roof once was with a camera, hoping to get some action photos of Bruce shooting a bear.

A bruin that my brother did not see approached the bait. The animal noiselessly slipped up to the edge of the opening and sat down. The distance that separated the bear and Bruce was less than 50 feet! Thick growth of leafed saplings on the edge of the clearing blocked the animal from Bruce's view.

After testing the breeze, the cautious bruin picked up my brother's scent and slowly faded out of my sight, never having made a single sound to give away its presence. If I hadn't been there, Bruce would not have known a bear had been within miles. Black bear have excellent hearing and a super sense of smell, often enabling them to detect the presence of a hunter watching a bait without giving the hunter any clue of their presence. Once bear sense a person at a bait they may leave the area entirely or revert to nocturnal visits, at least for a while.

When it comes to the animals' ability to detect and avoid the presence of a hunter, bear hunting over bait is very similar to ambushing them at natural food supplies. In fact, there is a greater chance of bear pinpointing hunters at bait sites than elsewhere because human scent is frequently encountered at bait sites and, for this reason, bear are apt to approach them more cautiously than sources of natural food.

It isn't unusual for bruins to circle a bait before approaching. Others may sit down just out of sight listening and testing air currents with their noses for up to 30 minutes before deciding to show themselves. In either case, if a bear picks up a hunter's scent or the hunter makes a noise that tips the bear off, such as slapping a mosquito or coughing, good-bye bear.

The next time the same bear visits that bait it will be even more cautious. If the wind is right, if the hunter is in the right position and doesn't blow it, there is a chance of scoring. As is turned out, Bruce eventually killed a bear at the site where one slipped away without him knowing it was there. What made the difference is that he changed positions to the other side of the clearing where the breeze was more favorable for him, considering the bruin's approach. There was an old outhouse on that side of the overgrown clearing that served as a blind. Two days after the bear slipped away on him, Bruce dropped a bruin, which may or may not have been the same one, in its tracks with a .30-30 Win. at a distance of about 15 yards.

Stand Location

Stand selection is obviously important when hunting black bear over bait. Select a position downwind from the bait, as well as from the area from which bear are expected to approach. Elevated positions like those in trees, where legal, can reduce the chances of bear winding hunters, but they certainly don't eliminate the possibility and won't if they aren't in the right location. Stands on the ground can be good, too, provided the wind is right and there is enough cover.

A black bear's eyesight is its weakest sense, so a lot of cover isn't necessary to remain unseen as long as movement is kept to a minimum. Bear see movement more readily than stationary forms and can easily identify its source. When hunting from the ground I use natural cover as much as possible, often simply sitting against a tree trunk to break my outline. Ferns, blowdowns, stumps, rocks, old buildings and more can be used as blinds that are part of the natural surroundings. If you prefer, a blind can be constructed.

When hunting from the ground, try to select a stand location where a bear isn't likely to approach from the rear. Some positions that are generally good for this are against a rock wall, along the edge of a lake or in an opening overlooking the edge of heavy cover. If hunting with a rifle and the cover is open enough, it may be possible to sit up to 200 yards

A bowhunter draws on a black bear angling away from him as it feeds on a bait. Bowhunters must place themselves close enough for a clean shot.

Treestands over bait must be comfortable enough to allow the hunter to remain quiet for long periods of time. A good seat is a real plus.

from a bait where the chances of being smelled, heard or seen are slim indeed. I know a number of people who have done this, setting up a rest to shoot from at their stand to ensure accurate bullet placement.

In many cases it won't be possible to wait for a bear to arrive at a bait from that distance. The terrain and cover usually dictates much closer shooting. Fifty yards is probably average for most shots at black bear over bait with rifles. I would want to be within 30 yards when hunting with muzzleloader, shotgun or handgun. Twenty yards is the maximum distance I recommend for bowhunting at bait sites. The closer the better is my philosophy when hunting with bow and arrow from baited stands, with 10 yards my preferred distance.

Blinds or stands should be constructed or positioned in advance of opening day to give bear a chance to get used to them. Hunters may even want to leave clothing with their scent on it in blinds, so bruins will grow accustomed to human scent in that location. If bait activity drops off when this is done, forget it. Don't worry if unable to put a stand up ahead of time. I've positioned them the day before I hunted as well as the same day I hunted and enjoyed success.

Climbing Bear

Some black bear become so accustomed to ground blinds and tree stands positioned ahead of the season that they take a liking to them, either crawling or climbing into them out of curiosity or to use them for taking a nap. I know of a number of cases where this has happened both before and during hunting seasons. When in tree stands I've had black bear stand up against the base of my tree a number of times, as if thinking about joining me, although they may have just been checking my scent out on the tree trunk itself. In none of the cases did the bear actually try to climb the tree. I attempted to photograph one of the animals and it simply walked off, pausing to look back at me over its shoulder before walking out of sight.

Black bear that do climb into ground blinds or toward treestands aren't necessarily interested in their occupants. The animals may simply be curious or may be repeating what they did before, using the stands that were previously unoccupied. I'm convinced that due to the poor eyesight of black bear, they sometimes mistake hunters in trees for other bear, especially if the wind isn't in their favor.

If in a treestand and a bear starts climbing your tree, the animal can often be stopped by revealing your presence. Attracting its attention by waving a hand is often enough. If that doesn't work, stand up or move to a position where you are in full view. Try hollering next.

Occasionally, a black bear will climb a tree aggressively and may be intent on attacking. On a spring hunt in Saskatchewan, Michigan, bowhunter Mike Bowers was attacked by a sow with cubs after one of the cubs climbed the tree he was in. Fortunately, he was able to fight her off and only suffered minor injuries to a leg.

Hunters who find themselves in similar situations are often forced to shoot the animal. Both a bow and gun can be carried afield while bear hunting in many Canadian provinces and I often do so where this is legal. A rifle is more effective than a bow when faced with an aggressive bear. Another reason I carry a rifle when bowhunting for bear, where this option is legal, is to fall back on in case I see a trophy bear I want that does not offer a bow shot.

Make yourself as comfortable as possible at your stand to reduce the amount of movement necessary during the long hours you may be there. It's okay to shift positions occasionally, just do so slowly and as quietly as possible. I sometimes take advantage of the noise created by a passing jet or a gust of wind to shift positions so if I do make some noise, it won't be real obvious.

Clothing

Camouflage clothing is a good choice for stand hunting, although any garments that blend in with your surroundings are fine. I've had excellent success with Realtree camo. Michigan is one state that requires bear hunters using firearms to wear a hat, vest or coat of fluorescent orange material. Both bow and gun hunters after bear in Saskatchewan even have to wear full suits of white, red or orange, and a red or orange hat. Bear do have color vision, so hunters wearing clothing that does not blend in with their surroundings can reduce their chances of being seen by utilizing cover as much as possible to stay out of an incoming animal's view. Wear garments made of soft, nonabrasive material that won't make noise when you move.

Biting Insects

Mosquitoes and black flies can sometimes be a problem when hunting over bait during warm weather, especially in the spring. Black flies are notorious for climbing up pant legs and sleeves, so be sure to take measures to prevent this from happening by closing them off with rubber bands or tape, or tuck pant legs in the tops of boots. Wear light cotton gloves that can pull over the ends of sleeves. Headnets will protect face and neck. Mesh jackets with headnets attached are designed to protect hunters from biting insects.

Repellent can be used as added protection, or by hunters who choose not to wear protective clothing. Many hunters prefer products with *Deet* that are relatively odorless because they are effective at keeping most biting insects at bay for long periods of time.

Cover Scents

Hunters concerned about their scent or that of an insect repellent they are using may want to use one of the many cover scents currently available. Skunk perfume is an effective cover scent because skunks are often attracted to bear baits, occasionally exposing black bear to their scent firsthand. Anise or anise extract can also be used as a cover scent while watching baits.

Treestands

I prefer portable treestands to permanent ones because if one position doesn't work, it's a simple matter to move to another. With time, bear using a bait may learn where hunters are usually stationed in permanent stands, and won't show themselves during shooting hours. A hunter who waits in a new place under these circumstances can sometimes harvest that bruin. Treestands for black bear hunting need not be more than 10 to 15 feet above the ground.

One problem with some portable climbing stands is that they can make a lot of racket going up and down the tree when hunters come and go. A way to avoid this is to install steps in or on the tree trunk so it is possible to climb in and out of the stand without unnecessary noise, especially at the end of the day.

When To Hunt

There is no question that more black bear are shot at bait sites during afternoon and evening hours than during any other time of day. Those hours are prime feeding times for bruins. However, another reason most bear are shot then is that's when most hunters are hunting. Morning hunting for black bear over bait is terribly underrated, in my opinion. I've seen bear at bait virtually every hour of the day and have had excellent success during mornings, and midday can be good, too.

Most hunters who don't hunt mornings claim they are concerned about scaring bear off the bait when approaching at that time of day. Hunters who follow my recommendations about whistling or talking as they approach a bait don't have to worry about that, regardless of what time of day it is. Yes, bear will leave the bait when hearing a hunter approach, but they won't be scared and they will return if nothing is different than when the bait was replenished before the season.

Do everything the same as you would any other time when checking the bait, only when done get in your blind or treestand and wait quietly.

As you approach your bait, whistle to move off any bear that might be feeding, then take your stand and wait. Most often they'll return when things quiet down.

If a bruin was there when you arrived, it may simply wait until it thinks you are gone, then return to check out what's new. If all goes well, the bruin will get an unexpected surprise.

I know this happens because I've seen it myself, and others hunting with me have also experienced it. One morning I dropped a bowhunter off at a bait and left whistling as I always do. The archer later told me that he could still hear me whistling when a black bear appeared to investigate what I left behind.

Baits that are routinely replenished during morning hours are most likely to be visited by bear during mornings and the same with baits checked during afternoons or evenings. It can work the other way, too, depending on each bear's feeding time. To take the best advantage of my hunting time, I always try to hunt three or four hours during the morning, take a break, then return sometime in the afternoon. If the bait has been hit during my absence, I make it a point to hunt through midday the following day, providing I don't connect before dark.

Timers

Timers make it possible to determine when baits are being hit without the hunter being there. A Trailtimer records the first visit to a bait and a Trail Monitor provides a continuous record of visits. Trailtimers are digital watches that record the time a bait is visited. When a bear pulls or breaks a thread running from the bait to the timer, the time is recorded.

This can also be accomplished with the type of battery operated alarm clock that has hands if it is rigged properly.

The Trail Monitor uses an invisible infrared sensor that covers an area 90 degrees wide out to a distance of 50 feet to detect black bear visits. The unit automatically records, in 15 minute increments, the time, date and duration of visits. The monitors are strapped to trees at the desired height and their sensitivity can be adjusted to only detect bear, ignoring visits by birds and small mammals. This may be the best way to gather information on a bait you are planning to hunt without actually being there yourself, and the device will save you time when you start hunting.

One of the advantages of timers is that they can help hunters determine which baits are being visited during legal shooting hours and which are the best ones to hunt. It can be a waste of time to hunt baits only hit at night. Keep in mind that bear don't always feed at the exact same time every day, so the information provided by timers should be used to get a general idea about when the best times to hunt might be.

If I had a choice, I would much rather shoot a bear during the morning than evening. The light is generally better and there's plenty of daylight remaining to track a bear, if necessary, and get the carcass out of the woods. Bait hunters who insist morning hunting is a waste of time can do what they like, but I can't help chuckling to myself when I hear or read words to that effect. I know better, and now you do, too.

Whenever I'm going to be occupying a bait stand for a long period of time I make it a point to carry a plastic bottle with me to urinate in. I refrain from urinating at a bait site either before or during hunting season. It makes little sense to use scents to attract bear to a spot, then deposit human scent that may be offensive to them.

Detecting Bear

While waiting at a bait station remain constantly alert. Become familiar with the sights and sounds of your surroundings. A black spot that wasn't there before may be a bear lurking just out of sight. An unusual sound may mean the same thing.

For animals of their size, black bear can be amazingly quiet while moving through thick brush. In fact, it isn't unusual to see them before you hear them, if you hear them at all. Their thick foot pads are like cushions, permitting the animals to walk noiselessly, if they choose to. A sound to listen for that can be a good hint that a bruin is nearby is a snapping twig. As black bear cautiously approach a bait they sometimes step on twigs or branches that won't support their weight, giving away their presence to hunters who know how to interpret such sounds.

Trailtimers are electronic devices designed to record the time of a bear's first visit to a bait. A set-string triggers the single recording.

The Trail Monitor uses infrared signals to make a continuous record of bear activity.

Occasionally, a bear will make a noisy approach to a bait, making no attempt at caution, breaking branches and rustling leaves with every step. As a general rule, these are dominant animals and have not had any bad experiences at that bait or any other. Bruins that are cautious and nervous may have been shot at before or are subordinates and want to avoid an unpleasant experience with a hunter or a larger bear that is also using the bait.

If a yearling to average-size bear shows up at a bait and is antsy, it may be because of other, bigger bear in the area. Some subordinate bear grab a mouthful of food and leave right away to avoid a confrontation. Hunters who hope to bag a better-than-average bear should be patient when observing this type of behavior. If hunting during June, a small to average-size bear may be a sow in heat and will soon be followed by a boar.

In situations where sows with cubs are involved, they are generally together during the spring, coming into a bait at the same time. By fall though, it isn't unusual for cubs to arrive at a bait before their mother. Jim Haveman, for example, had a pair of cubs come to a bait he was watching, and he was convinced they were orphans when their mother finally showed herself a full 15 minutes later. Keep this in mind when hunting a state or province where cubs are protected. The size of bear can be terribly difficult to judge at times, but if an animal looks small, it's best to be safe rather than sorry—don't shoot. Sows with cubs are almost universally protected during spring seasons.

Some cubs are mistakenly shot as legal bear every year due to the difficulty in judging the size of some animals in some situations. However, I think there are also some legal bear that have been mistaken for cubs. Size alone can sometimes be misleading. Some yearling sows are as small as male cubs.

The easiest way to tell the difference between a cub and yearling is to look at the teeth. If the animal has canine teeth in the front of both jaws, it's a yearling. Cubs have smaller milk teeth in place of canines.

There are other sounds to listen for besides those the bear themselves might make that may serve as clues that a bruin is nearby. Bluejays, for instance, have tipped me off about an incoming bear a number of times. A group of jays will make a big fuss when they see a black bear, although they will do the same when observing other predators, too, both the landbound and winged types. Red squirrels will also chatter and scold the bear from safe perches in trees.

Persistence Pays

If bait has been hit by one or more bear regularly before the season, but you fail to see a bruin after a day or two of hunting, try not to get discouraged. Persistence often pays off when black bear hunting. It may simply require a change in the weather before a bear presents itself for a shot.

If at all possible, don't hunt when there is a strong wind blowing and constantly changing directions. The odds of going undetected by a bear under these conditions are slim to none. It is also best to forget hunting during heavy rain because black bear seldom move during this weather condition. Days with little or no wind are great for bear hunting over bait. A little rain doesn't hurt, either. Times before and after storms or unsettled weather can also be terrific for bear hunting over bait.

One year I hunted a hot bait for five days in a row before I finally saw a bear and tagged it. The bait was only hit at night until the fifth day when an animal strolled into view two or three hours before sunset. If you are unwilling to wait for the weather to change, or are convinced bear are feeding primarily at night, the use of something appealing to the animals such as candy or honey, where legal, might lure them into view. Heating honey or grease on a Sterno or backpack stove while on stand, may lure bear in during shooting hours.

Nocturnal Bear

Another trick that might change the habits of nocturnal bear is to use a call to lure them in. Bear calls that imitate the cries of a dying rabbit or a

Black bear can approach a bait with all the stealth of a whitetail. They may sit just outside a hunter's view, testing the wind and looking for danger.

Black bear have excellent hearing and will pick up the slightest sound a hunter may make. This bruin sat out of bow range as he studied a bait.

fawn in distress can also be used to bring bear into view.

Feeding habits of nocturnal bear can also be changed by carrying bait out with you at the end of the day, moving the bait closer to a bruin's bedding area or changing stand locations. If bait sites are in open habitat where bear don't feel comfortable during shooting light, hunters will seldom see bruins. Moving the bait into heavy cover may help. Hunters can increase their chances of ambushing late-feeding bear by posting somewhere along the approach trail rather than at the bait.

Abandoned Baits

Baits are sometimes abandoned by bear for any number of reasons. A hunter's presence at a bait, or hunting pressure in the general area sometimes causes bruins to change their habits. Of course, if the bear you are hunting is killed by another hunter, you have invested a lot of time for nothing.

The sudden availability of a natural favored food supply may lure bear away from bait, too. In the spring, for example, bear may leave baits to feed on grass for about a week, then return to baits once their craving for greens have been satisfied. Availability of apples, acorns or beech nuts may affect baiting during the fall. During years of beech nut abundance, bear frequently abandon baits to gorge themselves on the nutritious nuts.

There is no question that baiting success is better during years with a scarcity of natural food. Bear will generally return to baits they've left after hunting pressure subsides, or their taste for natural food is satisfied, but it may take weeks for that to happen. It is normally a good idea to prepare one or two alternate bait sites on the chance that something happens at your preferred location to reduce the possibility of success.

Multiple Harvests

Most hunters like to hunt virgin baits, those that haven't been hunted before. However, previous hunting pressure may not make any difference, especially on baits being visited by a number of black bear. The bait I hunted with Jim Jarvis in Colorado one spring is a prime example. Another bowhunter bagged a bear from the bait I hunted the week before I arrived. I nailed one of four or five different bear seen on that bait in two days, and two days after I connected, another bear was taken from that bait.

All three animals harvested there were boars. Some locations are simply attractive to bear for one reason or another and hold lots of animals at certain times of the year. Bruins that are shot are sometimes replaced by others. On my Colorado hunt, a breeding sow may have been responsible for attracting boars to that particular bait. Good bait sites usually remain that way year after year, unless too many animals are harvested from the area or something happens to change the habitat. I know of some baits that produce at least six bear a year.

Michigan bowhunter Phil Grable probably holds the record for the most black bear shot at a bait in the shortest period of time. He bagged four bruins at the exceptional bait with bow and arrow over a span of 42 minutes. This took place in Ontario during 1969 or 1970, according to Grable, and there was no limit on black bear in the province, or at least where he was hunting, at the time. Grable was testing some new bowhunting tackle on that hunt, so he took advantage of the liberal limits to give it a good workout, and it performed well.

Two of the four bruins Grable arrowed that evening dropped where hit, and a third only ran a short distance before dropping when still in Phil's sight. Other bear that came in later smelled the dead bear, but the carcass didn't bother them. They continued on to the bait.

The fourth and last bruin for the action-packed evening was the only one that made it into nearby cover, leaving Grable's sight before going down.

Second Chance

If a black bear is hit at a bait, but not hurt seriously, the animal may return, giving the hunter another chance. I can think of two cases off-hand where this has happened. One year Bruce Wood hunted a bait with me on the opening day of Michigan's bear season. He was using archery equipment and hit a bear first thing in the morning.

We trailed the animal for a long distance with little blood and eventually lost the trail. The following evening I was hunting the bait myself when a bear cautiously stuck its head into view by the bait, then moved ahead so I could see its shoulder. I anchored the sow on the spot with a .30-60 and, upon examining the animal, found Bruce's broadhead embedded in the skull. It was in heavy bone where it didn't do any damage, not penetrating far enough to reach the brain.

Francis McCarthy hit a bear with an arrow that ricocheted along its ribs, although at the time he thought the arrow penetrated the body cavity. I tried, unsuccessfully, to locate that bear with one of my hounds. Some time later the same animal gave Fran another chance and he made good on it.

The End Of The Day

When shooting light fades and I'm ready to leave a treestand for the day I often whistle when climbing down on the chance a bear might be nearby. The whistle prevents the animal from approaching any closer than it already is without alarming it. If using a ground blind, I may simply walk away as quietly as possible. However, if I have reason to suspect a bear is nearby I will whistle as I depart. Arrangements can also be made for one hunter to pick up a partner, whistling as he approaches the bait, then both can leave together without making any bear in the area overly suspicious. The buddy system is especially useful in situations where a bruin appears as a hunter is getting ready to leave and it's too dark to shoot. The bear will leave when the partner approaches without the hunter having to give himself away.

Some seasoned black bear know what's happening at a bait at all times, aware that hunters are stationed there during hours of daylight, regardless of what precautions are taken. These animals may simply approach a bait so close, then wait for darkness and the departure of resident hunters before moving in to feed. One of the biggest black bear I've had a chance at did this to me.

The author used his bow to bag this fine black bear from a bait site in the province of Saskatchewan, a region known for trophy black bear.

It was late in the season when I started baiting him. An experienced hunter had seen him earlier and estimated his weight at 600 pounds. The animal was eating everything I put out on a daily basis. After several days of consistent action on the bait I decided to try for him, using a Hawken .50 caliber muzzleloader made by Thompson/Center Arms. It was loaded with a 370-grain maxi-ball.

I was sitting on the ground about 20 yards from the bait on the edge of a swamp. It must have been 20 to 30 minutes before shooting light faded when I heard subtle sounds that signified an approaching bruin. However, nothing showed, so I had to leave. The hammer on the rifle was cocked, with a cap in my hand ready to put on the nipple when, and if, the bear appeared.

Before standing to leave I lowered the hammer, which clicked twice. At the sound, the bear, which had been waiting just out of sight, made a bound or two deeper into the swamp, then started pacing back and forth, grumbling, growling and breaking branches. He was making a lot of noise in an effort to intimidate me. That bear was hungry and wanted me out of the way so he could eat. It worked. I left in a hurry with my hackles raised.

That was the closest I came to that bear. After that evening he either waited until full dark to approach the bait or patiently remained quiet when it came time for me to leave. However, he kept visiting the bait at night. I could have had another crack at that trophy if I would have organized a hunt with hounds. In fact, that may have been the best way to try for that bruiser in the first place, but the season ended before such a hunt could be arranged.

8

Introduction To Dogging Bear

T rophy black bear are bagged over bait and with hounds. But hounds are the best alternative to try for a big bruin that is stuck on a nocturnal feeding schedule. Hounds will follow him to his daytime lair and drive him out to where hunters can get a shot. Other times, dogs will bay him or tree him in a position where hunters can move in for the harvest, assuming, of course, that all goes as planned.

As with baiting, everything doesn't always happen the way it is supposed to. Black bear normally have plenty of opportunity to escape hounds, and they usually take advantage of it.

Black bear hunting with hounds is a darn exciting way of going about trying to fill a tag, whether trophy hunting or with any legal bruin. In fact, the excitement is often the same during any chase regardless of whether or not the bear is actually seen. The chase is the major part of the hunt. Some of the most exciting and enjoyable bear hunts with hounds that I've been on have been during training or pursuit seasons when just cameras, not guns or bows, are permitted, guaranteeing the bear's survival to run another day.

Enjoyment of the chase is really heightened when one or more of the dogs on a bear's trail is your's. Friendly rivalry among houndsmen, based on whose dog is alleged to be putting on the best performance, is a part of this type of hunting. It takes a special hound with the nose, endurance, courage, brains and speed to make a good bear dog. And it takes special people to raise and run these hounds. I'm pleased to say I've known both special dogs and special people who practice this particular approach to black bear hunting.

Dog Breeds

The breeds of hounds generally used to hunt black bear are Plott, Walker, blueticks, black and tans, and redbones. Plotts are among the most popular of these bear hunting breeds today, but there are some fine bear dogs representing other breeds as well. Not all of the best bear dogs are purebreds. A couple of the best hounds I've seen in action are owned by Lawrence Edwards, and they are part Airedale, although they look like Plott. Some houndsmen also breed a strain of pit bull into their dogs.

The best bear dogs generally weigh between 40 and 65 pounds. Hounds in that weight range are generally quick and agile enough to harass a bear at close quarters and dodge out of the way when necessary, plus they are usually fast enough to catch a bear in the first place. Hounds heavier than 65 pounds tend to be slower and have a better chance of getting hurt or killed in a bear fight. D. DeMoss claims to have harvested 2,000 black bear in front of hounds, most of them in Washington when working for timber companies on damage control programs. A couple of his better dogs were females weighing $42^1/_2$ and 43 pounds.

There are exceptions to weight limitations, though. A Plott named Tiger Two owned by Leo Dollins is an example. The male was a big dog, weighing 80 to 85 pounds, and he delighted in chasing big bear, according to Leo. It was a big bear that eventually killed Tiger Two when he was seven years old.

A perfect dog should have a nose good enough to smell scent that is at least 10 hours old and have the ability to follow an old trail until the bear is jumped. The dog should also be able to tree the animal and remain treed until hunters arrive, even if it takes them hours to get there. Such a dog should also have a steady, loud mouth, enabling hunters to locate the tree.

Some hounds used for bear hunting have these abilities, but they aren't encountered every day, by any means. Although one dog can tree a black bear, and it has been done many times, it usually takes teamwork on the part of a number of dogs to see a bear chase to a successful conclusion.

Anywhere from three to six dogs comprise a good pack size for chasing black bear. In situations where more than three hounds are used, one to several members of the pack are often young dogs in the process of learning from their more experienced packmates. It is possible to use too many dogs on a chase, sometimes resulting in confusion and a hunt

Plott hounds, like this one belonging to Lawrence Edwards, are one of the most popular breeds for dogging bears. Plott color is often brindle, but can be all black.

This black and tan hound is on the trail of a black bear where it crossed a road in Michigan. Most bear can stay ahead of dogs for great distances.

that ends sooner than it should, while the bear remains safe and sound. In cases where large packs of dogs bay a bear on the ground and there's a fight, a hound or two may be hurt unnecessarily because their packmates got in their way when trying to dodge out of the bear's way. States such as Michigan and Wisconsin have laws limiting bear dog packs to six, with no relaying of dogs permitted.

Treeing

A treed bear is the desired outcome of most dog races, but this does not always happen. Some bear simply refuse to climb, and in other cases the dogs don't have what it takes to force a bear up a tree. It generally takes pressure to make bear climb, which translates into constant barking on a bruin's heels or in its face and/or biting the bear's flanks whenever possible. The combination of hunters and hounds is sometimes what it takes to put a bear up. A bruin that encounters people ahead of it with dogs close behind may tree.

Lawrence Edwards has helped his dogs tree bear a number of times in an effort to help clients he was guiding bag a bear. He said the technique he uses works 60 to 70 percent of the time. Edwards employs this unique approach to treeing black bear on animals his dogs have at bay, usually after the client has tired and can't keep up with the chase. When the guide catches the hounds and bear, he charges at the bruin while hollering and firing a handgun in the air. That's more than most bear can take. As a result, they run as hard as they can, tire quickly, then climb a tree.

Unless pressured in this fashion, some bear, especially bigger-than-average animals, travel at a leisurely pace ahead of hounds, stopping occasionally to face the dogs, and never tire. Lawrence said he has helped tree 8 to 10 bear by pulling this trick. One of those bear was the heaviest any of his clients have tagged, weighing 540 pounds.

"That bear let me come from here to the tent (about 15 to 20 feet)," Edwards said. "All the time he was looking over his shoulder right at me. It looked like he was never gonna break. Then he just mowed a path out of there." The big bear went out of sight over a ridge and climbed an enormous white pine.

It takes an exceptional pack of dogs and hunters to consistently tree

Roger Gorham releases his Walker hounds on a bear track in Oregon. Most experienced houndsmen prefer a pack size of three to six dogs.

black bear. By consistently I don't mean on every race. Houndsmen who average a bear for every three chases, whether treed or shot on the ground, are doing terrific. A lot of training and conditioning are required to produce a top-notch pack of hounds.

Training

The more practice dogs get chasing bear before hunting season opens, the better condition they will be in once it's time to hunt seriously, and the better they will be able to perform. The same applies to hunters. Short of actual field experience, hounds can be conditioned for bear hunting by "roading" them, which involves letting them run ahead of or behind a vehicle for exercise until they tire. It is best to get dogs accustomed to running both in front of and behind hunting vehicles on roads that don't have much traffic.

The reason for this training is that in hunting situations a good way to start a chase is to let an experienced and trustworthy dog go ahead of vehicles to locate where a bear crossed. When roading dogs in front of a vehicle let them go at their own pace. Hunters can set a faster pace when roading dogs behind a vehicle.

There are opportunities to condition bear dogs in other ways. I've heard about one houndsman who hooks his dogs up to a merry-go-round type arrangement in his backyard for exercise. The hounds run in circles for hours at a time, toughening pads, plus building muscles and endurance.

When it comes to training pups to hunt black bear, the best approach is to turn them loose with seasoned veterans. Experienced hounds make good teachers. It is important for pups to get as much exposure to other dogs as possible so they will be accustomed to hunting as a team. Males that have a tendency to fight with other dogs at any time detract from a pack's effectiveness and can ruin a hunt. Fortunately, most hounds are easygoing.

In situations where a dog shows fighting tendencies, efforts should be made to discourage this behavior. One option is to expose the hound to others while on a long rope so a fight can be ended quickly and the dog disciplined should a fight start. A shock collar can also be used to discourage fighting. Such a collar can be employed to give a dog an electric shock when it shows an inclination to fight.

Training some bear dogs also involves discouraging them from chasing or showing interest in non-target animals such as deer and porcupines. Shock collars are widely used for breaking hounds on deer. To do this, dogs are often taken into areas where there are a lot of deer. This can be done during chance encounters, too, and houndsmen often carry shock collars in their vehicles for this reason. Dogs that show any interest in deer scent are shocked until they associate that smell with pain, and lose interest.

Pups that are taught the meaning of the word "no" can be discouraged from chasing species such as deer by repeated use of the word when exposing them to deer scent. I used this technique with success to break a Plott pup.

Bear dogs are often wrongfully accused of chasing deer when whitetails are seen running out of an area where hounds are driving. In most cases, deer are simply disturbed by the barking of dogs on a bear's trail and leave the area as the sound draws close to them. A bruin may cross a road a long distance ahead of hounds and when deer cross in the same area just ahead of dogs it is easy to get the wrong impression. Hounds that prefer chasing deer to a bear are of no value to bear hunters and are eliminated from a pack immediately.

Running Raccoons

Many a bear dog has gotten its start on raccoons. Raccoons are good for training pups because they tree readily and don't travel as far as most bear. The best time to train pups on raccoons is when there is snow on the ground, either during early fall or spring when raccoons are active. Under these conditions the dog handler can see tracks and encourage the hound to follow the right course, in addition to helping the dog get back on the right track if it wanders off the trail.

Once a raccoon is treed, the dog should be praised and encouraged to bark as long as possible. It helps to bring a treat to give the hound at that point. A way to train dogs to tree for great lengths of time after they learn to trail on their own is to delay arrival at the tree. Stop when still out of sight of the dog and wait 5 or 10 minutes before going to the hound to praise it and perhaps give it a reward. The time it takes to reach a tree can be gradually lengthened until a hound will stay treed for an hour or more. In real hunting situations it can often take that long for hunters to arrive. Exercises of this type builds the dog's confidence in its master, knowing he will eventually show up with a reward.

Scent Trails

A technique for getting pups interested in following bear scent is to leave a scent trail by dragging a piece of bear hide or head. Be sure to make several turns rather than going in a straight line, so that the dogs will learn to check for changes in direction, which bear in the wild do constantly. Make sure the hound is out of sight when leaving the scent trail, and hide the item at the end of the trail. Start the dog at the begin-

Not all treed bears are shot. Some are run during training seasons to help dogs and hunters gain condition and experience.

Some houndsmen employ open boxes in their vehicles to allow hounds to scent a bear trail while the entire unit is moving down the backroads.

ning of the trail and encourage it to follow, then reward the dog if successful in the trailing effort. Try to avoid leaving the scent trail in the same manner and the same place every time. Otherwise a dog may simply run to the location where it expects the head or hide to be hidden.

Most hunters don't have the space, time or money to train and keep large packs of bear dogs. However, if each member of a group of hunters houses one or two hounds, there should be enough dogs to hunt with, plus some reserves.

Getting Started

Hunters who haven't tried dogging bear, but would like to get involved, should try to arrange to go along on a hunt with someone in their area. Joining a bear hunting club or meeting a fellow NAHC member in *North American Hunter's* "Meeting Place" would be a good first step. Most groups of recreational hunters are willing to show a newcomer the ropes, and some guides may be willing to take a novice along in exchange for assistance with handling clients. If you don't live in bear country where hunting with hounds is permitted, you may want to hire a guide to introduce you to this fascinating and sometimes frustrating bear hunting technique.

I was fortunate enough to be able to tag along with a group of dog hunters in the Munising area of Michigan's Upper Peninsula to get my feet wet. I did, indeed, get my feet wet, as well as a camera, when wading across a river to follow the dogs on my introductory hunt. Hunts with Dan Flynn and crew were usually weekend family affairs with children and wives often going along, which is common among dog hunting groups. This fact reflects the universal appeal and satisfaction provided by participating in this form of bear hunting. Dogs aren't the only members of the chase that work as a team. The dog handlers and other members of the party do, too. It's one big team effort.

If a bear is solidly treed, word goes out to everyone on the hunt, and no action is taken until everyone who wants to be there arrives at the tree. As a general rule, the first hunter to the tree can claim the bear. However, on social hunts of the type, group members who have never bagged a black bear are often designated as shooters.

It isn't unusual for some houndsmen to lead their dogs away from a treed bear to let the animal run another day. In situations where the bear is taken, the harvest is generally earned. Even though only one tag is filled in such situations, all members of the party usually feel a measure of success, no matter what role they played. This is one way that bear hunting with hounds differs from most other techniques.

A bear bagged over bait, for instance, usually gives the greatest sense of accomplishment to one hunter, the person who tagged it, even though one or two others helped in the endeavor. The bruin bagged in front of hounds may be reason for celebration for as many as 10 hunters, which spreads the recreational benefits provided by a bear, no matter how intangible.

Transporting Hounds

There are plenty of ways to transport hounds on a hunt. Pickup trucks probably transport more bear dogs than any other type of vehicle. On rigs with cabs, dogs may simply be left loose in the back. More often, though, hounds are chained or tied in pickup beds whether or not they are covered, to prevent fighting and keep dogs out of hunting gear. One method I've seen used is extending chains across the width of the bed with clips extending from them, far enough apart to allow for spacing of dogs. Hounds in open pickup beds must be secured on short ropes or chains to prevent them from jumping out when a bruin is first scented.

Dog boxes of various sizes and shapes, with any number of compartments, are often fashioned to fit in pickup beds on the backs of hunting vehicles. Most of these are homemade to suit the owner's fancy. Some are even constructed for use in the backs of hatchback economy cars. Regardless of the design, it is critical that dog boxes have plenty of ven-

This is D. DeMoss with his customized bear hunting rig. A rig dog is in front. Dogs in back can stick their heads out of the holes in the tops of the compartments.

tilation if they will be used during hot weather to protect hounds from suffocating. If improperly ventilated, the temperature inside boxes can reach intolerable levels when dogs are placed inside after a hard run on a hot day. I know of a number of bear dogs that have died needlessly in boxes, and pickup campers can be a problem, too. Dogs should be checked regularly when in boxes during hot weather and then removed and chained outside as soon as possible when overheating develops.

D. DeMoss uses a specialized rig for hunting with hounds, consisting of a modified Volkswagen with a Pinto engine that has a fiberglass shell on the back for carrying dogs. The shell is divided into compartments, with holes in the top of each just big enough for hounds to stick their heads through.

Collars

Heavy, wide collars of leather or other sturdy material, with metal name plates attached, are used on most bear dogs for a number of reasons. The collars protect hounds from serious neck injuries if they tangle with a bear. More than one bear dog's life has been saved by its collar. Name plates also identify the dog's owner along with his telephone number and address should hounds become lost, which isn't unusual. Some collars are bright orange and/or have light-reflecting tape on them

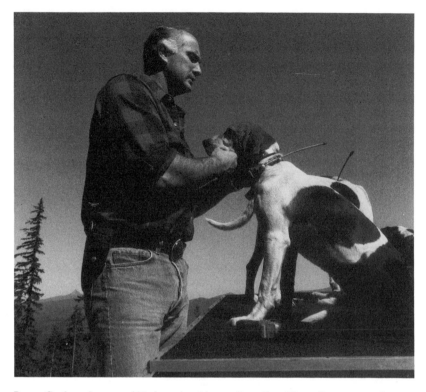

Roger Gorham fits one of his hounds with a radio collar. The collars prevent hunters from having to look for dogs for days.

to increase a hound's visibility during day and night, decreasing the chances they will be mistakenly shot in the woods or hit by a car on a road.

"We really appreciate it when someone picks up one of our dogs for us," Dan Flynn says. "It saves us a lot of time and effort looking. Even if they don't want to take a dog into their car, if they just tell us where they saw the dog, it's a big help. We're usually driving roads looking for lost dogs near where the chase ended."

Additional radio tracking collars are commonly used by houndsmen on their valuable bear dogs, in an effort to reduce the chances of losing dogs and to help relocate them when they become lost. The collars give off radio signals picked up as beeps by a receiving unit hunters switch on when hounds are lost. Receivers are attached to antennas that pick up collar signals. These collars are very similar to those used by wildlife biologists to monitor the movements of black bear and other wildlife.

Although some people are critical of the use of radio-collared dogs

Transmitters in collars give off a signal that can be picked up by an antenna and receiving unit carried by hunters in the field. They've helped recover many lost dogs.

to hunt black bear because they feel this gives hunters an unfair advantage, these arguments, in my opinion, have no more validity than criticism of CB radios and four-wheel-drive vehicles. It only makes sense for houndsmen to use tracking collars to protect their investments. Bear dogs can be expensive, with some hounds valued at thousands of dollars. Even if a dog is killed, radio collars enable owners to locate the carcass rather than anguishing over the hound's whereabouts and spending days searching in vain for the animal. Individuals who don't know much about this form of hunting and seldom take the effort to learn are often responsible for unnecessary criticism of helpful hunting aids or methods.

At least one Michigan hunter who had tracking collars on his hounds was able to locate one of them that was shot and killed intentionally. The collar also enabled him to determine who was responsible for the dog's death and, through court action, was able to recover damages for the lost dog in the amount of $2,000. In most areas where dogging bear is permitted, it is illegal to shoot hunting dogs. Individuals who commit such a crime, and that's exactly what it is, are liable for damages, as the case in Michigan illustrates.

9

Hunting With Hounds

F irst order of business on any black bear hunt with hounds is to find the freshest scent trail possible. In most cases, hound hunters try to locate spoor from the biggest bear, although it is sometimes difficult to control the size of bear that is run.

Starting From Bait

When starting from a bait, for example, it can be difficult to determine what size bear was there most recently, unless a track can be located or it is known that a big boy is frequenting the area. Hunters who hope to start a chase from baits should check them for activity the evening before the hunt. Then it should be easy to tell if a bear has been there when checked the following morning. One to three experienced dogs are normally led to a bait that has been hit, and released to sort out the scent and start the chase. If the bear scent is fresh enough and the veteran hounds start away on it, additional dogs are often released to join them for support. Support dogs learn to go to the barking of packmates.

Roading A Dog

There is usually even less opportunity to be selective about the size of bear that is run if the chase starts by roading a dog in front of vehicles. The hound will follow the first fresh bear scent encountered. Hunters should take note of where the dog left the road to look for bear tracks, as confirmation that the dog is going in the right direction. The scent is often strong on both sides of a road a bear crosses, and hounds sometimes start in the wrong direction, although smart dogs soon realize their mistake and return to the road to head off in the right direction. Confirming a track's direction prevents releasing support dogs to go in the wrong direction. Once a strike dog is headed in the right direction on good scent, additional hounds join the chase.

Striking From Vehicle

To save wear and tear on strike dogs, they're often positioned in the open bed of a pickup, or on the hood or roof of the cab. When the dog or dogs smell bear they bark. This method of starting a hunt enables houndsmen to be selective about the bear they chase. Once a dog strikes, bear tracks can usually be located where the animal crossed the road, and a rough idea of its size determined. We used this method with good success while hunting with Lawrence Edwards and his hounds in Ontario, passing by yearlings and sows with cubs.

D. DeMoss and a Plott named Lucky jointly developed the use of "rig dogs," which is what hounds that strike from a vehicle are called. After roading Lucky until he tired, DeMoss would put Lucky in the back of his pickup untied. When the dog smelled a bear he would jump out and start a chase, sometimes without his master realizing it until later. DeMoss then started tying Lucky in the truck bed to prevent this from happening and the hound responded by barking when he scented the bear. That's how the use of rig dogs developed.

Locating Tracks

Locating bear tracks for hounds to run is the hunter's job. A party of houndsmen may split up into small groups and each group is assigned a sandy road to drive slowly while looking for bear tracks. Spotters may ride on the hoods of vehicles for better visibility. As economic measures to save gas, some houndsmen use motorcycles, three wheelers or dune buggies to look for bear tracks. Once a good track is located and deemed runable, support is added.

Bear hunting parties who rely on visual location of tracks rather than strike dogs, often "drag" roads in the evening, so they can search for prints the following morning. This is usually accomplished by pulling a treetop, log, old bedspring or something similar behind a vehicle, sweeping the road of old tracks and making new ones easier to see. This practice has gotten out of hand in some cases, resulting in damage to some U.S. Forest Service roads, and could be outlawed if abuses continue. Portions of a letter I received from George H. Lyon, Jr., a district ranger in Michigan's Hiawatha National Forest explains the problem:

A hot–footing black bear heads across a Michigan back road as it attempts to elude hounds. Everything doesn't always go the way it is supposed to on these exciting hunts.

"*.... Many of the Hiawatha National Forest Roads on the Minstique Ranger District received significant damage. In an apparent effort to make annual tracks more visible, various types of scarifying devices (including spring tooth harrows) were dragged up and down the roadways. The results of this activity showed the following types of damage:*
  1) *Soil-holding grass sod is ripped up.*
  2) *Road surfaces are loosened and more subject to rutting and washing away.*
  3) *Road surfacing material is physically removed from where it was placed.*
  4) *Stone surfacing is mixed with dirt, destroying its strength qualities.*

Past practices by bear hunters were usually limited to dragging the roads with tree tops to produce a 'swept' appearance. We were tolerant of this practice because damages to the road were minimal. In the future, I would like to ask for greater cooperation in the use of National Forest road systems. Dragging of roads should be deferred to the 'sweeping' type of activity which will not damage the roads."

Spotting Bear

Occasionally, a bear will actually be seen crossing a road while hunters are looking for tracks or trying to strike bear scent, which ensures a hot chase. In situations where there is an opportunity to shoot a bruin on the spot, hound hunters normally pass up the shot in preference to running the animal with hounds. This happened on a hunt sponsored by the Michigan Bear Hunters Association a number of years ago.

Members of the party searched for a bear track fresh enough to run all morning and into the afternoon without luck. Finally, two hunters with the group saw a bear in a two-track woods road. The pair watched the animal amble down the road for some distance, during which time there was ample opportunity to take a shot at the bruin, until it finally disappeared into heavy cover.

The two assembled the party members as quickly as possible and the hunt was on. The dogs chased the bear until dark without anyone getting another glimpse of the quarry. However, there was a lot of excitement and anticipation involved in that chase, especially when several members got close to bear and dogs a couple of times as the bear temporarily stopped to fight. That experience, which everyone relishes after long hours with little activity, would have been missed had the party members harvested the bear when they initially saw it. This is but one example of how the chase is more important than the kill when bear hunting with hounds.

It is also worth noting that this form of black bear hunting is not all adrenalin pumping action and excitement. There are a lot of boring and frustrating hours spent trying to get a chase going and looking for lost dogs. On some days no chase develops at all, with the entire time spent looking for tracks to no avail. The next day hunters may have their choice of running four or five bear in the same area. Bear simply don't move or are relatively inactive on some days, and on other days they're everywhere.

Starting Time

Although most dog hunters start their search for a fresh track early in the morning, bruins or their spoor can be encountered at any time of day. However, it's generally not a good idea to start a race too late in the day due to loss of shooting light and the chances of lost dogs. While hunting with hounds in Ontario during the spring, we've frequently struck hot scent during the middle of the day. It is practically impossible to hunt with hounds on days when heavy rain is falling because scent is quickly washed out. Bruins will often be active after the rain stops, though. Windy days are bad, too, because the dogs can't be heard for any distance.

Strategies

Once a chase gets underway, members of the party often attempt to follow the dogs on foot, while others anticipate the bear's course of travel and intercept it ahead of the dogs.

At least one hunter usually stays where the chase started on the chance the race circles back in that direction or it abruptly ends for one reason or another and the dogs return to the starting point. Once the hounds fade out of hearing, hunters in the rear usually move ahead.

Hunters who attempt to follow a bear chase on foot must be in good physical condition, better than many people realize, because black bear often lead hounds for miles across some of the thickest, most rugged terrain in North America. Even hunters in the best of shape are sometimes left behind as the baying of fast-moving hounds moves out of hearing in minutes. In the event that happens, the best course of action is to take a compass reading on the direction the dogs were last heard and continue on that heading. Carrying a compass is a must when following bear dogs, and having a map of the area is a good idea, too. In mountainous country, the position of baying hounds can sometimes be relocated from a high point in the direction they were last heard. If contact with the hounds isn't regained by the time a road is reached, hunters usually wait to be picked up by another member of the party.

Bear hunters following hounds use radios, where they are legal, to help communicate the cross–country course of the hounds to fellow hunters.

Radio Use

Hunters on foot normally carry walkie talkies with them and can radio for a ride once on a road. Someone else in the group normally has contact with the chase, so runners can get back in the hunt once picked up. In situations where runners manage to stay within hearing of the action, they use radios to keep other party members apprised of how the chase is progressing. Runners routinely carry a leash or two with them, wearing them over a shoulder for later use if dogs have to be led out of the woods.

Two-way radios and four-wheel-drive vehicles are very much a part of bear hunting with hounds today, and houndsmen are sometimes unjustly criticized for their use. These modern conveniences give hunters an advantage, but not an unfair one.

Four-wheel-drive vehicles enable hunters with handicaps to take part in hunts that, otherwise, they might not be able to due to physical limitations. Trailing bear can be tough work. Even physically-fit hunters would be totally left out of some hunts without the use of vehicles, due to the distances traveled in short order by bear and dogs, which increases the difficulty of recovering dogs.

The biggest benefit CB radios provide is they save on gas consumption, enabling party members to communicate with one another. Usually, one participant always knows where the dogs are and passes the word along to others. Otherwise hunters out of touch with what is happening would be forced to expend the time, effort and gasoline to locate others in the group to find out what is gong on. On some hunts without radios, hunters could conceivably spend more time chasing after one another than bear.

Communication between hunt participants by radio is especially important when it comes to preventing those on foot from getting lost or injured. It's easy to lose track of your position when on foot, but a call on a walkie talkie can result in assistance in the form of honking horns or shots to direct hunters to the nearest road.

I recall one hound hunt on which a group of people could have been spared a sleepless night and a lot of worry when three hunters headed toward a treed bear without a radio. The trio became lost and ended up spending the night on a dry hummock in a large swamp. If they had taken a radio with them they could have either been directed out to a road, or, at the very least, notified other participants on the hunt that they were alright and would find their way out at daylight. As it was, those who searched or waited for the missing threesome feared the worst.

The fact of the matter is, radios and vehicles don't help houndsmen harvest many, if any, more black bear than they otherwise would. Good dogs and experienced hunters are the key ingredients. A fact worth noting is that in most sates and provinces where bear hunting with hounds is permitted, houndsmen using radios and four-wheel-drive vehicles seldom harvest enough animals to adversely affect black bear populations. Many experienced houndsmen estimate it takes 5 to 10 chases, on the average, for every black bear their group bags. Some groups do better than this, but they are the exception rather than the rule.

Ground Kills

There are probably as many black bear harvested on the ground ahead of hounds, either as they cross a road or when bayed, as there are taken from trees. It depends on who you hunt with, though.

Leo Dollins, for instance, is a houndsman who at one time felt if his dogs couldn't bay or tree a bear, it deserved to live. For years he did not allow hunters with him to shoot bear on the ground unless bayed, and some bear got away because of his personal conviction.

Black bear have favorite crossings on roads when pursued by hounds. For hunters familiar with them, these are perfect places to post to intercept bear. When hunting unfamiliar country, progress of the chase will generally dictate where to post. Bruins often cross roads in low areas where there's water or heavy cover, but they will travel through upland habitat, too.

Black bear may be a long distance ahead of dogs, so posted hunters should be constantly alert when hounds are headed their way. Hunters hoping to intercept a bear should wait on the edge of woods on either side of a road so shots can be directed into the cover as a bear enters a road or leaves it. Out-of-place noises can turn a bear intent on crossing a road, so all standers should remain as quiet as possible during their vigil.

Standers who hear hounds coming their way are often treated to excitement and suspense not knowing where, when or if a bear will appear. These sensations become more intense as the baying of dogs comes closer. In situations where a walking or fighting bear is involved, the animal may appear just ahead of the dogs or at the same time as hounds, and in some cases a dog or two may reach a road just before the bear. Hunters in this position shouldn't be overanxious to shoot, and should be sure of their target. If bear and dogs are together, a shot might not be possible if there is a chance of hitting a hound. Bear that approach a road can sometimes be heard coming, giving hunters a brief time to get ready to shoot.

In situations where a bear gets across a road unscathed and there isn't already a full complement of dogs on the chase, it can be a good opportunity to release one or more fresh hounds. The added pressure from new blood may increase the chances a bruin will make a fatal mistake. If the bear doesn't tree, it could stop to fight, or take refuge on the ground, with hounds baying excitedly while facing their adversary.

Bayed Bruins

Moving in on a bayed bear is a one-of-a-kind experience charged with excitement. Locations bruins pick to stop and face their pursuers are usually in extremely thick cover where visibility may be limited to a matter of feet. The trick is to maneuver into position for a shot without being detected. For this reason, the required approach is cautious, as quiet as possible and downwind from the action. Bear that hear or smell incoming hunters sometimes leave the scene, although they may not go far before baying again.

Hunters who get close enough to see a ground fight will generally be treated to a spectacle they won't soon forget. The bear will probably be

A hunter moves in on a bayed black bear. A bluetick hound is in the foreground. The shooter must wait for an opening when hounds aren't in the way.

in a mean disposition with ears laid back, hackles raised, jaws working and teeth snapping. Bruins are normally backed against something to protect their rear and may lunge toward dogs that get too close.

Once a bear is in sight, the trick is to take a shot that will miss dogs and kill the bruin instantly. Head shots are best for this purpose. Since most shooting in these situations is at very close range, many houndsmen prefer big caliber handguns, for their maneuverability. Under these circumstances, there is potential danger to hunters, as well as dogs, so they should have their wits about them, shooting fast and straight when an opening develops. In some cases it may be necessary to administer the coup de grace at point-blank range.

The closest call DeMoss had with a bear in his many years of hunting was one that was bayed. It was under a maple and he said he thought the animal was a yearling, so he wasn't as careful as he should have been. He moved in for a closer look and all of a sudden the bruin came at him. DeMoss had time for one quick shot from his .45-70 Gov. The shot clipped the bear's neck just as the animal plowed into the hunter and knocked him to the ground.

When the houndsman came to, the bruin was standing on his legs about to bite him in the stomach, when one of his dogs—Lucky—intervened, pulling the bear off him. Before DeMoss could shoot the bear again, it expired. The bullet had ruptured the jugular vein. DeMoss was fortunate to walk away with only puncture wounds in a leg and a scratched forehead from the bear's initial blow. That bear weighed more than 200 pounds.

Leo Dollins received a couple of scratches on a hand one time when he got too close to a big bear his hounds were fighting. In another close quarters affair, a bear grabbed the barrel of Leo's .444 Marlin rifle, leaving marks from its teeth in the metal before Leo freed the rifle and shoved the bore against the animal to kill it.

Houndsmen are sometimes more concerned about their hounds than themselves in a bear fight, and rightly so, because the dogs usually stand a better chance of getting hurt than hunters. If a hunter should get in trouble, dogs are usually quick to distract a bear, as DeMoss' experience illustrates.

Dog Injuries

Injury and death to hounds by black bear is one of the drawbacks of this type of hunting. Good dogs that are fast and smart may hunt for years without a scratch, but it's sometimes only a matter of time before they make a mistake. Fortunately, there's only a small percentage of bruins that choose to fight the dogs rather than run ahead of them. However, those few can be real hard on hounds, and it isn't just big boars that become defiant. Many a sow in the 125- to 150-pound class has left her mark on dogs across North America.

It isn't unusual for some experienced hounds to see their tenth birthday and beyond, but for every bear dog that lives that long, there are some whose lives were cut short by a bruin's teeth or claws.

I suspect, however, that hounds would prefer to go that way if they had to choose between not hunting at all and following a trail of bear scent to its source. Many of the best bear dogs live to hunt, which is what makes them so special. When you think about it, it is amazing that hounds are able, as often as they do, to intimidate a bear into fleeing or climbing a tree, especially in one-on-one situations. It doesn't take a very old black bear to be bigger and stronger, and in many cases faster, than the biggest hound. Fortunately, for hounds that chase bear and for the hunters who own them, most bruins apparently don't know that.

A Plott hound gets a nail trimming and good looking over by his owner. Keeping dogs in good condition improves their chances for safety and success.

Bear Leaving Trees

I've already made some comments about treed black bear, but there's more to be said—such as treed bear don't always stay treed. Shooting a bruin out of a tree may not be as easy as you think. A black bear sometimes climbs a tree, then reconsiders its options and bails out. The animals sometimes do this on their own or when detecting incoming hunters. For this reason, it is usually a good idea for hunters to approach treed bear the same way they would animals bayed on the ground, unless it's obvious the bear is way up a tree and isn't likely to come down.

I got an unexpected surprise when the first black bear jumped out of a tree on me. The chase had been going for about four hours when I got close enough to get my dog, a black and tan named Drew, in on the action. Not long after Drew joined the chase, the bear treed. I was carrying cameras and a walkie talkie. As soon as I arrived at the base of the tree and the bear saw me, it started to descend.

My voice joined that of the dogs and I beat on the tree in an effort to make the bruin change its mind. It kept coming, however, staring down at me with an unfriendly expression as it slid toward the ground. I started backing away from the tree when the bear got close. After taking a few steps backward I tripped and fell flat on my back. My eyes were glued on the bear rather than watching where my feet were going.

The bear leaped from the tree away from me, and as soon as it hit the ground, the dogs were all over it. From a sitting position, I tried to get my cameras into play, but before I got the straps untangled, bear and hounds faded into the swamp. About an hour later the dogs bayed the bear on the ground and a couple of other members of the party dispatched the bruin. It was a boar with a dressed weight of 175 pounds.

Clean Kills

Every effort is made to harvest treed bear as quickly and cleanly as possible, unless a decision is made to spare the animal. Head shots are generally the rule when shots are taken, unless a trophy bear is involved or the bear's position prohibits it. All dogs are customarily tied to trees in the vicinity away from where a treed bear is expected to fall and before any shots are fired to protect them from injury if a bruin isn't dead when it hits the ground. Hounds have been killed when bear fell on them under a tree, too. Backup shooters are usually designated to finish the bear if it's not dead when it hits the ground.

When Things Go Wrong

It is possible to miss or wound a treed bear. Lawrence Edwards had a serious problem with the marksmanship and behavior of a trio of hunters he once guided. Two of his best dogs were seriously injured and another badly shaken as a result. On the first day of hunting, the dogs treed a bear and a pair of hunters reached the tree before Edwards and the third hunter.

Without taking the time to catch and tie the dogs away from the tree, one of the two men at the tree took a shot at the bear and missed. The pair stood and watched as the bruin started down the tree toward the screaming pack of hounds. Lawrence arrived before the bear hit the ground and hollered at them to kill the animal. Another shot rang out and the black bear dropped among the dogs, very much alive.

The bear grabbed Buck, one of Lawrence's best Plott hounds (he was two years old at the time), and knocked him around. Then the bear broke the jaw of Bob, a key dog that was in his prime. Edwards had to wade in among dogs and bear to kill the animal before it did any more damage. Buck was scared, but not hurt. Bob's jaw healed after being wired together.

The next bear that treed on that hunt was only 10 feet up. The sow popped her teeth at the dogs as she glared down at them. Lawrence figured she would jump out if she heard or saw him and his hunters. He got one of the trio within 30 yards for a shot—another miss. The sow dropped out of the tree onto the dogs. Buck was there again and she grabbed him. Lawrence killed the bear at point-blank range after she released Buck. Fortunately for the hound, he escaped injury again.

As unbelievable as it may sound, two days later a similar situation occurred. This sow was only eight feet up in a birch tree, ready to make a quick getaway. The third hunter was about to take a shot offhand when Lawrence insisted he rest his rifle against a handy jack pine tree. His shot wounded the sow.

Guess which dog that bear got her paws on first? Buck again. Then the sow turned her attention to a female hound and relocated half of that dog's face. The guide had to kill that bear, too, to protect his hounds from further damage.

Once again, Buck escaped injury, but those three thrashings didn't do him any good. Buck would have been an "outstanding" bear dog, in his owner's estimation, if it weren't for those experiences. The hound is still better than most.

Always Carry A Gun

Hunters going into a tree or ground fight should always take a gun with them, even if they know someone else is carrying one. I violated that rule the time that bear jumped out of the tree on me, and that animal may have gotten away as a result. That alone wouldn't have been a major loss, but either the dogs or myself could have gotten into trouble, as happened in a couple of other cases.

One time Leo Dollins' dogs treed a small bear near a road in Canada. Not wanting to shoot the animal, he walked in without a gun to retrieve his hounds. The bear unexpectedly dropped out of the tree among the dogs and grabbed one of them by the neck. Leo beat on the bruin's head with a club in an effort to get it to release its grip, and it eventually did, running between Leo's legs.

As the bear was going between his legs, a dog grabbed the animal by the rear. At the moment, Leo was concerned his leg was really going to get chewed up. After the episode was over, however, he only had bite marks on a leg and lost part of a pant leg. The whole incident could have been stopped short had Leo brought a gun with him.

On another hunt that Lawrence Edwards was part of, a hunter and hounds were injured because the party of four or five hunters only brought one rifle to a tree. The bear was about 12 feet off the ground when the first shot was taken with a .30-30 Win., grazing the animal's neck. The bear moved out of the shooter's view to the opposite side of the tree. The hunter with the rifle was in a depression at the base of the tree and remained there when handing his rifle to another party member to shoot the bear again.

At the second shot, the bear dropped in the depression with the original shooter and the dogs. The bruin was still alive, so the rifle was passed back to its owner and he put the rifle up to the bear's ribs, firing the third and last round in the rifle. The shot didn't phase the bear, which weighed an estimated 260 to 280 pounds, so, when he realized the rifle was empty, the hunter threw it to Lawrence for reloading. The guy thought Lawrence also had a .30-30 Win. with him on that hunt, which he usually carries, and would have shells of that caliber in his pockets.

However, Lawrence had a different caliber rifle with him on the hunt. At the same time the gun owner threw his rifle, he tried to climb out of the bowl to get away from the bear, but the bruin grabbed his leg. Then Lawrence informed his partner in a none-too-casual tone that he didn't have any bullets, and the guy desperately dug one out of his pocket and threw it to Lawrence. He put that slug in the bear's head after loading it in the rifle, ending the episode. Fortunately, the hunter was not seriously hurt.

Carry Enough Ammunition

When following hounds or going to a treed bear, it's a good idea to carry plenty of shells or cartridges. The firearm becomes excess baggage without enough ammunition. Lawrence only carried three .30-30

Lawrence Edwards listens to the sound of baying hounds to determine the bear's course and rate of movement.

Win. shells with him on one chase to back up a hunter he was guiding. However, the hunter eventually tired and insisted on remaining where he was while Lawrence continued after the dogs. The hounds treed the bear once, but the bruin jumped out before they arrived.

Lawrence reached a point where he was sure he last heard the dogs, but all was quiet. So he hollered and fired in the air to get a response from the dogs. They did have the bear nearby and had quit barking because they were tired. The shot got them going again. Lawrence went to the tree with two shells left. He took careful aim at the 300-pound boar in an effort to break its neck, but missed the backbone. With the last bullet, he went for the head and connected. If that bullet hadn't done the job, Lawrence would have really been in a predicament.

What To Wear

The type of clothing worn on hound hunts isn't a major consideration as long as it conforms with the law, and is warm and comfortable. Try to avoid wearing noisy fabrics, though. Runners generally dress lighter than standers to avoid overheating, although a sweatshirt or coat can come in handy during cool weather after a chase is over.

Boots are a more important consideration for those who follow hounds. The best boots for this type of hunting are combat style with leather bottoms and canvas tops available at military surplus stores. These boots have holes on the insoles that are great for draining water after wading creeks, rivers, bogs or marshes while in pursuit.

Bean boots that are a little higher than ankle level are also good for dog hunts because they are lightweight and have rubber bottoms with leather tops. Waterproofed leather boots are another option, but don't wear all-rubber boots if at all possible. That's what I wore on my first bear hunt with hounds and they filled with water, doubling the weight I was carrying on my feet. Although tennis shoes can be worn, they don't offer any ankle support or protection.

Lost Dogs

In the event dogs are lost, they usually filter out to roads after they tire and quit the chase. If not picked up, they may stop at the first house they encounter. Some hounds routinely return to the point where the chase started. For this reason, at least one hunter usually remains at the starting point to wait for dogs while others drive roads, or home in on signals from tracking collars to look for missing hounds. If all canines aren't accounted for by the end of the day, a coat or blanket with a familiar scent is sometimes left at the staring point for homing dogs to lay on until picked up. These items are left inside the woods where they won't be visible to passing motorists or other hunters.

Fresh dog tracks going down a gravel or sandy road are a sure sign that hounds are out of the woods. Animals can usually be located by following the tracks. Hounds that are extremely tired when they quit may rest before venturing out to a road and may not turn up for two days or more. The use of tracking collars enables hunters to locate these dogs quickly and easily without spending days looking for them.

Ones That Get Away

There are more ways for black bear to escape hunters and hounds than there are for them to be caught. In many cases, bear are simply too tough for the hounds and will stay ahead of them all day until the dogs tire. Other times, bear might lead hounds into areas where hunters can't follow or aren't able to get into soon enough, and even if a bear trees, hounds eventually leave the tree before hunters arrive.

These hunts are team efforts, not only among members of a dog pack, but between hunters and hounds, too. Dogs and hunters work together to occasionally accomplish something that neither could do alone. If one segment of the team isn't able to come through on their end of the hunt, the bear benefits. Sometimes hunters or hounds are simply beaten by the bear that has control of the situation.

Black bear have plenty of tricks up their hides that they use to throw hounds off their trail. They may swim across a river, pond or lake, or

When following hounds you may have to cover some country yourself. A good pair of lightweight combat boots with vented insoles can keep you going longer.

walk down a creek using water to erase their scents. Sometimes this happens when it starts to rain during a chase. Bruins frequently walk on logs, either jumping off the side or up in the air to reach them where it can be difficult for dogs to piece together what happened. Some bear are also good at backtracking, retracing their steps then jumping off to the side. A good way for hunters to get an idea of how tricky black bear can be when pursued is to follow their tracks in the snow, which is a hunting technique covered in the next chapter.

Sometimes when a chase blows up or fizzles out, hunters can only guess at what happened. A hunt I shared with Lawrence Edwards and Gary Lohman in Ontario is an example. We were using Lawrence's hounds, and were trying for a big bear we knew was in the area. We found his huge tracks on two different days, but they were too old for the dogs to follow. The third time we found his tracks they were fresh enough to run.

The bear was jumped in short order and my two partners got a glimpse of it as it bounded across a road in front of the dogs. The chase sounded so good they went in after the hounds and bear, only to have the experienced canines quit. Lawrence made an unsuccessful effort to re-start the race, leaving us all scratching our heads about what happened. It seemed as though the bear vanished into thin air. We knew that didn't happen, of course. The bruin obviously pulled a sneaky maneuver that baffled the hounds, or, as Lawrence theorized, a moose may have crossed between the bear and the dogs, throwing the canines for a loss.

I could go on recounting anecdotes about black bear hunting with hounds, but I've covered the essence of this most interesting and excit-ing, yet controversial, technique. There are more hunting methods equally as important to examine, so it's time to move on. However, I hope there never comes a time when chasing bear with hounds is no longer possible. I worry that such a time may come.

10

Other Hunting Techniques

S ome states and provinces prohibit hunting black bear over bait or
with dogs. Under these circumstances, hunters intent on bagging a
bruin must resort to other tactics. There are several proven techniques,
including hunting natural feeding areas or waterholes, bringing bear in
with calls, making drives, and tracking them in the snow.

Before we examine these "alternative" hunting techniques, it's
worth pointing out that the effectiveness of these approaches to bear
hunting are often underrated. The effectiveness of baiting and dogging
bear, on the other hand, are more often overrated. I'm probably as guilty
of that as anyone because these two popular methods are legal where I
do most of my black bear hunting, and I have a tendency to rely on them.

What I'm working up to is that these other techniques can also be
used in areas where baiting and the use of hounds are legal, either instead of them or in addition to them. The results can be as good, and
sometimes better, when trying something different. The fact that baiting
and dogging bear is not legal in some areas doesn't necessarily put hunters there at a disadvantage. Watching natural food supplies is certainly a
lot less work in terms of time, effort and money than baiting or hunting
with hounds.

Hunting Feeding Areas

Understanding the types of food black bear prefer at different times
of the year, and where supplies of these foods are located is vital to suc-

cessfully hunting black bear in their feeding areas. Food sources in or near bear habitat are naturally those most likely to be visited by the animals. The presence of black bear sign will be the final evidence hunters need to determine exactly where bruins are feeding, and perhaps the approximate size of the animals involved.

If a spot with an abundance of sign is located where there's still plenty of food, it is usually a good idea to select a stand nearby and post there early and late in the day, although other times of day can produce action, too. Before selecting a stand, look for trails indicating bear approach directions, and use this information, plus the prevailing wind direction, to make the best stand site selection.

Hunters who feel bear aren't arriving at feeding grounds until after shooting hours can try to sit somewhere along their approach path, trying to get closer to what might be a bedding area. This practice, incidentally, can also be used to ambush night-feeding bear on baits, or those that wait for darkness to fall just out of sight from a bait. Refer to the chapters on baiting for more advice on the positioning of stands, use of cover scents and what to listen for when waiting for a bear.

As an example of how effective watching natural food sources can be, consider the success of Michigan hunter Dave Pietro, who bagged a trophy black bear one fall by building a blind overlooking an apple tree where the animal was feeding. Before bear season opened, Pietro actually saw the bruin several times, not far from his home. The size of the bruin impressed him and he decided to try for it once the season opened.

He located the apple tree where he figured the animal was feeding. There were other apple trees in the area, but this one contained the freshest and most plentiful sign. It was also closest to a swamp and had plenty of fruit left on its limbs.

Dave saw an average-size bear on opening day and passed it up, hopeful he would get a crack at the big one. He eventually got the shot he wanted on the fifth evening of his vigil. When the bear was weighed it tipped the scales at 499 pounds.

Don't overlook farming areas in bear country as potential magnets for hungry bruins. Black bear love corn and grains such as oats and wheat when they ripen. Hunters who can locate farmers with corn or oat fields being raided by bear stand a good chance of getting permission to hunt. Local game wardens or conservation officers can be good contacts to learn which farms might be getting hit, because these men often handle such damage complaints.   .

Ray Juetten bagged a better-than-average bear that was visiting a cornfield. After scouting the area for sign and places to take stands, Ray and his hunting partner estimated there were eight bruins using the field.

Black bear can be hunted successfully by locating a choice food source, then setting up an ambush either at the site or along a trail leading to it.

There were a lot of trails entering the corn, but most of them ended in short order. Juetten finally found the main trail and watched it one evening. He bagged a bruin that dressed at 280 pounds. Ray's partner got a shot at a bear, but missed. Another person hunting that cornfield tagged a trophy that had a dressed weight between 460 and 470 pounds.

If bear sign is distributed over a wide area in correspondence with scattered patches of food, a better way to get a look at a bear may be to stillhunt into the wind or crosswind from one patch of food to another, perhaps stopping to watch each spot for a few minutes before moving on. A group of four friends of mine enjoyed tremendous black bear hunting success in Michigan one fall by stillhunting through stands of beech and chokecherry trees. The group included Mike Hogan and his son, Brian, Dr. Tom Porn and Paul Myron. They saw a total of 20 bear between them during five trips afield, with the father and son connecting and the other two getting shots.

Myron stumbled on one of the hotspots for bear while grouse hunting. He was walking along a wooded road when he saw a bruin climb down a beech tree. Black bear often climb beech trees to get at the nuts. A short time later, Paul saw three more bear. Those sightings were enough incentive for Paul to exchange his shotgun for a rifle, and upon returning to the area he eventually heard a fifth bear descend a beech tree, and took several shots at it, but missed.

Brian was the first member of the party to score. He and his father came upon four bear feeding on fallen cherries in an opening. The young Hogan sighted on the largest of the four, which was 50 yards away, and filled his tag with a 150-pounder. Mike got a bear the same size as his son's the following week as it slid down a beech tree and started to run off.

Dr. Porn was nearby when Mike connected, and when Tom heard his partner shot, he headed that way. Before he reached Mike's position he jumped two more bear, missing one of them. On another hunt that season, Tom had a cub approach to within feet of him. He didn't shoot, of course, because cubs are protected in Michigan.

Spotting And Stalking

Stalking can also come into play when one vantage point offers hunters a viewpoint of a large area where bear may emerge to feed. Once a desired animal is spotted, the hunter moves into position for a shot. Variations of stillhunting and stalking are possible from boats or canoes on protected bays off oceans or lakes, plus rivers, and from trail bikes or all-terrain vehicles on logging roads or woods trails. Be sure to check state game regulations before going afield.

*Stalk and glass hunting, whether in the spring or fall, offers all the challenges and enjoy-
ment of any big country hunt.*

In Ontario during the spring, black bear graze on grass in openings
along hundreds of miles of logging roads. While driving these trails in
search of bruins, motorcycles or ATVs can be a better choice than four-
wheel-drive rigs because they use less gas, and they can go places 4X4s
can't. If hunters riding motorcycles or ATVs happen to see a bear they
should try to drop a marker at that point as they go by. Then, once a safe
distance away, the vehicle can be parked, enabling the hunter to sneak
back and take up a position overlooking where the bear entered the
woods to watch for its return. The animals will sometimes reappear
within an hour, although if they don't the hunter has a good idea where to
post on succeeding days. ATVs can be great to scout for bear sign in rugged terrain even if no bear are sighted. When rifles are carried on them
they should be in scabbards or cases, according to local regulations, of
course.

Is stillhunting or stalking to within bow range of black bear possible? You bet it is. Bob DeJong from Sitka, Alaska, can tell you all about

it. He and friend Bill Burgess each bagged a 200-pound bear on the same fall evening while bowhunting along a stream where salmon were spawning. The bruins were feeding on the abundant fish.

In Bob's case, he was fortunate enough to have the bear close the gap to within bow range after he started a stalk toward the animal. He made his killing shot at 30 yards. Bill crept to within 20 yards of his bear before arrowing it, having covered the last 100 yards on hands and knees. Bill was able to put a second arrow into his bruin at 40 yards.

Black bear feeding on berries in alpine areas or clearcuts during the fall in Alaska, according to Bob, can also be stillhunted or stalked. The same can be done in other areas where the same conditions exist. During spring seasons, Bob said he stalks black bear on beech fringes and tideflats where they graze on grass. On one spring evening he counted 13 bruins on a large tideflat. "There's nothing more exciting than to stalk within bow range of a bear on an open tideflat in knee-high grass," he said.

One of Michigan's longtime bowhunters—Loren Willie—has bagged a number of black bear while stillhunting or stalking them as they fed on blueberries or cherries. When stillhunting among cherry trees he always listens for the telltale sound of limbs breaking to give away a bear's location. Then he takes off his shoes or boots and pulls on heavy socks over those already on, to protect his feet during the stalks. The socks make walking quieter than with normal footwear. The bear are so preoccupied with filling their bellies, in many cases, and making lots of noise in the process, that Willie can sneak in close enough for a shot.

Gun hunters as well as bowhunters should use their ears plus their eyes when looking for black bear. They are noisy eaters, often breaking limbs on all type of fruit and nut trees as they feed. When grazing on grass, the sound of them biting or pulling mouthfuls of the green stuff can be heard, although not from far away. Bear feeding on spawning fish usually make plenty of noise by splashing in the water.

Hunters who anticipate glassing large areas for feeding bear should carry a good pair of binoculars or a spotting scope. And before setting out on a long stalk, first check out the animal's location carefully by noting landmarks to help guide you. Surroundings are going to look much different when closing in on your quarry. If hunting with a partner or two, work out a set of hand signals to they can help direct you to the bear. Always try to keep the wind in your favor on a stalk.

Watching Waterholes

In the arid southwestern U.S., where water is limited, black bear are

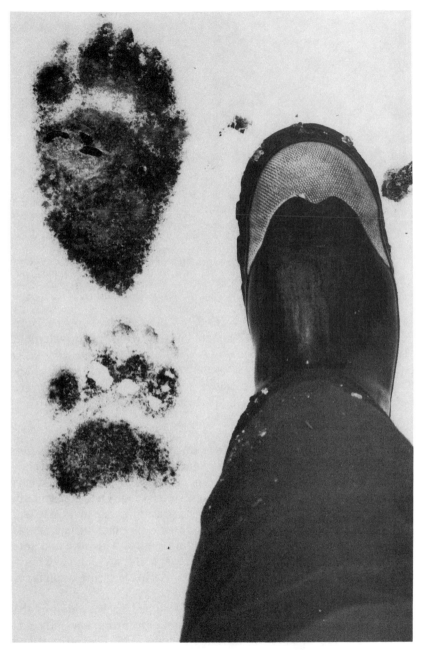

Tracking bear in the snow can be a particularly exciting method of hunting. It is most often used in the spring when late storms catch bear out of their dens.

Luring black bear within range by blowing a predator call is becoming a popular technique for taking trophies, especially in the open country of the West.

sometimes ambushed at waterholes. Leo LaPaz, Mescalero Apache Indian hunting guide from New Mexico, told me that watching waterholes is a good bear hunting tactic there. As it so happens, D. DeMoss killed his first black bear while it was "taking a bath" in a pothole in New Mexico. DeMoss was raised in that state and was 14 years old at the time. He said he saw a lot of bear sign in the area of the potholes.

Calling

As predators, black bear will respond to calls of animals in distress such as rabbits and fawns as well as young elk and moose. Calls that imitate the screams of rabbits, and bleats of fawns or calves, can be and have been used to bring bruins to hunters, both intentionally and accidentally. Most successful hunters who call bear do so early or late in the day with calls that imitate the cries of rabbits, either cottontails or jackrabbits. However, DeMoss said he knows of some hunters who have had good success luring black bear into view with deer calls that sound like fawns in distress. Deer calls would be most effective in the spring when fawns are present.

At least one company makes a call designed for bear hunting that imitates the screams of a dying rabbit when blown from one end, and a fawn in distress when blown from the opposite end. They also make a call that imitates a cub bear. Sows with cubs may be attracted to a cub call, as well as boars looking for a meal, so hunters should be careful

A black bear comes to a predator call alert and hungry! The hunter must stay ready at all times, because his quarry is likely to show up at close range.

about shooting bruins attracted to this call. On spring hunts especially, sows with cubs are protected; this is true during some fall hunts, too.

For calling to work, a bear obviously has to be close enough to hear the call. Select calling sites in areas with lots of bear sign or try calling bruins that are spotted and are too far away or go out of sight before a shot is possible. A call could be the ticket for producing a chance at a bear that might otherwise have been missed.

The only bear I called in was at Montana's Glacier National Park. I was trying to locate some of the animals to photograph, when one crossed a road in front of my vehicle. I visually marked the spot where the bear left the road and pulled over with my window open and cameras ready. I called like an injured rabbit. A couple of minutes later I heard, then saw, the animal returning. It came close, but was mostly screened by brush, then started circling me and walked back onto the road behind me.

Because I knew this bear was close, probably 100 yards or less, I cupped my hands over the call to muffle the sound so it wouldn't be too loud. This wouldn't be necessary when animals are farther away. It can take as much as an hour or more for bear to reach a caller in some situations because they usually approach slowly, often stopping between calls; hunters serious about trying to call a bear shouldn't leave stands too soon.

Callers should also make sure they have good visibility around them to prevent a bear from sneaking in close without being detected. Hunting with a partner, sitting back-to-back, reduces the chances of being surprised by a black bear looking for a meaty meal. Calling black bear from a treestand is also a good idea, where legal, especially when using a bow and arrow.

Since black bear sometimes bed down fairly close to bait sites, calling has the potential to work well at or near these locations, perhaps late in the morning or during early afternoon. In situations where no bear have been seen at active baits after several days of hunting, calling might be worth a try during prime feeding times. The calls may just get an animal or two to abandon their normal caution and show themselves during shooting hours. Although I've tried calling from bait sites a few times without success, I haven't done it enough to determine the technique's effectiveness at these locations.

Drives

Drives are a popular method of trying to fill bear tags in Pennsylvania, although other tactics are also employed. Groups of hunters usually drive swamps in the same fashion they would when deer hunting. Some members of the party post in locations where they think jumped bear will go, while drivers move toward them trying to move any bruins they may encounter toward standers. Pennsylvania bear biologist Gary Alt said black bear normally leave a swamp at a point closest to the next patch of security cover. Locations that fit this description make good stand sites during drives.

Young bruins are more susceptible to drives than older animals, according to Alt, because they tend to panic and run into hunters. He said older, more experienced bear tend to stay put during drives or circle back behind drivers, refusing to leave a swamp. A hunter following behind drivers stands a good chance of getting a crack at bear that try to circle drivers.

Black bear that are old-timers may also seek shelter in small patches of thick cover not normally hunted. One of the biggest black bear tagged in Pennsylvania, bagged during the 1983 season, was pushed from a small pothole swamp after larger swamps were pushed without success. That bear, a boar, proved to be 18 years old and had a dressed weight of 572 pounds.

In states and provinces where deer and bear seasons are open at the same time, some black bear are shot on deer drives. The first bruin I bagged was pushed into me by my brother during gun deer season in Michigan. Bruce spooked the yearling boar as it was rummaging for acorns. The bruin stopped some distance away from my stand with its head behind a tree when I took the first shot, which I think missed the animal. Confused about which direction the shot had come from, the bear ran toward me until he was about 20 yards away. He turned broadside, and my second shot was on target. He stayed on his feet, but my third shot dropped him before he traveled another 10 yards.

Snow Tracking

Trailing bear is certainly a viable technique for filling a tag in areas where the season is open when snow blankets the ground. A lot of snow isn't necessary to see tracks to follow, although when there is an inch or more of snow on the ground the white stuff usually makes for quiet walking, deadening the sound of leaves and twigs underfoot, increasing the chances a hunter can get close enough to a bruin for a shot before being detected.

However, it's no easy task to successfully trail and tag a healthy black bear regardless of how much snow is on the ground. It may be necessary to follow a bear for miles through thick, rugged terrain before catching up with him. With this in mind, hunters who hope to try for a bruin in this fashion should be in good physical condition and be comfortable in the woods. They should carry a compass to find their way and be prepared to spend a night in the woods, if necessary, with waterproof matches and snacks in a pack or pockets.

Black bear that know they are being followed often pull tricks that test a hunter's tracking ability. Gary Alt tracked a mature boar that was wearing a radio collar a distance of $14\frac{1}{2}$ miles in two days and got some insight into how difficult it can be for trailing hunters to get a look at their quarry. On the first day of tracking, Gary got close enough to hear the animal run off through a swamp when he jumped it at one point, but he didn't realize it was the bear at the time.

The bruin had made a loop and was resting 50 feet from its backtrail, watching it. Gary didn't realize it was the bear he heard until he followed its tracks around the loop. By then the animal was well ahead of him. Several times during the second day of tracking, Gary's father monitored the bear's location from his airplane to check how far the animal was from the tracker. The average distance between Gary and the bruin was 1.4 miles.

Looping back to watch his backtrail was only one of the tricks the bear pulled. On the second day, it went so far as to circle in Gary's tracks, leading him to wonder who was tracking whom. The bear also entered a stream a number of times. Sometimes he left on the same side he entered. Other times he walked in the water before returning to dry ground. Occasionally he walked in the water, then headed back in the direction he had entered the water. The bear also backtracked a number of times, then jumped off to the side of his original trail before continuing on. The first time this happened, it caught Gary by surprise and it took him awhile to figure out what happened.

"He went over this hill into open woods and all of a sudden his tracks just ended," Alt related. "I thought he probably jumped up a tree or something...but there weren't any trees around. Then I thought I was on Candid Camera and I was waiting for Allen Funt to turn up. Finally, I concluded that Captain Kirk had beamed him aboard his Starship Enterprise. I was looking around and I was laughing to myself and I thought, 'Where the hell did this bear go?' His tracks went nowhere. Then I got down on my knees. I was thinking of praying, but I wasn't that bad, yet. I looked in the tracks and saw toe marks in both ends of the tracks. Then I realized he had turned around. But in the process of turning around he never slid sideways or anything. His tracks were perfect."

One last trick the large boar pulled was to jump from one snowless rock to another, resulting in an absence of tracks until the bear ran out of the rock pile.

Although tracking and tagging a black bear can be difficult, it isn't

Trailing bear in the snow is extremely exciting. The size of the tracks give a good indication of the bruin's size, and he could be around the next bend!

impossible, especially if the animal doesn't know it's being followed until it's too late. Michigan hunter Jerry Weigold has bagged seven bruins after tracking them to their beds. Each bruin was harvested at the time it was initially jumped or encountered, when the element of surprise was in the hunter's favor. Jerry said he has never been able to connect on a bear that was jumped and got away because it knew it was being followed. He said bear that knew they were being trailed pulled tricks similar to those that Alt experienced.

Jerry was just as puzzled as Gary had been when a bear started backtracking on him. One particular animal that did this didn't want to leave the swamp Weigold jumped it in.

"He would walk up to trees and scratch the bark off to confuse me," he said. "That bear would always go up to a great big white pine tree so you'd swear he would be way up in the top where you'd never see him. He had me going back and looking up in those trees for a long time. The first two times he did this I figured he had to be up there for sure, but he walked so carefully backwards in his tracks that you couldn't see where he turned around or anything. He walked about 40 feet back and made one big jump on the other side of a windfall so you couldn't see his tracks."

In addition to walking on rocks, the bear Jerry tracked frequently walked on logs, jumping or stepping from one log to another when possible. Most of them were jumped in swamps at a distance of 20 to 25 feet, although some bear were found bedded in stands of hemlock trees. The bruins Jerry shot while tracking them averaged 200 pounds. In addition to the animals he shot, he has tracked others to dens and left them undisturbed. Shooting denned black bear is unsportsmanlike and unethical; in many states it's illegal.

11

Guns And Loads

S hot placement is often more important than caliber selection. However, there are certain calibers of rifles and handguns that are better than others for bagging a black bear. The same is true for shotgun gauges. A .22 Magnum rifle, for example, will bag a black bear, but bullets from this small caliber don't have what it takes to do the job quickly, cleanly and consistently. Guns and loads that consistently produce a clean harvest are those that will be recommended for black bear hunting in these pages.

Rifles

Many popular rifle calibers meet these requirements. Basically, any centerfire rifle .30 caliber or larger is a good choice for bagging a black bear. This general rule can be broadened just a bit to include the .270 Win., a versatile and widely used caliber for big game hunting, and the 7mm Rem. Mag.

Most of the bear I've bagged with a centerfire rifle have fallen to a .30-06. In my opinion, that caliber is among the best for collecting the makings for a rug. Wayne Bosowicz, who operates black bear hunting camps in Ontario and Maine, and whose hunters have tagged hundreds of bruins, says, "There's no match for the .30-06, period."

Leo Dollins, another veteran bear hunter and guide, often uses rifles reamed for .44 Mag. and .444 Marlin. D. DeMoss views the .358 Norma Mag. as the best rifle for big black bear, although he has also used the

This hunter used a .30–06 to bag his black bear. The cartridge is considered king of the black bear calibers by a lot of good hunters.

.350 Rem. Mag. and .45-70 Gov. with good results. Lawrence Edwards, another bear guide, has shot plenty of bear with a .30-30 Win. Additional centerfire rifle calibers that are proven bear-getters are the .300 Sav., .300 Win. Mag., .308 Win., 8mm Rem. Mag., .32 Win. Spec., .338 Win. Mag. and .35 Rem.

There are other lighter rifle calibers such as the .243 Win. that have accounted for black bear, and will probably continue to do so, but the light, fast bullets available for that caliber and others like it are not best suited to consistently penetrate layers of muscle, fat and bone to reach a black bear's vitals. A hit on the shoulder blade of a bruin with a 100-grain .243 Win. bullet, for example, may break the shoulder, but stop short of the chest cavity. A 150-grain slug from a .30-06, on the other hand, will break the near shoulder, take out the lungs and damage the opposite shoulder as well.

Is it possible to be overgunned for black bear? Yes, if a hunter goes to such a big caliber that he or she is afraid of the recoil, resulting in flinching and poor or inconsistent accuracy. Bear are easy to kill if hit properly. The caliber rifle used will not compensate for bad hits. A poor hit is a poor hit whether made with a .458 or a .30-30. Hunters who wrongly believe one of the magnums is required to anchor a black bear may be more likely to make a bad hit with them than a rifle they can handle more easily, such as a .270 Win., .308 Win. or .30-06.

Here's an example of how some hunters get the wrong impression about what it takes to kill a black bear. I talked with a bear hunter who was convinced after his first successful bear hunt in Nova Scotia that a .30-06 was not adequate for black bear. He did bag an average-size bear on the hunt with an ought-six. However, the bruin went about 100 yards after the shot before dropping. He admitted the hit wasn't the best, missing lungs and heart, but for some reason felt it was the rifle's fault.

As a result, he returned the following year with a rifle reamed for .460 Wthby. Mag. Fortunately, he practiced with the rifle, becoming proficient with it. The guy eventually got a shot at a bear, hit it in the chest and dropped it on the spot. He was pleased with the performance of the big bore, of course, but failed to realize a .30-06 would have put that bruin down just as quickly with the same type of hit.

The versatile .30–06 (left) is flanked by some other adequate, albeit more specialized, bear cartridges: .30–30 Win., .35 Rem., .308 Win and .44 Rem. Mag.

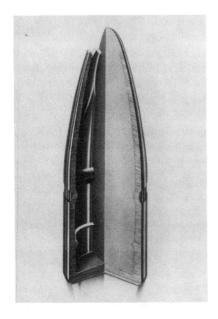

Regardless of the cartridge chosen, good bullet construction is of primary importance for handling tough, heavy–boned animals like big black bear.

Bullets

I've used both 180- and 150-grain soft nose bullets in my .30-06 and have gotten the best results with 150s. The heavier bullets sometimes go completely through the bruin without expanding inside. The slightly faster 150s expand more and are often found just under the skin on the side opposite entry, expending all of their energy inside the carcass. Put another way, I've flattened more black bears in their tracks with 150-grain bullets than 180-grain bullets, and would recommend their use in any caliber.

For calibers in which 150-grain or a similar-weight bullet are not available, heavier bullets will have to do. Bullets for .44 Mags. are available only in 240-grain size, for instance. However, there are two bullet styles available, soft point and semi-jacketed hollow point. Soft points are the better choice because hollow point bullets sometimes mushroom too fast, not producing enough penetration.

There's more to rifle selection for black bear hunting than caliber. A rifle's weight, sights and type of action also enter the picture. The primary hunting method you plan on using will dictate, to some extent, what choices to make. If you will be hunting with hounds, for example, you will want a light, fast-handling rifle that will be easy to carry, because it's not unusual to follow hounds for miles over rugged terrain covered with thick brush. A sling makes carrying a rifle easier on these

In stalk and glass hunting, shots can stretch out to 200 yards or more. These shots are the forte of cartridges like the 7mm Rem. Mag. and .300 Win. Mag.

types of hunts and will leave your hands free to handle the dogs, should the need arise, so keep this in mind when selecting a rifle for this type of hunting.

Sights

Iron sights are adequate for most hound hunts, but telescopic sights are a good choice for stand-hunting, plus spotting and stalking. Scopes are invaluable for their light-gathering ability early and late in the day, plus magnification and ease of aiming at medium to long ranges. Some shots at bruins feeding on grass during the spring in western states and Canada can be at hundreds of yards, while most shots when watching baited sites are 75 yards or less. Either fixed or low-power variable scopes such as $1^{1}/_{2}$-5X are fine for stand-hunting where shots are expected to be 100 yards or less, while the $2^{1}/_{2}$-8X or 3-9X power variables are better suited for use in areas where shots can be longer.

Other Considerations

Rifle weight isn't as important when stand or still-hunting and stalking as it is when chasing after hounds. Bolt action rifles are generally more accurate than other actions, and will be most beneficial when hunting openings. Beyond that, rifle actions are a matter of choice.

Flat shooting rifles such as the .270 Win., .30-06, .308 Win., 7mm Rem. Mag. and .300 Win. Mag. are good all-around rifles for any type of bear hunting, but are especially well-suited for medium- to long-range shots possible while spotting and stalking. Other rifle calibers such as the .30-30 Win., .32 Win. Spec., .35 Rem., .44 Rem. Mag. and .45-70 Gov. are best suited for close shooting, when hunting with hounds or over bait.

Muzzleloaders

Black powder rifles in .50 caliber and larger are recommended for hunting black bear. Percussion cap models are better than flintlocks because it's easier to keep the powder dry, and when taking a shot the powder charge ignites instantly. With flintlocks there is a split second delay between hammerfall and discharge, during which time the rifle must be held on target to ensure accuracy.

Two bruins have fallen to my Thompson/Center .50 caliber Hawken. Fellow outdoor writer Dave Richey also killed a black bear with a similar muzzleloader while hunting with me. All three black powder bear were shot with 370-grain maxi-balls propelled by 100 grains of FFG powder. Two of the bruins ran 50 yards before piling up. The third dropped on the spot.

One type of percussion cap muzzleloader, the Knight MK-85, is designed to shoot modern rifle bullets with sabots (pronounced say-bos), a type of plastic patch, in addition to round balls and maxi-balls or bullets. Hornady sells boxes of bullets complete with sabots for use in these rifles. Jacketed hollow point .44 caliber bullets are available for use in .50 caliber front loaders, and jacketed flat point .44 caliber bullets can be obtained for use out of .54 caliber MK-85s.

Today's muzzleloaders have one other major feature that sets them apart from replica front-loading rifles. They have double safeties that dramatically reduce the chances of an accidental discharge. The nipple is also recessed in an action similar to that a bolt action rifle would have, reducing the chances that moisture will affect firing of caps or powder charge.

Projectiles

Although we used bullet-shaped maxi-balls made by Thompson/Center to bag our bear, round balls should also do the job. Ballistically, round balls are faster and have more energy than maxis. We decided to use maxis due to their greater weight. Round balls for .50 caliber muskets weigh 175 grains.

Maxi-balls propelled by 100 grains of FFG black powder have a

A lever–action with a low power scope like this Marlin .45–70 Gov. and its Leupold Alaskan 2 1/2x make good rigs for shots at treed bear.

Though its roots are founded in tradition, the future of muzzleloading is in modern inno-vations like this Knight MK–85 rifle and other in–line action guns.

Muzzle loader bullets like these from Hornady have a modern, conical shape. Trios (from left) include 425-grain 54 caliber, 385-grain 50 caliber, and 285-grain 45 caliber.

muzzle velocity of 1,418 feet per second and 1,652 foot-pounds of energy, according to a Thompson/Center booklet. Round balls with the same powder charge leave the muzzle at 2,052 feet per second and have ballistics comparable to the .45-70 Gov., and round balls come closest to the .44 Mag.

Hornady makes a "Great Plains" maxi-bullet that should also prove effective. These bullets have hollow bases compared to the maxi-ball's flat base. They come prelubricated, too. Great Plains .50 caliber bullets are available in both solid and hollow point designs. Hollow points weigh 385 grains and solid points weigh 410 grains.

Powder

Most muzzleloaders come with owner's manuals that list the best loads to use for hunting. As a rule of thumb, they state the amount of powder to use for big game hunting loads can be determined by multiplying the caliber by two (powder charge in grains = caliber x 2). For .50

calibers then, a good load would be 100 grains and for .54 calibers, 108 grains (actually 110 grains for ease of measuring).

Some owner's manuals suggest optimum powder charges for target shooting rather than hunting. Based on my experience, 90 grains of powder should be the minimum charge used for bear hunting with a .50 caliber front loader and 100 grains should be a minimum for a .54 caliber. Lighter charges often do not produce enough velocity for projectiles to pass through bruins, which is important in yielding a blood trail to follow should a bear run off after the shot. Be sure to consult the specifications provided by manufacturers before preparing any load.

Residue from burned black powder builds up inside the barrel of a muzzleloader after several shots, making it increasingly difficult to load. For this reason, it is a good idea to bring a cleaning rod and patches to the range to swab the barrel between shots.

There are several types of black powder that vary in size of individual granules. FG powder has the coarsest granules and is generally used in shotguns. FFFG has fine granules and is often used to charge handguns and prime the pan of flintlocks. FFG powder is in-between and is generally recommended for use in rifles. Pyrodex, a modern version of black powder, is also popular among front-loading rifle users.

Patches

No patch is required between powder and maxi-balls or bullets. Lubricant is added directly to maxi-balls and a ramrod is used to seat them on top of the powder. When using round balls, patches are required, either lubricated cloth patches or plastic cup-shaped patches made by Butler Creek Corporation in Jackson Hole, Wyoming. I've used both and have had more consistent groups with plastic patches, but test them yourself to determine which works best in your rifle.

Other Accessories

It's necessary to carry plenty of accessories with you when hunting with a muzzleloader. Besides powder and maxi- or lead balls and patches, you will need a powder measure, a ballstarter to start round balls or maxis down the barrel, plus percussion caps or flints, depending on the type of muzzleloader used. If using a percussion cap model you will also want to carry a nipple wrench and an extra nipple. Leather pouches, called possibles bags, are often used to carry these accessories, but a couple of big pockets will also do.

To speed up reloading, I generally carry two or three premeasured charges of powder with me. I used to put each charge in empty, plastic 35mm film containers and pre-lubricated maxi-balls in other containers.

A rifle, handgun, muzzleloader or a shotgun loaded with slugs could handle this shot. Leave the buckshot at home; it's not up to the task.

Now I use double-ended plastic tubes with caps on each end made by Butler Creek Corporation. The powder charge goes in one end and the maxi- or lead ball and patch in the other.

Shotguns

What about shotguns for hunting black bear? A 12-gauge, shooting slugs, is okay. But if you have a choice between using a shotgun and a rifle of one of the calibers recommended earlier, use the rifle. Generally speaking, buckshot should not be used for black bear hunting. Buckshot does the job sometimes, usually at close range, and fails at other times. Because buckshot does not produce consistent results, I do not recommend its use.

I was with a friend of mine who shot his first black bear with a 12-gauge shotgun. Jim had a slug in the chamber and 00 buckshot in the magazine for backup. A bruin gave him a perfect chest shot at 20 yards when it stood up on its hind legs to reach bait in a tree, and Jim made a

Used properly and loaded with good ammunition a scoped shotgun is a fine bear hunting tool under some conditions—particularly at short range in tight cover.

good hit. However, the bear dropped down on all fours and rather than going down, ran away. Jim hit the bruin twice with buckshot as it ran. The bear only went 50 yards before piling up.

The slug had done the only damage, hitting the lungs. The buckshot that was recovered didn't make it through the bruin's heavy layer of fat. Buckshot loads have been improved since then, but I still think they are a poor choice for bear hunting. Hunters who decide to hunt black bear with a 12-gauge shotgun and slugs, should use a slug barrel with iron sights or mounted with a scope, for accuracy.

Handguns

Hunters serious about bagging a black bear with a handgun have two proven choices—the .41 Rem. Mag. and .44 Rem. Mag. The .357 Mag. will kill black bear, but it's not a bear gun. Either soft or hollow point bullets can be used for black bear hunting with handguns. Bullets in 210-grain size can be used with the .41 Rem. Mag. and 240-grain loads with the .44 Rem. Mag.

Many hound hunters elect to carry handguns instead of rifles for a number of reasons. Sidearms are lighter and easier to carry than long guns when following dogs. When holstered, a hunter's hands are free to handle hounds. And more importantly, handguns are easier to handle than rifles when in the middle of a bear and dog fight. At close quarters, which often exist in such a situation, a handgun is more maneuverable

Big bore handguns are potent bear medicine in qualified hands. Stick with the .44 Rem. Mag or the .454 Casull in revolvers.

than a rifle to put a bullet in a bear without endangering dogs or fellow hunting partners.

The area of big game hunting with handguns was revolutionized with the advent of single shot models such as Thompson/Center's Contender, which handles cartridges formerly reserved for rifles. Contenders are available with 10- and 14-inch, interchangeable barrels in a number of calibers suitable for black bear hunting. The .30-30 Win. with 150-grain bullets is a prime example. Rick Powell shot a black bear with a Thompson/Center Contender in that caliber one fall. The bear was treed by Lawrence Edwards' hounds. Other calibers to choose from are the .35 Rem., .41 Rem. Mag. and .44 Rem. Mag. Faster velocities and more energy are obtained with the same bullets from 14-inch barrels than 10-inch barrels.

One of the best calibers in single-shot handguns for black bear hunting is not available from Thompson/Center, but barrels can be custom-made by J.D. Jones from SSK Industries. The caliber is the .375 JDJ, named after Jones. Cartridges are handloaded from .444 Marlin brass with 220-grain soft nose bullets.

If you are considering using a .45 Colt handgun for black bear, you might be better off leaving it at home. A fellow hunting with some friends of mine shot a treed bruin with a .45 Colt. None of the slugs penetrated into the bruin's body cavity. The bullets spent all of their energy plowing through hide and fat. That 200-pound boar was killed with a .44 Rem. Mag. handgun when the .45 Colt proved ineffective.

Well, there you have it. Solid recommendations for choosing centerfire rifles, muzzleloaders, shotguns and handguns, plus the best loads for each. If you follow these recommendations and place your shots properly, you shouldn't have any trouble bagging a black bear.

12

Bows And Broadheads

S electing a bow for black bear hunting is not as simple as it used to be. I'm not referring to the draw weight, though. That's still easy. What makes bow selection difficult today is that there are so many designs from which to choose. When I started bowhunting, bow styles were limited to recurves and long bows, with recurves being the more popular. Since then the compound bow has taken over in popularity. There are still archers hunting with recurves, and there has been a resurgence in the use of long bows following the same trend as gun hunters turning to muzzleloaders from centerfire rifles. Bows with a draw weight of at least 50 pounds are generally accepted as minimum tackle for bowhunting black bear. Women and youngsters who are serious about bear hunting, but who can't handle bows of that poundage, should try to get as close to 50 as they can.

Comfort and accuracy are the two key considerations when selecting a bow. It is always a poor choice to sacrifice accuracy and comfort for speed and power with a bow. If you have to strain to pull a bow back to full draw on the practice range, you may not be able to draw it at all when a bear walks into view and you become tense, excited, nervous and anxious all at once. Shot placement is more important than power and speed when it comes to bagging a black bear, whatever the hunting tool.

Long Bows

Long bows represent the simplest and oldest form of bowhunting

Some hunters find the greatest enjoyment in hunting black bear with traditional tools. That's probably why this hunter stalks the woods with his long bow.

A quality recurve offers the advantages of light weight and simplicity. An added advantage when hound hunting is that many recurves are takedown designs.

equipment, with long limbs that have a slight or gradual curve in them. These bows are appropriately named because they are usually more than 70 inches long, with many measuring 76 to 78 inches. Long bows of this length are required to propel hunting arrows at desirable speeds of 170 to 185 feet per second.

Recurves

Recurve bows use shorter limbs to achieve faster arrow speeds of up to 190 feet per second. Limbs of recurves bend inward at sharper angles than long bows, then curve outward near their tips. Recurve bows vary in length from 50 to 68 inches. Longer recurves shoot faster arrows and are smoother in the draw and release than shorter models, making them more desirable for hunting. Sixty inches is a good average length for recurve bows used for hunting, with those a little longer probably being better choices than bows four or five inches shorter.

My favorite recurve, with which I bagged my first bow-killed black bear, measures 60 inches in length and has a 52-pound draw weight. The bow was made by the American Archery Company in Wisconsin. I claimed three bear with that bow before switching to a compound.

Takedowns

Recurve bows are available in takedown as well as one-piece models. Takedown bows have distinct advantages over one-piece recurves or compounds if you intend to hunt with hounds. Takedowns can be strapped to a packframe, leaving hands free to fend off brush, climb slopes or handle dogs before, during and after the hunt.

Long and recurve bows can and should be unstrung at the end of the day, as well as for transport by airplane, in vehicles and on horseback. In some instances hunters carry the strung bow by hand when on horseback.

The more simple designs of recurve and long bows reduce the chances that something will go wrong with them. Limbs can, however, be twisted if they aren't strung and unstrung properly. For this reason, a bow stringer should always be used for stringing and unstringing stick bows.

Compounds

Pulley-operated compound bows, which combine cables with the string, increase arrow speed, producing flatter arrow trajectories. In addition, compounds make it possible to shoot heavy draw weights while only holding a fraction of that weight—40 to 65 percent—at full draw. By comparison, long bows and recurves become progressively harder to pull back the farther they are drawn, with maximum force exerted on fingers at full draw. This makes it difficult to hold heavy hunting bows of either recurve or long design at full draw without getting shaky and making a sloppy release.

Compounds, on the other hand, are hardest to draw when the arrow is only part way back to your anchor point. When the string is pulled far enough so the pulleys "roll over", the holding weight drops off or relaxes a certain percentage, depending on the bow used and the number of pulleys it has. The difference between draw weight and holding weight of most two-wheel compounds is 50 percent, but some are available with as much as 65 percent letoff.

Another advantage some compounds have over recurves and long bows is that they are available in adjustable draw weights, usually in 10- to 15-pound increments. Beginning bowhunters can purchase compounds with draw weights of 50 to 60, 45 to 60, or 60 to 70 pounds, for instance, and may elect to start shooting at the lighter draw weight for

Regardless of what type of bow and accessories you choose, matching them properly is of the greatest importance.

The newest advances in bows for the hunter are the compound bow and the overdraw. This hunter has elected to employ both to his advantage.

target practice, eventually working up to maximum poundage for hunting. Compounds average shorter in overall length then recurves, but are generally heavier, due to the materials used in their construction.

Cams And Overdraws. Cams and overdraws are modifications to compounds that increase arrow speed. Replace round pulleys with programmed cams and the result is faster, flatter shooting and a more powerful bow. The only other difference is that bows with cams, rather than round wheels, are often a little harder to draw. The string has to be pulled farther back before the bow "breaks" or relaxes in draw weight. This is something that is easy to get used to with practice, though. I've bear hunted with a cam bow, the PSE Vector, for a number of years. When I first got the bow I had difficulty drawing it at 60 pounds, being used to a 50-pound round wheel compound. However, after a couple of weeks of drawing the bow around the house several times a day, my muscles adjusted to the added strain.

Overdraw bows are compounds modified to shoot shorter, lighter arrows. Arrow rests are moved back behind the sight window to accommodate shorter arrows. Light arrows fly faster than heavy ones, producing flatter trajectories. However, because of the arrow's light weight smooth releases are a must. For this reason, most bowhunters who have overdraw bows use release aids instead of gripping the bowstring with fingers.

One school of thought claims that overdraws have shown that penetration on big game is not exclusively dependent on arrow weight as was formerly thought. For many years the majority of bowhunters have favored heavy arrows to achieve maximum penetration on big game animals. Arrow penetration on big game with shafts released from overdraw bows has been terrific, suggesting that arrow weight isn't the only factor affecting penetration. Arrow speed is probably important, too, along with other factors.

Tom Nelson at Anderson Archery in Grand Ledge, Michigan, said a friend of his consistently gets 254 feet per second with 25-inch 2013 shafts out of his overdraw bow. Tom said his friend's bow is set at 70 pounds. Before modifying his bow for overdraw use, this bowhunter was shooting 31-inch, 2219 shafts at 210 feet per second.

For comparison, Tom said that cam bows shoot arrows at 220 to 230 feet per second, while round wheel compounds average 200 feet per second. It should be understood, however, that arrow speed varies tremendously from one bow to the next, even among the same make and model. Another maxim to remember is that arrow speed alone will not harvest a bear. Arrow placement and sharp broadheads combined with sufficient arrow speed will drop a game animal. Fast arrows and flat trajectories are more important bowhunting considerations when pursuing mule deer, antelope and caribou—those species requiring longer shots at unknown distances.

Accessories

With the exception of long bows, most modern bows are designed to accommodate sights and accessories such as stabilizers, string trackers and more. Nonetheless, if you plan on using these items, or others like them, be sure the bow you choose for bear hunting has places for them.

If at all possible, obtain a bow that is camouflaged at the factory. Otherwise, you will have to camouflage shiny limbs yourself. Camo tape is handy for doing so, or spray paint can be used. The job doesn't have to be fancy. The objective is simply to dull the bow's finish and reduce its visibility to game when in the woods.

Recommendations

All of the bow designs discussed are satisfactory for black bear hunting within the draw weight suggestions mentioned at the outset. However, I would recommend round wheel or cam compounds for most bowhunters for bagging a black bear. After taking half a dozen bear with my PSE cam bow, I switched back to a round wheel compound set at 60 pounds. The Bear Super Magnum 44 I'm now using draws smoother and is easier to hold at full draw, and it still gives me plenty of arrow speed. I prefer a 60-pound draw weight over a 50-pound draw for bear hunting because it increases the chances for complete arrow penetration on bruins. The presence of entry and exit holes increases the chances of having a good blood trail to follow.

If you are a traditionalist and like to keep your equipment simple, long or recurve bows are good choices. Steer clear of stick bows with fiberglass limbs. Instead, select recurves and long bows made of layers of wood and glass, with glass as the outer layer. Long bows are suited for bowhunters with good instinctive shooting ability, although there's nothing that says you have to put a sight on a recurve or compound, either. Recurves are slightly better for black bear hunting than long bows because they are shorter and easier to handle in thick cover where black bear are often found; they also throw a slightly faster arrow.

Hunters who are interested in more arrow speed than is available from cam bows, and who are willing to use a release aid, should select an overdraw bow. Most bow manufacturers have overdraw bows on the market, or at least kits that can be used to convert conventional compounds to overdraw capability.

Hunters who get a compound and don't know how to tune it themselves should have someone knowledgeable do it for them. A compound that is out of tune is difficult to shoot properly. While you are at it, have the draw weight checked to be sure it is accurate. The actual draw weight of a bow is sometimes different than what it is labeled.

Draw Length

Hunters need to know their draw length to select the proper bow and arrows of the appropriate length. An easy way to determine draw length is to hold the end of a yardstick on the center of the chest so it parallels the ground. Reach out toward the end of it as far as possible with both arms. The measurement at the tip of fingers is the draw length.

Arrows

It is important to shoot arrows matched to a bow, which is why hunters should know the actual draw weight of their bow. Fortunately, arrow manufacturers make it fairly easy to make the right arrow selection. Easton Aluminum has an arrow selection chart for aluminum shafts that clearly shows what shaft sizes to choose for stick and compound bows in respect to draw weight. The weight of broadheads you will be hunting with is also important in determining which arrows to use. This variable is also shown in the chart.

I hunt with a compound set at 60 pounds and shoot 4-blade broadheads weighing 145 grains. My draw length is 28 inches, but I hunt with 29-inch shafts to allow for clearance of heads. According to the arrow selection chart, I could use five different shaft sizes, with 2314s and 2216s the most commonly used. However, 2117s fly well out of my bow and are one of the five choices. That is the shaft size I shoot.

If I were hunting with a 60-pound pull recurve, the recommended shaft sizes, according to the chart, are 2315, 2219, 2413 and 2512. Most stores that specialize in archery equipment have these selection charts available and can tell you which size shafts will perform best out of your bow, based on your draw weight, length and choice of broadheads.

Draw weights of long and recurve bows are based on a 28-inch draw length. Long and recurve hunters who shoot arrows less than 28 inches in length should subtract three pounds draw weight for every inch less than 28; they should add three pounds draw weight for every inch the bow is drawn beyond 28 inches.

Aluminum shafts are the choice of most serious bowhunters because they are light and strong, plus they are usually closely matched from one shaft to another in the same size. Shafts are also made from cedar and carbon. Some wooden arrows have a tendency to warp, but are often the preferred shaft material among traditional bowhunters. Cedar arrow

Camouflage arrow shafts are a great asset in hiding from game. Use bright fletchings to help you find your arrow after a shot.

shafts, I believe, should never be used with compound bows.

AFC is one of the major manufacturers of carbon arrow shafts and they have arrow selection charts to help hunters choose the correct size shafts. Their chart shows that 2200 shafts would be the best choice for use with my 60-pound compound. Arrows in size 2400 are recommended for hunters shooting 60-pound recurves.

Carbon shafts are slimmer than those made of aluminum, so hunters who will be switching to them may need a new quiver or may have to adapt the one they already have to hold carbon arrows. Bear Archery makes a quiver that can be adapted for aluminum or carbon arrow shafts.

Fletching

Arrows are fletched with plastic vanes or feathers. Vanes are waterproof and feathers aren't, although they can be waterproofed to some extent by spraying them with hair spray or a spray made specifically for the purpose. Feathers can be shot off arrow shelves and vanes can't, requiring the use of an arrow rest. Feathers are also more forgiving of a poor release than vanes, but are noisy if bumped or brushed against anything. The choice between the two is simply a matter of what shoots best with your setup.

Broadheads

There are a lot of different broadheads to choose from, many of which are adequate for bear hunting. The two basic types of broadheads available today are those that require sharpening before use and those with presharpened, replaceable blades.

Popular choices in the former category are Bear Super Razorheads, Zwickey Black Diamond Deltas or Eskimos, and Rothhaar Snuffers. Bear heads have two main blades and they are designed for the addition of razorblade inserts to give them four blades. The Zwickey Deltas and Eskimos are available in either two- or four-blade models, with the Deltas being the larger of the two. Snuffers are large, heavy three-bladed heads that, due to their size, should only be used with bows pulling 60 pounds or more.

Examples of broadheads with presharpened blades that have proven themselves on black bear are Bears, Rocky Mountains, Savoras, Brute Fours and Razorback fours and fives. As the names imply, Razorbacks are available in either four- or five-blade models, and Brute Fours have four blades. Rocky Mountains and Savoras come in three- and four-blade models. Bear makes a wide variety of replaceable blade heads that have either two, three or four blades.

Small, two-bladed broadheads are required for use with overdraw

Enough variables like elevation come into play on every shot. You don't need to impose any more because you neglected to target shoot your broadheads.

bows. Tom Nelson said Zwickey Eskimos and Satellites are used by some bowhunters with overdraw bows. The Hunter's Edge is another small head that works with overdraw bows. Muzzy products manufactures excellent broadheads.

The Bear Razorhead has bagged most of my bow-killed bear. Recently I switched to their four-blade Bruin. Even though the Super Razorheads are supposed to be ready to hunt with, right from the package, a touchup is often required to make them razor sharp. Hunters who aren't willing to take the time to sharpen heads like the Razorhead, Delta and Snuffer should use presharpened models.

There are a variety of sharpening tools available on the market to aid in effectively sharpening broadheads. Most bowhunters use a file and/or whetstone to put smooth, sharp edges on their heads. The key to putting the best edge on broadheads is to maintain the same angle between sharpening tool and edge as it is being sharpened. I've had excellent success with a Razor Edge kit.

The importance of using sharp broadheads for bear hunting with bow and arrow cannot be overemphasized. I've mentioned proper shot placement with both rifle and bow in these pages in an effort to emphasize the extreme importance of this final step in shooting a black bear. For a bowhunter, especially one who must penetrate the thick hide and layers of fat on a black bear, razor sharp broadheads are a must!

Broadheads with replaceable inserts (top, with string tracker collar visible) and those with fixed, resharpenable blades are both adequate for black bear hunting.

Other Accessories

Bow quivers are required for carrying broadheads afield. Be sure to use one that has a hood or case to cover broadheads and prevent accidental contact between cutting edges and your anatomy. Quivers that attach to bows, plus those worn on the back or on belts, are available. I prefer bow quivers myself because extra arrows are readily available, should they be needed.

Bowhunters will need a glove, tab or release aid for holding the bowstring during the draw and release. I've always shot with a glove, but tabs may give smoother releases. Release aids provide the most consistent, smoothest releases. Try them all to determine what suits you best.

Don't forget to put a nocking point on your bowstring so arrows are nocked in the same place for every shot. Small metal rings with rubber cores that clamp on strings make great nocking points. These should go $1/8$- to $1/2$-inch above a point on the string at a 90 degree angle to the arrow rest, and arrows should be positioned underneath them.

Other optional bowhunting accessories include armguards, sights, silencers and string tracking devices. If you have a problem with your bowstring slapping your forearm or hitting loose clothing, an armguard is obviously a wise choice.

You won't need a sight, consisting of one to several pins set for different yardages, if your arrows group consistently without one. However, if your accuracy is inconsistent without a sight, I recommend using one, which should improve matters. I tried instinctive sighting the first year or two I bowhunted, with terrible results. Then I tried a sight and my shooting improved tremendously. The aiming points made me pick a specific spot at which to aim on game animals, rather than aiming at the entire critter.

Silencers can be added to bowstrings to reduce noise. Rubber bands sometimes work as well as those available commercially.

I highly recommend the use of string trackers for black bear hunting, because bruins simply don't bleed as freely as deer, and can be difficult to trail as a result. String trackers don't always work perfectly. When they do, though, they can make the job of recovering a bear easier. I've had good luck with trackers. If you do use a string tracker, test it beforehand to see how arrows fly and to make sure the string pulls out freely. More on string trackers can be found in the chapter on trailing bears.

For more information on bowhunting equipment and specific information on how to select an anchor point and shoot a bow, refer to books on the subject. It's also a good idea to join a local archery club. Most experienced members are usually willing to help beginners.

13

Taking The Best Shot

Regardless of the hunting method used to put you in position for a shot at a bruin, if the shot is blown all other aspects of the hunt become insignificant, at least it will seem so at that moment.

Several factors are responsible for misses or bad hits on bear. One of the two that a hunter controls is his confidence in his gun or bow, meaning he has it sighted in, and knows where bullets or broadheads hit at different distances. The second factor that a hunter controls is shot placement, knowing where to put a bullet or broadhead to produce quick, clean, one-shot kills, then doing it when the time is right.

Emotions are more difficult to control, and account for their share of blown shots. Most hunters become excited upon seeing a black bear; that's why we hunt. But some hunters are anxious to take a shot quickly, sometimes too quickly, perhaps concerned that the long-awaited opportunity might not last. A few hunters get so excited when a bear is within range that they lose track of what they are doing, either failing to aim when they shoot or not shooting at all.

Another emotion that grips some hunters, although it may be more subconscious than conscious, is fear—fear of what might happen if they hit the animal. Consequently, these hunters sometimes miss. Bear fever is the best way to label misses caused by emotions. It's similar to buck fever, but is more complicated. We'll explain why later. First, let's cover the basics.

Shot placement is everything! The way to gain confidence in your skills is to practice and practice some more. Test broadheads to learn about their flight.

Sighting In

There's no good excuse for not having a gun or bow sighted in. All guns and bows should be tested for accuracy before they are used on a black bear hunt. Hunters who hope to use a recently-acquired gun or bow, or one that hasn't been shot for a long time, will probably have to adjust the sights on it so it consistently shoots where it is aimed.

To sight in an untested gun or bow, make the first shots at close range—10 yards for bows and 25 yards for rifles—so that if sights are way out of whack bullets and arrows should still hit the target. Hunters who don't have access to a target range should go to a location with a suitable backstop where it is legal to shoot. Gravel pits are good choices for testing firearms, and clean sand banks that are free of rocks are great for stopping arrows.

It is important to sight in a bow with the type of broadheads you plan to hunt with, because arrows tipped with field points won't necessarily fly the same when broadheads are in place. One type of broadhead may fly differently than another, too. In fact, this is often the case.

Blocks of Styrofoam make good target material for broadheads, although paper or cardboard targets serve the same purpose as long as there is a good backstop directly behind them.

When sighting in guns, use the same bullets and loads that you will be hunting with. In most cases, different weight bullets will have different points of impact. Even the same weight bullets made by different manufacturers may not group the same.

I generally use large paper grocery bags as targets for handguns and rifles. A round bull's-eye is inked in the center of one of the widest sides of the bag or paper plate and the bag is placed in front of a sandbank with rocks in the bottom to hold it in place. It's nothing fancy, but it serves the purpose, as will any number of other materials.

Guns. Before attempting to sight in a gun with telescopic sights, make absolutely sure all screws are tight on scope mounts and the scope is solidly secured. If it's not secure you will be wasting your time trying to sight the gun in because recoil from each shot will move the scope. I know of at least two people who shot up a box of cartridges trying, unsuccessfully, to sight in scoped rifles on which the mounts were not se-

Sight in rifles and handguns from a steady rest, but practice shooting from all kinds of field positions before you hunt.

Whenever possible shoot from some kind of rest. In the field, that might be a tree limb, a fallen log or your knee.

cure. If a scoped gun shoots erratically, regardless of reticle adjustments, check for loose screws holding the scope in place.

To properly sight in any gun it should be shot from as steady a position as possible, meaning from a rest. A benchrest is best, but lacking that, use a tree, rock, post or the ground (from a prone position) to steady guns so sights aren't moving across the target during shots. Always use a pad of some sort between the rest and the firearm. Sand bags, cushions, rolled-up coats or gun cases are all satisfactory. Never rest a rifle directly on something hard. When shooting a handgun, a rest is generally used to steady hands and arms.

Once a gun's sights are steady on target, it's up to the shooter to squeeze the trigger slowly and steadily until the gun fires. If the trigger is jerked or pulled, sights will move, affecting where the bullet strikes. To reduce the chances of jerking or flinching, use some type of ear protection, whether ear plugs or headsets; some shooters use both. To get the feel for the trigger squeeze of a particular gun, dry fire it a couple of times before loading it.

Fire three-shot groups to determine where a gun is shooting, aiming at the center of the bull's-eye and squeezing the trigger each time. If the sight picture and trigger squeeze were basically the same for each shot, all three shots should print fairly close together, indicating whether the gun is shooting left, right, low or high. Erratic shot placement can be blamed on flinching, if sights or the scope mounts aren't loose. Try three more rounds if the first shots don't show a pattern, but mark the exiting holes in the target first by circling them with a marker so they won't be confused with others.

Once a determination is made where the gun is shooting in relationship to the target's center, sights can be adjusted so they hit where you're aiming.

A scoped gun is easiest to sight in if it is clamped in place during firing and sight adjustment. If this is possible, simply turn elevation and windage adjustments for the scope's reticle so the intersection of crosshairs moves the center of your three-shot group to the center of the bull's-eye. That's all there is to it. The rifle should be sighted in for the distance, but always shoot another three rounds to make sure. Further adjustments may be necessary.

If anchoring a scoped gun in position isn't possible, make reticle adjustments until satisfied they are on. To adjust iron sights, the rear sight is usually moved. Move the rear sight the same way you want your shots to go. In other words, if your first group is low, raise the rear sight to bring following shots closer to the center. When shots group to the left and you want to move them to the right, move the rear sign to the right.

After a gun is sighted in at close range, move out to 50 or 100 yards to make final adjustments. Handguns, muzzleloaders and shotguns can be sighted in at 50 yards and most rifles can be, too. However, if you expect to be black bear hunting in open country where shots might be 200 to 300 yards, sight in your centerfire rifle so it prints two inches high at 100 yards. Sighting in centerfire rifles such as the .30-06 and .270 Win. with 150-grain bullets in this fashion should cover you on shots from 50 all the way out to 250 yards by aiming at the center of the shoulder. Make sure by shooting your firearm at those distances. Setting sights on shotguns and muzzleloaders to hit two inches high at 50 yards should cover you out to 100 yards.

Bows. When sighting in a bow, adjustments are made to front sights. To correct bowsights, move them in the direction arrows are hitting. If arrows are right of center, move sight pins to the right. This will shift point of impact to the left.

Since arrows released from bows don't have anywhere near the trajectory of bullets, individual sight pins are commonly used for different distances, usually in 10 yard increments. My bowsight normally has a maximum of three pins set for 10, 20 and 30 yards and I seldom take shots beyond 30 yards. *All* of the black bear I've shot with bow and arrow have been less than 15 yards away. Once movable sight pins are adjusted properly, their positions should be marked with tape or a felt-tipped pen so that they can be easily repositioned if they move.

Shooting From A Treestand

If you plan to hunt black bear from a treestand, either with gun or bow, take some test shots from an elevated position. When shooting downward, the point of impact may be higher than when shooting from a position level with the target. If at all possible, take some shots from the stand itself, at least with bow and arrow. The point of impact of center-fire rifle bullets doesn't change a great deal when hunting at 50 yards or less, which are often the distances of most shots taken from treestands.

Shooting Up

When shooting at an upward angle, bullets and arrows also have a tendency to hit higher than they would on the level. This is important to keep in mind if you plan to hunt with hounds and may have a crack at a treed bruin. Practice this type of shot by putting targets on a steep bank above you where there is an adequate backstop. Shots taken at a steep downward angle often produce similar results. Targets can also be hung from trees at an upward angle for target practice, as long as there is a safe backstop behind the target to stop bullets and broadheads.

Keeping It Sighted

Once sighted in, most guns and bows will continue to hit where you aim. However, never take this for granted. Your eyes can change from one year to the next or the wood in a rifle stock may change. Perhaps your spouse or kids or hunting buddies accidentally bumped your bow or rifle and it fell, knocking sights out of alignment. Anything can happen. Always check to be sure sights are true. It only takes a few shots to find out if the gun or bow is on target. If the sights are out of alignment, they can be readjusted. Either way, you should always feel confident that if you get a shot at a bear your bow or firearm can deliver a clean one-shot kill.

If your bear hunting trip involves travel on commercial airlines, one last check of sights should be made at your destination. Most baggage, including rifles and bows, receive rough handling when traveling by air. A metal pin guard on my bowsight was bent and broken after my flight home from a spring bear hunt in Colorado. I hate to think what would have happened to sight pins if that metal guard wasn't there. Put as much padding as possible in cases to protect against damage when traveling.

Where To Aim

Now that sights are set you know you will be able to place a bullet or broadhead where you want it. That brings us to shot placement. That factor is the key to quick, clean kills; timing of the shot is also an important consideration, especially for bowhunters. Gun hunters have more freedom than bowhunters when it comes to taking killing shots at black bear. Bullets can plow through heavy bone that may stop or deflect an arrow.

Gun hunters can make killing shots on bruins from just about any angle, but the classic broadside and head-on shots are preferred. The best way to put a black bear down quickly is to break one or both shoulders. An animal that is broadside to the shooter is perfect for this type of shot. Aim for the center of the shoulder blade. A bruin hit in this location isn't going far, if anywhere. I've dropped numerous black bear in their tracks with this hit. The outline of the shoulder blade may be visible, but if it's not and the bear is broadside, aim for a point in the center of the body directly above the front leg.

Don't aim for the shoulder blade if shooting a light, fast bullet out of a .243 Win. or similar caliber. This shot is only for guns and loads recommended in Chapter 11. If using a rifle lighter than those mentioned in this chapter, aim for a point behind the shoulder to ensure penetration into the chest cavity.

If a bear is on all four legs with its head up, facing the hunter, or is sitting on its haunches, a bullet in the center of the chest or where neck and chest meet will quickly anchor the animal. The same holds true on bear that stand on their hind legs for a better look around. Aim for the center of the chest. A frequent hunting partner of mine, Jim Haveman, shot a bruin in that position on a rainy day as it stood up to check for food in a tree. A stream of water squirted from the bear's chest when Jim's slug hit home. The bear ran, leaving a steady trail of blood, but barely covered 50 yards before dropping.

On bear that sit or stand with their backs to the hunters, aim for the center of the back between the front shoulders. A hit there will break the backbone and put the animal down on the spot. The same aiming point can be used when hunting black bear with a rifle from a treestand, where legal. For bruins that are standing on all four legs and facing away from the hunter, hold for the center of the back between the front shoulders.

Shot placement will be slightly different on bear angling away or toward hunters than when broadside or head-on. Forget about aiming at the near shoulder blade on bruins that are angling away. On bear angling at a gentle to moderate angle, aim for a point behind the near shoulder in line with the far shoulder. When facing away at a sharp angle, aim for a point behind the ribs so the bullet will penetrate the chest cavity. On bear

This bear is in a fine position for a shot by either a firearms or a bowhunter. It just doesn't get any better than this.

angling toward you from left to right, put a bullet in the right side of the chest, and in the left side when moving toward you from right to left.

The head shot is an instant killer, but the kill zone isn't as large here as most hunters might think. Discounting the snout, jaws, muscle and hide, the brain cavity of an average black bear is no bigger than a grapefruit. I measured the braincase on the skull of an average black bear and it was approximately three by four inches. A hit around the edges is undesirable, so subtract an inch from each measurement and you end up with a two by three-inch target. Such a shot doesn't leave much margin for error. An unsteady rifle, jerking the trigger or the slightest movement of the bear's head and you've missed your chance—worse, you've wounded a big game animal. Head shots, most hunters feel, are best avoided except when hunting with hounds and an instant kill is required to save dogs from injury.

For all practical purposes, chest and shoulder shots are the ones to rely on most often when black bear hunting. There is a respectable mar-

This angle should say no to the bowhunter, maybe to the firearms hunter. If the bullet clears the buttocks and smashes the right shoulder, you've got a bear.

No shot. If he's this close, you'll get your chance when he turns one way or the other. There is no need to risk a shot now.

gin for error with either one. Bullets that go a few inches high or low, left or right of center should still kill cleanly. If you aren't certain you can make a killing shot, don't shoot.

To reduce, if not eliminate, the chance of losing a bear once it is hit, be ready to follow the first shot with a second and third. No matter how well you think a bruin is hit, if it shows any signs of life, shoot it again.

If the bear is no longer visible, listen for any sound that may indicate its whereabouts, such as crashing brush or a death moan. It isn't unusual for a downed bear to moan one to several times just before expiring. I've heard them do it numerous times. Mark carefully the location of any sound that might give away a hit bear's location. Then, after waiting at least 20 minutes, proceed cautiously to that point.

There's a whole different set of rules for bowhunters to follow when it comes to shooting a bear. Archers have to be much more selective about shot placement than gun hunters. The best shots with a bow on a bear are when an animal is angling away or broadside so an arrow can be placed behind the shoulder blade and into the lungs.

The point of aim when a bruin is facing away at a slight angle should be directly behind the shoulder blade. If at a sharp angle, bowhunters should aim for a point behind the ribs where the arrow will enter and angle forward into the chest cavity.

If the bear is angling sharply away from you, don't shoot. I know of several cases where a broadhead hit the ribs of a bear that was angling sharply away and ricocheted along the ribs just under the skin rather than cutting through them. These shots resulted in nonfatal hits.

On broadside shots, arrows should hit behind the shoulder blade as close as possible to it. On a vertical axis, bowhunters should aim for a strike zone including the center of the body, extending three to four inches low of center and an inch or two above. Archers in treestands may want to try for a point of entry slightly above center, allowing for downward trajectory of the arrow.

Bow shots at bear at all other angles should be avoided. The strike zone for chest shots is too small to hit consistently, with lots of bone to deflect or stop arrows. There are even more bones to cause problems on bear directly below bowhunters in treestands. It often takes patience to wait for a bear to move into the proper position for a bow shot, but the wait is generally worthwhile. If a bear is nervous, it sometimes helps to wait for the animal to relax before taking a shot, too. A relaxed bear seldom travels as far as one that was uptight when arrowed.

Bear Fever

It's an entirely different problem when the bear is relaxed and the

Take him! That bullet or arrow can go right behind the back rib, angling toward the off-side shoulder. If you can shoot accurately, he's yours.

hunter is uptight, struck with a case of bear fever. I'm not totally immune from the malady myself, but I happen to be the type of person who usually gets excited and shaky after the shot rather than before. Lawrence Edwards is the other type person.

Lawrence got a bad case of bear fever when hunting over bait on a guided hunt. As it turned out, a big bear showed up at the bait, presenting Lawrence with a broadside shot at close range. Rather than taking time to aim, he pointed his rifle in the general direction of the bear and fired. The bullet missed the bruin, of course. However, there's more to the story. There were three unfired rifle shells found on the ground next to the spent case. Smitten with bear fever, Lawrence was unsure whether he ejected the three cartridges before or after he fired the shot.

There are different intensities of bear fever. Hunters usually shake with excitement, which is perfectly normal. More often than not, black bear hunters have the time to wait out an initial surge of excitement or the shakes, then take a shot. I generally become more relaxed the longer

Treed bear can make surprisingly difficult targets. Take your time and check out all the options to find the best possible shot.

I watch a particular bear, especially one at a bait station.

Overall, the more exposure a hunter has to black bear the less likely he or she is to have an attack of bear fever when the opportunity to shoot finally arrives. It is to a beginning bear hunter's advantage to take every opportunity possible to observe bear prior to hunting them. For many people, that means going to a zoo. If you live in bear country, perhaps you know a place where bear can be watched in the wild or at a dump. Spend time watching or photographing the animals if you can. Pay particular attention to their actions and anatomy so you will be better able to judge when and where to shoot when hunting. If nothing else, study photographs of black bear like those in this book to get a feel for where to shoot on a bruin.

If your contact with bear is limited and you think you may have a problem with bear fever, hiring a guide who will be with you when you shoot may be the smart decision. Or, maybe a friend is willing to hunt with you for moral support and back-up.

Bear fever is primarily a mental condition, so the more secure and confident a hunter feels about facing a bear in a hunting situation, the less likely it is to be a problem. Bear hunters who have sighted in their guns and bows, plus know where to place their shots, have every reason to feel confident about making a kill should the opportunity for a shot present itself. The next five chapters contain information on hunting techniques that can help you get that shot at a black bear.

14

Trailing Wounded Bear

Most bruins bagged with bow and arrow disappear from sight before expiring, and some shot with firearms do the same. The purpose of this portion of the chapter is to provide helpful information on how to follow and locate these animals.

If shots are placed properly, the hunter will be trailing a dead bear. However, there will be situations in which killing shots are not made due to hunter error or circumstances beyond his or her control, and a wounded black bear must be tracked down and finished.

Shot Placement

Many hunters may not realize it, but the most important aspect of trailing wounded bear comes as the shot is taken. The factor that determines how easy or difficult a trailing job will be and how far a black bear will have to be trailed is shot placement. This may sound familiar by now. It certainly should. If I accomplish nothing else in this book other than impressing upon readers the importance of only taking high percentage shots at bruins, I'll be happy.

Part of the problem is that many bear hunters are already successful deer hunters and they assume shots that put deer down will work on black bear. This is true to some extent, but not in every case.

One major difference between deer and bear is the size and position of the lungs. The lungs of most black bear are smaller and positioned farther forward in the chest cavity than they are in deer.

Before going on a black bear hunt, hunters should be positive about where to best place their shots. Chapter 13, on shooting, is a good reference.

String Trackers

Bowhunters can do one more thing to prepare for a tracking job by obtaining and using a string tracker. In most cases, these tracking aids enable bowhunters to follow arrowed bruins even if there is no blood, and I highly recommend their use. The reason is that black bear do not bleed as freely as deer, and sometimes leave no blood trail for the first 50 to 100 yards. Blood flow is retarded by the layers of fat on a black bear's body, especially during the fall, and their long-haired hides.

There are a number of string trackers on the market, but the best one I've found for bear hunting is a Game Tracker. This tracker is available with either white or orange line in 17- or 30-pound test. The heavier line is best for bear hunting, and white line is easier to follow at night.

The tracker line is fastened to the forward end of the arrow shaft by holding it in place between the back of the screw-in broadhead and the shaft. The line should be taped to the end of the shaft for added insurance on the chance the head unscrews as a bear runs. Arrow trajectory isn't affected out to about 30 yards on bows of at least 50-pound pull, which is well within the range of most bow shots at black bear. However, hunters should test the devices before hunting with them to make sure they work properly.

If using a string tracker with small capacity spools of line be sure to hunt with a full spool or one that is almost full. A bowhunter who was bear hunting with me one year was using a model containing a small spool of orange line. He had taken several practice shots with the spool he hunted with, leaving little line on the spool. When the guy took a shot at a nice bear the remaining line balled up and was too large to feed through the opening in the container. The arrow had enough force to snap the line and went on to hit the bear. However, the arrow used so much energy breaking the line that there was insufficient penetration to yield a one-shot kill.

String trackers are not infallible. Sometimes the line breaks soon after a bear is hit, or the arrow may pull out and the line comes with it. But when they do work properly and the line proves helpful in locating a bear, they are worth their weight in gold. This potential advantage outweighs the disadvantages by a long shot. They prove valuable even on missed shots by enabling bowhunters to quickly and easily locate their arrows. Also, when a bear is arrowed, hunters need not worry about

The author feels string trackers are a virtual necessity for bowhunters. They better the odds of locating downed black bear quickly.

Keep your wits about you when you're following a wounded black bear. Pay attention to details and check ahead carefully before you proceed.

finding their way back to where they started from. The string will lead them to their trophy and back to their stand.

I used a string tracker when I connected on my black bear in Colorado while hunting with guide Jim Jarvis. The device worked perfectly, feeding line out with the running bear for the 50 to 75 yards it covered before piling up. My arrow passed completely through the bear leaving a double line to follow. The line went from my bow through the bear and to my arrow, which was embedded in a tree trunk at the bait.

Hunters who use string trackers must accept the responsibility for picking up used string at the conclusion of a hunt. Failure to do so creates an eyesore. It might also lead someone to your proven bait station.

After The Shot

Bear hunters who familiarize themselves with proper shot placement, taking only shots they should, and bowhunters who employ string trackers are a step ahead of those who don't when it comes to trailing a bruin they hit. The procedure to follow immediately after a hit varies, depending on whether a firearm or bow and arrow was used. As a general rule, gun hunters should follow up shots immediately and aggressively with another shot, with the exception of those using single shot firearms such as muzzleloaders. Bowhunters should be passive, waiting before taking up the bear's trail.

With A Firearm

Gun hunters should be ready to put a second slug into a bear after the initial shot, and should do so if the animal shows any sign of life. If the animal drops, rolls or runs out of sight after hit, move up to the point where it was last seen as quickly as possible or at least to a spot where the bear is once again visible, and use a second bullet if the animal is not yet dead.

Hunters using firearms will have to rely on their ears to determine the next course of action when bear are out of sight. Upon reaching the point where the animal was standing when shot, listen carefully for any sound such as crashing brush, coughing or moaning that may give away a bruin's location or line of travel. Visually and mentally mark the location of any telltale sound by picking out a distinctive feature such as a nearby tree for reference.

If there is a lot of commotion in one location, the bear is probably down, but not yet dead. Proceed to that spot quickly and finish the animal. As black bear die, they sometimes moan loudly when air is expelled from their lungs. The sound isn't pleasant, and has sent chills up the spine of more than one novice black bear hunter, but hunters who know what it means can proceed directly to the spot where the sound came from to claim their kill. Lung-shot bruins will sometimes make coughing or gurgling sounds as they expire.

Sounds of a running bear may also be heard. Black bear usually crash through branches and brush on a dead run when shot, making lots of noise. Mark the spot where the last sounds are heard. The animal either dropped at that point, slowed to a walk, reached an opening or stopped to lay down. If sure of a good hit, the animal is probably dead and the hunter can move to the spot where the animal was last heard to find the carcass. Hunters who are unsure of the hit or uncomfortable about following a bear by themselves, should make sure the spots where the bear was hit and last heard are carefully marked, then go for help.

When returning to recover the bear, make sure you have something with you to mark a blood trail, such as tissue, surveyor's tape or a spool of string tracker line. This line is the best choice, in my opinion, because the line leaves a continuous trail rather than a broken one to refer back to when looking ahead for new blood sign and can be followed out more easily once done tracking. There are 2,500 feet of line on a spool of 17-pound test. This is one way that gun hunters can make use of archery equipment.

If it is dark, or will be soon, bring flashlights with fresh batteries or a lantern to help in locating a bear. Under these circumstances, leave guns and bows in the vehicle. It is illegal to have either in the woods after shooting hours end.

If a dead bear is not located where the animal was last heard, search the surrounding area for sign. Blood will have exited both sides of the animal if the bullet went through, but only on the side of entry if it didn't. A running bear often leaves noticeable scuff marks on the ground where it lands between strides. If there are not clearly defined tracks, freshly broken branches, bent or broken saplings, turned leaves, crushed logs and damaged stumps may be other sign.

Mark the bear's trail once it has been located, then move ahead, marking each additional track or spot of blood, unless there is a steady flow that is easy to follow. Frothy blood is a sure sign of a lung hit and a short blood trail. Bright red blood may mean a heart shot or arterial wound. Dark red blood usually originates from the liver. Intestinal matter mixed with blood is an indication of a gut shot. If hit in the evening and the weather permits, trailing a gut-shot bear should be resumed first thing the following morning. If hit in the morning, wait at least four hours.

In situations where the bear's course of travel can't be located in the vicinity where it was last heard, return to where it was hit and try to work the trail out from there, circling back-and-forth across the bruin's probable path until locating blood. There should at least be hair at the spot where the bear stood when hit, and blood is often present, too. Follow blood trails as far as possible, keeping noise to a minimum to avoid scaring the bear off if it is still alive, and to hear the animal should it move. If trailing during hours of daylight and a bear is jumped, try to shoot the bear again to finish it. If it stays too far ahead, wait several hours or until the next day to resume trailing.

If a bruin is hit with a firearm, and goes one-quarter mile or more without laying down, it is probably not seriously hurt. One that is properly hit usually won't go that far. Nonfatal injuries may leave plenty of blood initially, then gradually taper off to nothing. A poor blood trail may not be an indication of a poor hit though. Most bleeding on a hit high in the body will be internal, so don't give up too soon.

Under circumstances where no blood can be located or the blood trail ends after a short distance, hunters must do their best to relocate the

Trailing a wounded bear in dense cover, this hunter switched to a shotgun loaded with slugs. It's a tough combination to beat at short range.

trail or find the animal by covering as much ground as possible. Criss-cross the terrain in the direction the animal was headed until it is covered thoroughly. When they have a choice, wounded bear often travel downhill, and may go to water, but not always. Keep this in mind when coming to a dead end on a blood trial. If there are clearly-defined trails where the blood stops, follow these as far as possible for further clues.

Using A Dog

The best way to find a bear when there is little or no blood to follow is to rely on a hound. One that will follow bear scent doesn't need blood to determine where a bear went. I've used a hound on a leash as an ace in the hole to locate downed bear for years and have recovered some that would have been impossible to find any other way. By following the animal much farther than would have been possible going on blood sign alone, my dogs have also made it possible to determine that bear not found were healthy enough to recover from their wounds.

I feel very strongly that all serious black bear hunters should own at least one hound for trailing purposes. In states and provinces where hunting with hounds is not permitted, allowances can be made for tracking dogs restrained on a leash, provided the hunter first notifies and gets permission from the game warden. Most wardens will probably permit the practice, but hunters must inquire ahead of time to protect themselves. Wardens may want to go along, or at least be notified each time a dog is used to trail a bear.

When trailing a wounded black bear with a hound, proceed as you otherwise would. If the animal is still alive and jumped, mark the location and return later. The next morning, hounds with good noses can follow bear scent that was left the previous evening. The two dogs I've used for this purpose have done so. If more than one bear dog is available when a bear is jumped, and if hunting with hounds is legal, then both hounds can be released in an effort to bay or tree the bear. A single dog stands a better chance of being hurt or killed by an injured bruin than two or three, but sometimes one hound can successfully tree or bay a wounded bear.

One fall I brought my Plott hound, Charlie, along to help trail a bruin that had been hit with a broadhead. The animal was shot at a bait in the evening and we took up the trail the following morning. There was plenty of blood to follow initially, but when we eventually jumped the animal where it had bedded for the night, the bleeding had stopped. I was convinced there was no way we would catch the bear with the dog on a leash because the bruin was healthy enough to move out ahead of us without us hearing or seeing it, so I let Charlie go on the bear's trail.

If a good dog is available, use him! Well–trained dogs take the guess work out of locating wounded black bear.

The dog was in good shape and I figured he would be able to stay out of the bear's way long enough for us to catch up and finish it, if the bruin bayed on the ground. As it turned out, the bear treed after about a half-mile chase and was finished with a firearm. There is no way that bear would have been trailed and harvested successfully. As it turned out, the arrow wound wasn't fatal. If it weren't for Charlie, I'm sure that bear would have recovered from the injury.

On another occasion, a fellow I was guiding shot a bear with a .44 Mag. caliber rifle during the morning and was unable to find the animal. I put Drew, a black band tan, on the trail several hours later. The dog led me toward a steep, rocky hillside several times, but I didn't think an injured bear would climb it, so I kept stopping the dog short and went back to the bait to start over again. Eventually, I let the old hound have his way. He went right back to that hillside. There was the bear, hiding among the rocks.

There were a number of downed trees on the hillside, too, and when we got close to where the bear was hiding, Drew lunged ahead and jerked me into one of the trees where I fell and lost my grip on the dog's leash. The hound ran ahead and I got back on my feet just in time to see the bear run downhill ahead of him. I took one shot at the bruin, but missed. Drew bayed the injured bear at the bottom of the hill, behind some big boulders.

I hobbled toward the action, having injured a knee, only to hear my dog start to move off before reaching the bottom of the hill. When I rounded the last boulder and saw what was happening, I discovered the tables had been turned. The bear was chasing Drew at that point and the dog's leash was dragging on the ground. If the leash hung up on a branch, the hound would be in trouble.

My next shot had to count, and it did, but I don't even remember aiming. When I shot, the bear dropped with a broken shoulder and I pumped two more rounds into him to make sure. Drew's chances of being hurt were increased because of the leash, but even a single hound without such a handicap may be hurt by a wounded bear.

On that particular day I was carrying a 12-gauge shotgun and slugs. Since then I started carrying a .44 Mag. handgun, freeing both hands to handle the dog.

All of the wounded bear I've jumped, with or without a dog, day or night, have run away. However, it always pays to be cautious. Wounded bear that are cornered have been known to turn on their pursuers, both hunters and hounds. If bear did attack when trailing with a hound, it would make sense to release the dog to distract the bear. When trailing without a dog, always keep an eye out ahead and to the sides in an effort

Approach downed bear with caution. Move in from the rear, then work around to the head and check the eyes for reaction.

to avoid close contact with a bear that may still be alive.

Hunters who have access to a bear dog and hit a bear they are unable to trail shouldn't wait too long before putting the hound into service, especially if other bear are in the area. The presence of bear scent fresher than that from the wounded animal may distract a hound, reducing its effectiveness in following the right animal. Scent fades, too, with time. Rain and wind accelerate the process. Even under favorable conditions, trailing a bear with a dog should be started within 12 hours, but only if permission to do so has been granted by the game warden. If I'm having trouble with a blood trail, I try to put a dog in action within three to four hours so the scent is as fresh as possible.

If more than 12 hours elapse before a dog can be put on the trail of a wounded bear, or if the blood trail has been washed out, all is not lost. If a bruin is down within a reasonable distance of where it was shot, a hound can locate the carcass by winding it. A dog worked into the wind to check for the animal will sometimes find it.

The first black bear I shot with black powder rifle didn't leave a drop of blood, although I was sure I connected. I aimed for the bruin's chest as it sat facing me. Since I was hunting close to home, I got Drew and we were on the bear's trail in about an hour. The bear had only gone about 50 yards before expiring. My maxi-ball hit a little lower than aimed, but still did a good job. The reason there was no blood was that the slug didn't exit and the hole of entry was plugged.

I probably would have found that bear without the dog, but it would have taken longer, and there was a chance the carcass would have gone undetected. The animal went down in extremely thick cover in a swamp. With the dog, there was no question I was going to locate the bear, as I did; any bear hunter can up his odds of finding bear he hit in the same way.

Any type of bear dog can trail a wounded bruin. Hounds that are on the small side, such as females, are best suited because they are easier to handle on a leash.

Charlie was Drew's replacement, and the Plott hound weighed in around 80 pounds. Charlie was sometimes hard to control on a hot trail because of his size.

Not all hounds take to a blood trail willingly, so a little training is helpful. Take the dog on the trail of a number of bear that you may have already located or ones that leave an easy-to-follow blood trail. Then praise and reward the hound once the carcass is reached.

Whenever the carcass of a black bear is located, always approach from the rear and look for signs of breathing. Also look at the eyes. The eyelids are always open on a dead bear. If they are closed, the animal is probably still alive and should be shot again. Whether the eyes are open or closed, every downed bear should be approached with extreme caution.

Hunters using single shot firearms should reload quickly, then follow the same procedures for trailing bear outlined above. Front-loading rifles can take minutes to reload, so hunters using them may want to listen to determine what course a bear takes, before starting to reload.

With A Bow And Arrow

In most cases, a black bear hit with a broadhead runs off so fast there is no time for a second shot. However, on occasion a second shot is possible, and bowhunters should be ready to take advantage of the opportunity. Fellow bowhunter Dave Bigelow hit one of the first bear he tagged with two shafts, dropping it in sight. When hit with the first arrow, the animal spun around in a circle, giving Dave enough time to nock a second arrow and put it in the bear's boiler room.

Michigan bear hunter and taxidermist Jim Haveman, from Traverse City, once grazed a nice boar with his first arrow and it ran a short distance then stopped, giving him a 10-yard broadside shot. Haveman's second broadhead sliced through one of the animal's lungs, redeeming the bowhunter.

When a bear is arrowed, bowhunters should try to see where the shaft hits. Although this is not always possible, the knowledge can be useful in deciding how long to wait before beginning tracking. Bright fletching, especially orange and yellow, show up well against a bruin's black fur and can help you judge shot placement. Solid chest/lung hits will kill quickly. Hunters should wait at least an hour after a liver hit, which is located about in the middle of a bear's body. At least four hours should elapse before following a gut-shot bear.

Archers using string trackers will get an idea of how good a hit they made by watching how the line pays out, provided the device works properly. If line uncoils rapidly for a number of seconds, then stops and moves again, but at a much slower pace before stopping for good, that's a good sign. It's not a good sign if the line keeps unraveling until the spool is gone. In situations where the animal is still heard running, and the line has stopped moving, the arrow either pulled out or the line broke. Under those circumstances, hunters should mark the location where the departing bear was last heard.

Bowhunters not using string trackers should note at what point a bear goes out of sight, the direction of travel the animal is taking, and the location where the bruin is last heard. Bowhunters should remain completely quiet for at least five minutes to look and listen for any further clues to where the bear may have gone. Then, the bowhunter should wait for an additional 15 minutes. If he hears no new sounds, he should leave the area as quietly as possible. It is important to be quiet on the chance that the bear is bedded nearby. Any disturbance may cause it to get up and move off, making the recovery process more difficult.

An exception to the wait-in-place philosophy when a black bear is arrowed is when the animal is paralyzed from a spine shot, but still alive. Try to get another arrow into the animal from your blind or stand, but if the animal starts dragging itself off, carefully go after it to put an arrow into its lungs immediately. But keep your distance! A black bear with the use of only its front quarters can still cover ground in a hurry, and he won't be in the mood to chitchat. Lawrence Edwards guided a hunter one fall who hit a bruin in this fashion and didn't attempt to finish the animal. It was hours later before the guide arrived and they followed blood to where the bear stopped to rest. From that point on, there was no blood and the bruin was lost. The paralysis was apparently temporary, the rest giving the animal an opportunity to recover.

Once an appropriate amount of time has elapsed (20 minutes for a heart/lung shot, four hours for a gut shot), return to the spot where the bear was hit and begin trailing the animal by following the string or blood trail. If your tracking string begins to move, the bear may still be alive. The best thing to do is back off for an hour or more before starting after the bruin again.

Since both firearms and archery equipment are legal during most, but not all, bear seasons, bowhunters can often have a partner carrying a gun accompany them when tracking—provided it's during legal shooting hours. My brother Bruce was my back-up when trailing the first couple of black bear I shot with bow and arrow. A gun is most useful if a bear is still alive and a follow-up shot with a bow is not possible.

Under these circumstances, it is the hunter's responsibility to finish the bear as quickly as possible with a bullet. Hunters who insist on pursuing a wounded bear with a bow when the odds of getting a decent shot are against them are unethical and unsportsmanlike. They are more concerned about their ego than the quarry and the sport. The chances of recovering wounded black bear are reduced by relying solely on bow and arrow.

If hunting during a bow-only season, the hunter has little choice, and must try to finish the job with archery equipment, unless a game warden or conservation officer can be contacted and is willing to assist with a firearm or give the bowhunter permission to use a gun. When night trailing, hunters must leave guns and bows behind, of course. The best course of action to follow when a bow-shot bear is jumped, whether day

Good trailing techniques produced a quick recovery on this black bear for NAHC Publisher Mark LaBarbera.

or night, is to mark the area carefully so it can be located again and quietly back off, waiting a number of hours before returning. The animal probably won't go far if pursuit is broken off right away.

Blood Trailing

In situations where there isn't much blood, hunters can sometimes better see what little there is by getting down on hands and knees. Rust spots and red pigment on leaves can sometimes be mistaken for blood. Blood spots that have dried wipe off easily with a wet finger. Rust and red pigment won't. Crushed berries sometimes leave blood-like stains on vegetation, too, so be aware of it and try not to be led astray by these possible distractions.

Three people are ideal for following a blood trail. One person carefully scouts for sign, another marks the sign and remains on the last clue until another is located, and the third person keeps a watchful eye on the surroundings. When only two people are present, one searches for clues, while the other remains at the last one and watches the surroundings. If more than three people are on hand to follow a wounded bear, one person should take charge to conduct an organized search. Too many hunters, with perhaps some who may not know what to look for, can trample blood sign or tracks before they are recognized.

Bowhunters who have made good hits should find their bear within 200 to 300 yards, but keep trailing as far as possible until the bruin is either located or you are convinced it wasn't seriously hurt. Even minor wounds may yield a long blood trail, but bleeding may be heavy at first, then taper off or be sparse the entire time. Bow hits can sometimes be difficult to judge based on blood sign. Arrows that look like they go into the chest cavity sometimes slide along the outside of the ribs, especially on shots at bear angling away from a hunter at an extreme angle. In most cases, the lungs were missed if a bear goes beyond 200 or 300 yards, but the bear can still be found.

There are several reasons why I feel it is important to locate bear as soon as possible after they are shot, which sometimes results in trailing them during hours of darkness. There's always the chance of rain, and sometimes snow, to wash out a blood trial. Dead bear that are left in the woods overnight may be eaten by other bear or wolves. I've only had this happen once, but Wayne Bosowicz reports that it has happened a number of times to kills made by his hunters. In some cases, the entire carcass has been devoured.

In addition, the longer a bear carcass sits without removing the viscera and allowing the meat to cool, the greater the chances of spoilage of both meat and hide. Heavy bear hides hold heat in, resulting in spoilage extremely fast in warm weather. If handled properly, bear meat is excellent eating, and hides are great trophies. Both are worth preserving. The following chapter covers how to best care for your trophy from dressing it to getting meat in the freezer.

15

Trophy Care

F ield dressing black bear is relatively simple, and is very similar to field dressing deer. Hunters should carry sharp knives afield with them to be prepared for this chore. A long-bladed knife isn't necessary. Pocket knives work just fine, as long as the blade is sharp. The knife I use is a folding model made by Buck with a $3^3/_4$-inch locking blade. I've dressed lots of black bear with that knife and look forward to doing many more.

There are a couple of ways to open the body cavity for removal of the viscera. Before you start, roll up your sleeves and put your wrist watch and ring in a pocket to protect them from blood. If possible, the animal should be resting on its back with the head uphill.

Start cutting in the center of the abdominal area where the hair is thin. Make a small horizontal cut through the skin, fat and muscles until into the body cavity. Be careful not to cut too deeply or you will damage the intestines. Hold the body tissue above the viscera and start a vertical cut that will open the body cavity, keeping the knife blade between two fingers as you slice toward the chest. At the ribs, grip the knife with both hands and continue cutting through them to the neck. Blades on pocket knives may not be suitable for cutting ribs, and if that is the case, this step can be skipped. Cutting the ribs, however, makes it easier to remove the heart and lungs and aids in cooling the carcass. After ribs are cut return to the abdominal area where you made your first cut. Extend that cut downward to the pelvis. If it's a boar, remove the penis and testicles.

Some states, such as Colorado, require that proof of sex be left intact on a bear carcass, at least until the animal has been registered. If that is the case, the genitals will have to remain until later.

Another way to open the body cavity of black bear for gutting is to start the cut at the sternum, which is at the bottom of the ribs in the center of the body. There is a gap at this point between viscera and the body cavity wall, enabling hunters to stick the knife point downward into the cavity without damaging internal organs or the stomach. Then extend the cut to the pelvis, using two fingers to guide the knife and hold the tissue above the viscera. If possible, once done with the lower part of the body, slice through the ribs.

After the carcass is open, cut the diaphragm, which is a thin muscle separating the chest cavity from the lower body cavity. Cut it as close to ribs and backbone as possible. The stomach generally has to be held out of the way to get at the diaphragm. Stomach, liver and intestines can be pulled to the side and rolled out on the ground after the diaphragm is cut. There may be other strands of connective tissue holding the viscera, which should be carefully severed.

Next, reach up above the heart and lungs into the neck, grasping the wind pipe. Pull it tight and cut the windpipe above your hand. Be careful to avoid slicing fingers in the process. Once the windpipe is cut, pull it out and the heart and lungs will come with it.

The final step in the dressing process is to cut around the anus and remove the lower digestive tract. After the bowel is removed, check the passageway to make sure it is free of obstructions to allow blood to drain out and heat to escape. If fat is present, remove it. Some hunters take care of cutting around the anus before removing the viscera.

When all of the viscera has been removed and the anal area cleaned, take a few minutes to remove kidneys, excess fat and any of the diaphragm remaining. Successful black bear hunters in some states leave part of the diaphragm in the body cavity because pieces of this muscle are usually taken at the check station to test for trichinosis. If stomach or intestines have been ruptured, clean as much of the material out of the carcass as possible. Meat that has been soiled should be cut away and discarded. Always keep the carcass in a cool location. Wrap it in cheesecloth or a mesh bag if flies bother it.

The heart and liver are good to eat, provided they haven't been damaged by bullets or broadheads. Bear livers are reddish-brown in color—much lighter than those from deer, and have green, fluid-filled gall bladders attached. The liver is separated into several lobes and is connected to the diaphragm. A plastic bag is handy to put heart and liver in to carry out of the woods.

Begin field dressing by making an incision from the sternum to the pelvis. Try to make the cut as straight as possible to help the taxidermist.

Capture those photo memories before skinning out your trophy. Take time to set up shots that you'll cherish for years to come.

Photographing Bagged Bear

One of the best ways to preserve the fond memories of a successful black bear hunt is to have some photographs made of the hunter with his trophy. If possible, have photographs taken in the field before the bruin is dressed. Photos taken at or near the kill site when the carcass is still fresh and limber often look the best.

If a bear goes down in the open where there's good light, that's great. Under circumstances where a bruin drops in thick cover where there's poor light, you might consider moving the carcass into the open for photographs. Try to position a bear for photographs to eliminate most, if not all, blood from view and make sure the animal's tongue isn't hanging out of its mouth.

It is usually possible for the hunter to stand or kneel next to the carcass to block blood from view. When this isn't possible, frame pictures in the camera's viewfinder that exclude bloody portions of the carcass.

Some of the best bear and hunter photos are closeups of just the animal's head or front quarter and the hunter.

Make sure both hunter and bear are clearly visible through the viewfinder and evenly lit. Avoid shadows. Since most black bear are a dark color, using a flash will give best results when photos are taken in the shade, early and late in the day or under overcast skies. A flash is unnecessary if taking photographs in direct sunlight.

If you don't have a flash when sunlight isn't available and you are using a 35mm camera, take a number of photographs at different settings to compensate for poor lighting. As an example, let's say the light meter in your camera read f5.6 with available light. Take one to several photographs at that setting, then change the f-stop ring to 4 to allow more light to enter the camera and take another set of photographs. This overexposes the film by one f-stop and sometimes produces better results than the exposure suggested by the camera.

In situations where a camera isn't available until a bear is dressed and out of the woods, follow the same basic guidelines mentioned above. Try to take photographs in settings that looks as natural as possible, eliminating buildings and vehicles from view.

Transporting Carcasses

The prevailing circumstances will determine what course of action to take next. The carcass will have to be transported from the spot where it fell to a point where it can be loaded into a vehicle. If a road is nearby, dragging the animal the short distance may be the best option. When there's a long haul, however, and it's late, the best option may be to hang the bear in the woods and return to get it out the following morning.

That is how we handled two bruins bagged one fall. One was dropped about an hour before dark, but by the time two of us had dragged it up a steep hill it was dark and there was still $^1/_4$-mile to go, so we hung the animal with a rope from the sturdy limb of a hemlock tree. A piece of wood was used to prop open the chest cavity to aid in cooling the carcass. That was a gun kill.

The second bear was bagged about one-half hour before dark with bow and arrow using a string tracker. We returned to our cabin and ate dinner, then the five of us hunting together went to trail the arrowed bear well after dark.

We found a 300-pounder at the end of the line within 100 yards of where it was hit. Rather than trying to manhandle the carcass out of the woods that night, we hung it from a nearby tree and got it out of the woods the following morning. Coincidentally, the fellow who tagged that bear is Bob Eastman from Flushing, Michigan, a long-time

A small block and tackle is useful for hoisting bear off of the ground for field dressing and skinning chores.

bowhunter and owner of the company that makes Game Trackers.

When hunting alone, or in the event you bag a big bear that you want to hang in the woods overnight, a block and tackle is the best way to hoist carcasses off the ground. We had to use a block and tackle to hang a big boar bowhunter Gary Lohman got one year. We were never able to have the carcass weighed, but I estimated the dressed bruin weighed over 400 pounds.

If there is concern about bear or wolves tampering with a carcass, the best thing to do may be to get it out of the woods right away. A piece of clothing or item with human scent on it will keep wolves away from a carcass, but I'm not sure about other bear. One fall a big boar made off with a small bear a group of hunters camping in Michigan's Upper Peninsula had hanging near their tent.

In the event temperatures are warm, above 60 degrees Fahrenheit, bear should be taken out of the woods and skinned as soon as possible. Under circumstances where a big bear is involved and there is no way to reach the carcass with a vehicle, the best thing to do is skin the animal first, then quarter the carcass and carry it out piece-by-piece, provided that this is legal in the state or province in which you are hunting. All-terrain vehicles are great for hauling bear out of the woods, provided one is available and it can reach the carcass.

Most bear hauling is done by hand, either carrying or dragging the carcass. Small to average bear, those that weigh less than 150 pounds, can be carried with front and back legs draped across shoulders. If someone isn't along to help get the bear on the carrier's shoulders, the carcass may have to be pulled up on a stump or log to get it in a position to carry. I watched one hunter carry over his shoulders a bear that weighed at least 150 pounds.

Jim Jarvis did the same thing, except that he had each front leg over a shoulder and leaned forward as he stood up to get the hind legs off the ground behind him, then walked toward the road with the load. In the same fashion, last fall we carried out a bear that Charlie had treed, and which was killed with a bow and arrow. That bruin had a dressed weight of 160 pounds.

Another way to carry small bear is to tie a hind foot to a front foot on the opposite side of the body, forming a sling. This bear-leg sling can be slung over either shoulder to carry an animal out of the woods.

Still one more method of carrying bear out of the woods is to tie them to a pole. A strong pole longer than the bear is necessary so the ends can be put on the carriers' shoulders. When tying a carcass to the pole, secure it between the legs next to the body to prevent it from swinging back and forth. My brother and I once carried a 140-pound bear he

Three hunters can walk a dressed bear out of the woods like this trio is doing. However, it's best to talk loudly and cover the bear with orange material.

shot by simply tying its feet to a pole. The weight of the swinging carcass constantly upset our balance, and we ended up dragging the bruin most of the way to the road.

I do not recommend carrying bear in areas where there are other hunters, for reasons of safety, unless it's after dark or the carcass is wrapped with hunter orange material. Such precautions are always a good idea.

To drag black bear, use a strong rope with one end around the bear's head and the other attached to a sturdy stick or pole to hang onto when dragging. The shorter the length of rope between the drag stick and bear the better. That way, part of the front quarters can be lifted off the ground while dragging to reduce friction. If a pole is used, hunters can push against it at waist to chest level like a yoke.

Rather than putting a rope around a bear's head for dragging purposes, Leland Stice puts a thick piece of wood in a bear's mouth long enough to protrude from both sides of the mouth, behind the canine teeth. Then the mouth is tied shut and the middle of a rope or chain is secured to the protruding stick around the muzzle, leaving both ends for pulling. This works well in thick cover where spaces between trees are too narrow for two people to get through together.

A third person can help drag in thick cover by attaching a second rope to a front or hind foot. Another way for three hunters to pull a bear at once in thick cover is to use three separate lengths of rope with one

You've bagged your bear, and posed with pride. Now it's time to begin the hard work of dragging the beast out of the woods.

secured to each front leg and the third on the head. When dragging in open hardwoods or along a trail, three or four people can pull simultaneously by using a long drag stick.

Take frequent breaks when dragging or carrying a bear out of the woods to avoid overexertion. It's surprising how easy even long drags can be if taken a short distance at a time. Solo hunters should always try to obtain help to get a bear out of the woods, unless planning on skinning and quartering the carcass.

Skinning

A bear can be skinned just as easily in the woods as at camp or home, and the sooner it's done the better, to allow maximum cooling of the meat. Start skinning with the animal on its back. If still laying where it was field dressed, try to move the carcass far enough away from the viscera to avoid soiling hide or meat. A spot where the ground is level is best.

If the pelt hasn't been split from the neck to the tail for dressing, extend the main cut the full length of the body. Then slice the hide along the inside of each leg, following the longest hairs, either starting or ending at the main cut along the middle of the body. Some hunters prefer to start at the base of the legs and cut upward until reaching the bear's paws.

Incisions on hind legs should extend to heels and can be continued through the center of the pad to toes. End the cuts on the front legs part-way into the center of the pads forward of wrists. Once these cuts are complete, start working the skin free from the carcass one leg at a time. Use a sharp knife to cut tissue between hide and meat, with one hand pulling the hide from the carcass. Skin the inside of each leg first, re-move the feet from the legs, leaving them attached to the hide. Then the skin can be quickly peeled from the back side of the legs.

Front feet can be removed easiest at wrist joints. A knife is adequate for cutting connective tissue at the joints, but a saw can also be used. If a saw is employed, take care not to cut the hide on either side of the joint. Once the bone is severed with a saw, complete the cut with a knife to avoid cutting the skin on top of the wrist.

Skin hind feet as far as the toes, then cut across toe joints, leaving toes and pad attached to the hide. If in a hurry, hind legs can be skinned to the heel and the entire foot removed by cutting at the ankle joint.

Attention can be turned to the body after the legs are skinned. Re-move the hide from one side first, as far as the middle of the back, by rolling the carcass on its side. Then do the other side. The already skinned hide protects the carcass from dirt and vegetation to some extent as it is rolled from one side to the other.

Eventually, the entire pelt will be free from the carcass with the ex-ception of the head. At this point, the head can be removed from the car-cass with the hide attached by either cutting or sawing through the neck.

Black bear can also be skinned while hanging by their hind legs. The lower portion of the hind legs and feet must be skinned first before a bear can be hung in this fashion. Take care not to cut the tendons that attach to the back of the heels while skinning hind legs. Once hide is removed from lower legs, make a cut between those tendons and the leg bone for insertion of a sturdy pole. The pole or branch used doesn't have to be long, but it will have to be strong enough to support the weight of the bear carcass.

Put one end of the pole through a gambrel, then hoist the carcass to a sturdy tree limb, meat pole or some other support so the pole can be placed over the top of it and inserted through the remaining gambrel. Hanging a bear in this way is relatively easy from the bed of a pickup truck.

A block and tackle can also be used to hang a bear for skinning, as Oregon guide Rodger Gorham does. I hunted with Rodger and his hounds one fall and we harvested a bear at least two miles from the near-est road in a creek bottom. It was late in the day when we got the bear, so we left the carcass in the creek overnight after field-dressing it to keep it cool. The following day we hung the carcass and Rodger removed the

The white lines roughly mark where cuts should be made to skin a black bear. Follow your taxidermist's recommendations for the best results.

hide and deboned the meat. We packed out the meat and hide.

Once hung, skinning can be completed. The job is often easier on a hanging bear than one on the ground because it is possible to work all the way around the carcass. It is also possible to peel some of the hide from the carcass once there is enough loose skin to hang on to. In addition, there is less chance of getting dirt on the carcass when off the ground.

Caring For The Hide

Now that the meat from your bear is taken care of, let's return attention to the hide. Thus far it has been skinned, with the exception of the head. If the hide is to be turned over to a local taxidermist for processing the day it is skinned, no further work is necessary. If more than a day will elapse before the head and hide can be left with a taxidermist, place them in a freezer right away and bring them to the shop frozen. Fold hides loosely and put them in one or two garbage bags for freezing. It helps to turn freezers up to their coldest settings, if they aren't already, to ensure that hides freeze solidly. Don't apply salt to bear hides that are to be frozen, because salt will keep it from freezing.

Hunters who plan on shipping bear hides to taxidermists or a tannery will have to skin the head and flesh the hide themselves. Remove the skull first. If you are interested in having a rug made, cut the hide along the underside of the neck and throat to a point two or three inches short of the end of the lower jaw. Hunters who are considering a full or head mount should not cut the head skin any farther than the base of the neck. The head can be skinned by inverting the skin over the skull.

Skinning The Head

Be extremely careful when skinning the head. When the ears are reached, cut them from the head flush with the skull. The skin around the eyes must also be cut flush with the skull around the eye sockets, as should the lips. Cut the cartilage on the nose an inch or two back from the tip.

Once the head is skinned, the entire hide must be fleshed and salted. Bear hides contain large quantities of fat. All of it must be removed in order to protect the pelt from spoilage.

Paws and a number of points on the head require special attention. Scrape away all flesh and cartilage from the paws. Also remove flesh from the base of ears and skin the back of the ears, being careful while doing so. Then shave the lips down as thin as possible without cutting the hide.

Once all of these steps are taken care of, the hide is ready for a liberal application of salt. Use table or pickling salt to rub into all parts of the

If you can't freeze the pelt or get it to a taxidermist immediately, rub it thoroughly with coarse salt.

pelt. Make sure plenty of salt is applied to paws, ears and lips.

Then let the hide dry in the shade outside or on the floor of a shed or basement while resting on newspapers to absorb moisture. Keep hides out of direct sunlight because the sun will burn a bear hide. Moisture will come out of the pelt as it cures. The hide can be shipped, preferably in a burlap bag, but some carriers require that hides be contained in plastic bags after they are completely dry.

Cleaning Skulls

Flesh should be removed as soon as possible from any bear skull that is to be measured for record book consideration. Carve off as much muscle as possible with a knife first. Once that step is complete, there are several ways to finish the process.

The skull can be boiled to soften the remaining tissue for removal. This is a relatively fast method, but may result in some shrinkage of the skull if it is boiled too long.

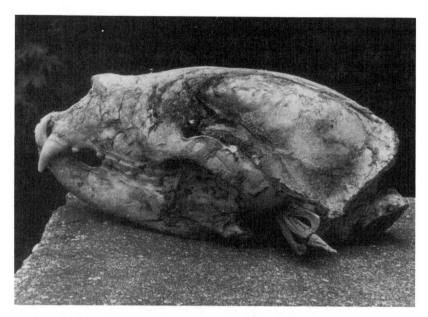

Skulls can be cleaned by a number of methods. (Note the broadhead embedded at the base of the jaw. A vivid reminder of the importance of shot placement.)

A good method of cleaning bear skulls was developed by Donald Smith with the Minnesota Museum of Natural History.

1. Boil the skull until the meat is soft (the consistency of stewed meat). Make sure that the skull is completely covered with water; any part exposed to air during the boiling process will become permanently discolored. Adding a small amount of potassium carbonate will speed up the softening process. Beware of adding too much, as an excess will decalcify the bone. Use about $^1/_2$ teaspoon per gallon of water.
2. Remove the softened flesh with fingers and a toothbrush.
3. Immerse the skull in a clear *glass* jar filled with a solution of pure Clorox or Hilex bleach. Chlorinated bleach has a corrosive effect first on the cartilage, then on the bone. Cartilage such a s in the turbinates and on the occipitals will dissolve off in a stream of bubbles. As soon as the cartilage has dissolved, the skull should be removed from the bleach and rinsed in cold water. If the skull is immersed in the bleach for more than 10 minutes, the bone itself will be attacked.
4. Place the skull in a 50-50 solution of 3 percent hydrogen peroxide and water in a clear glass jar. Adding a small amount of ammonia will speed up the bleaching process. If greater whiteness

is desired, put the jar containing the skull and peroxide on a white piece of paper and set it in direct sunlight. Let the skull bleach for about six hours.

5. Rinse in cold water and dry.
6. Immerse the skull in carbon tetrachloride or gasoline to remove grease.
7. Dry.
8. Spread Duco cement on the teeth to prevent them from cracking, as they dry out with time. This *must* be done with carnivore skulls because their teeth are especially prone to crack.
9. Spray the skull with clear acrylic plastic (such as Krylon). This seals the bone surface and makes it impervious to dirt and oils which would otherwise stain it.

Hunters who decide to boil bear skulls should remember to remove the brain. It can be taken out in pieces through a hole in the base of the skull where the neck was once attached.

The other methods of skull cleaning leave the final process of flesh and cartilage removal to insects and decay. Skulls can be buried in a convenient, well-marked location allowing the remaining tissues to break down naturally with the help of bacteria in the soil. The same thing will happen faster if the skull is left above ground, but it should be put in a location where it will be safe, yet the smell won't be offensive. If either of these alternatives are chosen to finish cleaning a skull, it should be enclosed in a wire cage or porous box to prevent neighborhood dogs or other animals from carrying it away or damaging it. Rooftops often provide a safe resting place.

Some museums and universities have still one other method of cleaning skulls. Some of these institutions maintain domestic beetle collections, which quickly clean flesh from bones. Establishments that have beetle collections may be able to save bear hunters the time and trouble of cleaning skulls themselves. If a university or museum is nearby, a phone call is all it takes to inquire about the possibility.

Safety

While skinning a black bear or fleshing the hide, there is always a chance of cutting finger or hand. However, the odds of doing so are reduced by working slowly and carefully. If the job gets tedious, it is better to take a break rather than risk injuring yourself or the trophy you worked so hard to get.

Any cuts that are suffered, small or large, while working on a black bear should be thoroughly cleaned and disinfected once the work is done. Germs have a way of getting into the smallest of cuts. I once neglected to take care of a small nick in one of my fingers after skinning a bear in hot weather. A serious infection developed as a result and a hospital visit was necessary to clear it up.

Hunters who follow the steps outlined in this chapter to care for their black bear can look forward to a beautiful rug or mount to remind them of a memorable moment in their big game hunting experience, as well as some fine eating.

Quartering The Carcass

After a bear is skinned, the shoulders and hams can be removed to carry out of the woods. The same process is followed when butchering a bear yourself. Cut hind legs or hams from the carcass at the end of the heavy leg bone where it joins the pelvis. A knife is sufficient to cut through connective tissue at that joint. Front legs with shoulders attached can be removed from the carcass by cutting between the shoulder blade ribs with a knife.

These hunks of meat can be put in meat bags or garbage bags to carry on a packframe or in a large canvas pack. The canvas packs I use to carry bait are large enough for this purpose. If meat is put in garbage bags, be sure to remove it upon reaching your vehicle, especially in warm weather. The meat will not cool and may even spoil in plastic bags. Lay meat on top of plastic in the shade, either in a vehicle or outside until ready to leave the area.

Hunters who wish to bone bear meat on the spot will be able to reduce the weight of their load considerably and may be able to carry it all in one trip. Cut as much fat as possible from the pieces of meat before boning to reduce the weight further. Hindquarters especially will have thick layers of fat on them during fall months.

Two other cuts of meat, which will be boneless, are the loins and tenderloins. There will be two of each. The tenderloins are long, narrow muscles that taper to a point at each end. They are on the inside of the body cavity along the lower part of the backbone. These choice pieces of meat may be covered with fat, which will have to be trimmed off to see the tenderloins clearly. Remove tenderloins by cutting along them next to the backbone. I like to eat tenderloins when they are fresh, refrigerating them until prepared for a meal.

The loins, or backstraps, are long, narrow muscles on both sides of the backbone. Loins extend from near the rump to the base of the neck. Remove as much fat as possible from that portion of the back before extracting the loins. Follow the same procedure used to free tenderloins to obtain the longer loins. Cut as deeply as possible on both sides of the backbone, slice one end of the loin free from the carcass and pull away

As soon as possible after a bear is down, the meat should be cut up and cooled. Bear meat is delicious if it is handled properly.

from the body while making final cuts along the length of the loin.

The four quarters and the loins comprise the bulk of the meat on a black bear, other than the neck. Ribs are usually too fatty for my liking, but there is some meat on them. Ribs and other undesirable scraps from a bear carcass usually get cooked for my dog to eat. I boil bear meat intended for my dog because he is as susceptible to trichinosis as I am. Odd pieces of usable meat salvaged from the carcass are used for stew, casseroles or ground into burger.

Transporting Meat And Hides

When transporting meat and hide long distances by car or airplane, dry ice is best for keeping them cold. It helps if they are frozen when starting out. Heavy duty boxes available from moving and storage companies are great for packing meat, hide and dry ice together. Pat Jarvis and I packed the meat and hide from my Colorado bear in such a box with 10 pounds of dry ice. Newspapers were used to fill in empty spaces before sealing the box with heavy-duty tape. When I got home late the following day, everything was still frozen solid.

One or two large coolers can also come in handy for transporting meat and hide. If dry ice isn't available to keep those items cold, chunks of regular ice will have to do, although the supply will have to be replenished at regular intervals depending on the temperature. Plastic garbage bags can be used to transport meat and hides with ice for day trips, if coolers or boxes are not available.

If a black bear carcass is taken out of the woods whole, and if the weather is cool (daytime temperatures less than 45 degrees Fahrenheit) or the animal can be put in a cooler, it can be hung several days without skinning. When it's warmer, the carcass should be skinned and butchered within 24 hours. If a bear is hung outside, make sure it stays in the shade. Direct sunlight will ruin bear meat and hides in no time. If it's warm enough for flies to be a problem, don't delay skinning and butchering. Flies can be discouraged from laying eggs on the meat for a short time by liberally sprinkling pepper inside the carcass, as well as on any open wounds, in the anal opening and in the nostrils. If flies do lay eggs on bear meat in little white clusters, the eggs should be removed as soon as possible to avoid damage to the meat.

Butchering

The first step in butchering a black bear after the major pieces have been removed from the carcass is to slice away as much fat as possible, while getting rid of hair and dirt. Fat will reduce the effective freezer life of meat, so it is important to eliminate it. Less freezer space will be re-

In remote areas the most convenient way to get out a bear is to skin it and butcher it in the woods. Be sure it's legal in the area you're hunting, and wear safety orange.

Hanging a bear by the hind legs and skinning toward the head makes the job go easily, especially for an experienced hand.

quired for defatted meat, too, and de-boning is a good idea for the same reason. Fat will be trimmed throughout the butchering process, as deposits inside the meat become easier to reach. Due to all of the fat trimming necessary on bear meat, especially in the fall, it is helpful to have a couple of sharp knives to work with or a sharpening tool to touch up the blade on a single knife.

Before starting to cut hams and shoulders into steaks, roasts and other cuts you should also have a supply of freezer paper, freezer bags or heavy-duty aluminum foil in which to wrap meat. I have used heavy-duty foil to wrap bear meat for years with excellent results. A large cutting board is handy to work on, and two big bowls are helpful to separate meat that will be used for stews, casseroles and burger.

When butchering a bear, try to cut away bloodshot meat. I usually give these pieces to my dog after boiling them with ribs, but meat that isn't too bloody can be salvaged by soaking it in saltwater.

Hunters should also have an idea what cuts of meat and how much of each they will want to use. Some people I know grind most of their bear meat into burger or have sausage made, using only the choicest pieces of meat for steaks and chops. That's a far better way to go about it than the person who puts roasts in the freezer, but never finds the time to prepare them. My wife and I reduce a carcass to roasts, steaks, chops, stew meat and burger because we like it prepared in a variety of ways.

Meat that is firmed up from being chilled or partially frozen is easiest to work with for butchering, but that isn't always possible. To speed up the butchering process, one person can trim and cut the meat while another separates it into meal-size packages and labels them. You should typically get two roasts from a bear. One from each ham. Roasts are also possible from the neck and shoulders, but neck and shoulder muscles are often best in stews or burger. If in a hurry, leave the shoulder blade in shoulder roasts, boning everything else. Steaks, instead of roasts, can also be cut from shoulders.

Meat from the lower portions of all four legs (below the knees) is used for stews or burger. Thin, outer muscles on hams are used the same way. Larger muscles on hams are separated and cut into steaks or left as roasts.

Loins can be cut into small chops or separated into larger steaks. Remove as much fat and connective tissue as possible from cuts before they are wrapped. It isn't necessary to get every scrap of fat from steaks, chops and roasts, though. Final trimming can be taken care of once thawed and ready to prepare. However, all fat should be eliminated from meat that will be ground into burger. Call ahead to be sure, and find out when it's convenient for the butcher. Some hunters insist that beef suet or pork fat be added to burger in a ratio of one pound of fat to anywhere from five to 10 pounds of meat. It's okay to do this, but it is not absolutely necessary. I leave my burger as pure, lean bear meat and it tastes just great.

Because I'm normally in a rush when butchering bear, I generally freeze two or three pounds of stew meat in chunks. Then I cut it into bite-size pieces before adding it to a stew or casserole. Hunters who prefer to have ready-to-cook stew meat in the freezer can take care of final cutting before freezing.

Whichever material is used to wrap bear meat, be sure it is wrapped tightly around the meat, eliminating air pockets. One layer of heavy-duty aluminum foil adequately protects meat. Some hunters double-wrap their meat in freezer paper or use freezer bags for one layer and freezer paper for the other. All packages of meat should be labeled as to the type and cut along with the date. I use masking tape to label foil packages, writing the information on the tape in ink before putting it on the foil. I simply use "B" for bear rather than writing out the word, followed by steak, roast, stew or whatever, and the date.

When packages of meat are put in the freezer try to spread them out initially, to accelerate freezing, rather than stacking them on top of one another. The colder your freezer, the faster meat will freeze. Storage life of frozen meat can be extended the colder a freezer is. A temperature of 0 degrees Fahrenheit is better than 10 degrees Fahrenheit, and readings below zero are better yet.

Cooking Bear Meat

People who try meat from a black bear that has been properly cared for are often surprised at how good it tastes. A fellow who got his first bear remarked about how great the meat was after having had several meals of it. He said it tasted like beef. Other hunters like bear meat better than venison.

Sound different from what you've heard? There's as much misinformation floating around about the meat from bear as there is about the animals themselves. The truth is bear meat can be great eating, whether from a spring or fall bear. But first a warning. Some black bear have trichinosis, which results from trichina larvae in their muscle tissue. This disease can be passed on to humans who eat infected black bear meat that is not cooked properly. Pigs are also carriers of trichinosis, along with raccoons, red foxes, coyotes and wolves. The percentage of black bear with trichinosis in hunted populations is very low, between two and three percent. In remote areas, the rate of occurrence may be slightly higher.

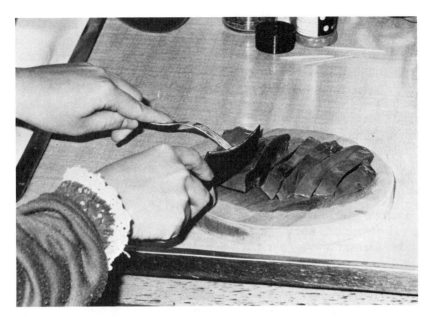

Save the liver! Sliced and prepared just like beef or venison liver, bear liver is every bit as tender and delicious!

The odds of bagging a black bear that has trichinosis are not high. To be on the safe side, though, all bear meat should be cooked so the inside of the meat reaches a temperature of at least 140 degrees Fahrenheit for a few minutes. To ensure that the inside of steaks and chops are properly cooked, they should be sliced thinner than venison.

There is no information available on how freezing affects trichina larvae in meat from wild game, according to Dr. Jerry Shad in Pennsylvania. However, he said that the larvae are killed in pork after being frozen solidly at 5 to -10 degrees Fahrenheit for two or three weeks. Three weeks are required if the meat is kept at 5 degrees Fahrenheit.

Black bear are fatty animals, especially during the fall. That fact turns some people off. I can't understand why, because you don't eat the fat, just the lean meat. Like any other big game, it is important to remove every speck of fat possible from black bear meat before it's cooked. Most of the fat should be removed during the butchering process before meat is packaged and frozen. Fat does not freeze well and will reduce the quality of meat the longer it remains frozen. When meat is thawed for a meal, any last little bits of fat should be removed as a first step in preparing the meat.

It is difficult to cut off all the fat from roasts. What I usually do is break a roast down into smaller chunks of meat to get at as much fat as possible. However, there is an easier way to remove the last traces of fat from roasts—parboiling. By parboiling a roast for 20 to 30 minutes at medium to high heat before putting it in the oven or crock pot, fat marbled in the meat is boiled off.

The age and weight of black bear doesn't appear to affect the quality of the meat, either. A fellow I know who killed a boar that dressed over 500 pounds said the meat was so tender he could cut it with a fork. That animal had been eating apples. I ate meat from another male that weighed more than 400 pounds, that tasted as good as any bear meat I've eaten. A friend of mine bagged a sow that was about 16 years old and the meat proved to be fine from that one, too.

Keeping Meat Moist

Because bear meat should be cooked thoroughly, steps should be taken to ensure that it stays moist. Sauces, soups and broths all work well for this purpose. In some cases, small amounts of water can be used to steam meat. No moisture at all is necessary when broiling steaks, including tenderloins, or chops. It doesn't take long for these cuts to cook thoroughly at 375 to 400 degrees and the inside of the meat retains plenty of moisture.

Most black bear recipes are quick and simple. My wife and I use very little seasoning, enjoying the natural flavor of the meat rather than trying to mask it, although we do use a lot of soups. When frying steaks and chops, a little butter or margarine is melted in the fry pan, then the meat is browned. Once the meat is browned, a cup of water or beef broth is added and the pan covered to keep steam in while the cooking process is completed at medium heat for about 20 minutes.

16

Record Book Bear

Many black bear hunters interested in bagging a trophy animal are weight conscious. I'm no exception. When I'm caught daydreaming about that once-in-a-lifetime bruin stepping in front of my sights, he usually weights at least 500 pounds on the paw...often more. That's the fun of daydreams.

Such an animal would indeed be a trophy in the eyes of almost every bear hunter. But, in fact, its weight would have no bearing on whether or not it qualified for "record book" status.

Record book black bear have to have big skulls. Weight and hide measurements of black bear, although of interest to many hunters, are not a fair way to judge all bruins one against another. It is simply impossible to accurately weigh carcasses that must be skinned and quartered to get out of the woods, or butchered on the spot because they are in an inaccessible location. Also, the weight of individual animals varies considerably between spring and fall seasons. Hide measurements are not the best comparison, either, since it is impossible to stretch all skins consistently. Body size, hide size and skull size of bear are sometimes related, but not always.

There are two national record books maintained to recognize outstanding big game trophies. Bow and arrow harvests are monitored by the Pope & Young Club. Exceptional animals harvested by any legal means or picked up from animals which died of natural causes are listed in *Records of North American Big Game* published by the Boone &

Crockett Club. A black bear skull has to have a minimum score of 18 to qualify for listing in Pope & Young's *Bowhunting Big Game Records of North America* and 21 to be considered for the Boone & Crockett record book.

Black bear skulls are scored by measuring their length and width with the lower jaw detached, then combining the measurements. All muscle and tissue has to be removed from a skull before it can be scored, of course. A 60-day drying period is also required before the skull can be officially measured. The drying period doesn't start until the skull is cleaned. Some shrinkage is bound to occur during the drying period.

Measuring Skulls

Calipers are usually used by official scorers to accurately measure the length and width of bear skulls to the nearest one-sixteenth of an inch. However, I watched Michigan measurer Duaine Wenzel score a black bear skull by placing it on a ruler, then using two straight edges to determine measurements. Hunters can do the same thing themselves. Hunters can also get a rough idea how skulls will score with a tape measure or ruler and a couple of blocks of wood.

Simply put the skull, minus the lower jaw, on a flat, level surface.

A Boone & Crockett scorer measures a skull with two straight-edges and a yard stick. Calipers are often used by measurers to score skulls.

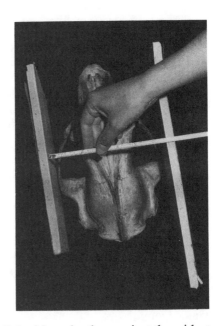

Hunters can get a general idea of how a skull will score by taking measurements between two blocks of wood.

Then place the pieces of wood parallel with each other against the widest points of the skull. The blocks of wood should be about as long as the skull but taller, and should be upright when resting.

Measure from the inside of one block to the inside of the other across the widest point. Once the width has been obtained, the pieces of wood can be positioned parallel to one another with one at the nose and the other across the back of the skull to determine the length. If the cumulative total comes close to 18 or 21, depending on whether the bear was bagged with bow or gun, an official scorer should be contacted for an accurate measurement.

A list of official scorers in the hunter's state can be obtained from Pope & Young and Boone & Crockett. On gun-killed bear, address inquiries to: Boone & Crockett Club, P.O. Box 547, Dumfries, VA 22026. On bow-killed bear, address inquiries to: Pope & Young Club, Box 548, Chatfield, MN 55923.

Large black bear skulls that are found by hunters while afield, and those turned up in barns, garages and attics are eligible for record book listing. Damaged skulls will be considered, but it is still to the advantage of hunters interested in having bear skulls measured to avoid shooting the animals in the head. Bear must be taken under rules of fair chase for the skull to qualify for listing in either record book.

Some Of The Biggest

The present world record black bear skull was found by Alma Lund and Merrill Daniels seven miles from their home in Ephraim, Utah during 1975. The skull scored 23^{10}/$_{16}$. That official score made it 1^4/$_{16}$ inches better than the previous record holder, which also came from Utah five years earlier. Rex Peterson and R.S. Hardy collected the former world record black bear while hunting with hounds. That skull scored 22^6/$_{16}$.

Two more black bear skulls scoring 22^6/$_{16}$ are now on record. One was collected in Arizona by Roy Stewart during 1978. The second was bagged by John Whyne in Pennsylvania during 1983. Whyne said he was making a drive with companions on a mountain when he stopped to take a drink of water from a spring and got behind the other drivers. As he moved ahead after taking the drink, he spotted the record book bear 50 to 75 yards ahead looking downhill toward one of the other drivers. The animal had a dressed weight of 580 pounds, according to a scale at the check station, and it was determined to be nine years old. The skull from Whyne's bear was measured by a member of the Pennsylvania Game Commission.

At the end of the Boone & Crockett's 18th awards program during 1983, those three skulls scoring 22^6/$_{16}$ became third largest. A bruin bagged in Saskatchewan during 1977 by Calvin Parsons is ^{2}/$_{16}$ of an inch larger with a score of 22^8/$_{16}$.

Ray Cox holds the honor of having arrowed a black bear with the largest skull on record for a bowhunter at 22^4/$_{16}$. The old male was treed by dogs in Colorado during 1978. Cox reported that the animal didn't have any teeth left. The number two bow-killed black bear was collected by Robert Faufau in Wisconsin during 1981 while hunting over bait. The skull from that bruin scored 21^{14}/$_{16}$.

Record Book Sows

Sow black bear seldom grow heads large enough to qualify for record book recognition. Consequently, most of the skulls listed in the record books are from boars. However, there are 11 skulls from sows listed in the third edition of *Bowhunting Big Game Records* out of more than 1,500 black bear entries. Record book sows were taken in Wisconsin, Utah, Idaho, Minnesota, New Mexico, Quebec, Saskatchewan and Alberta. The score of the largest sow skull is 19^{15}/$_{16}$.

Characteristics Of Book Bear

Age, genetic background and diet are probably the three major factors that determine if any given bear will have a record book skull. There

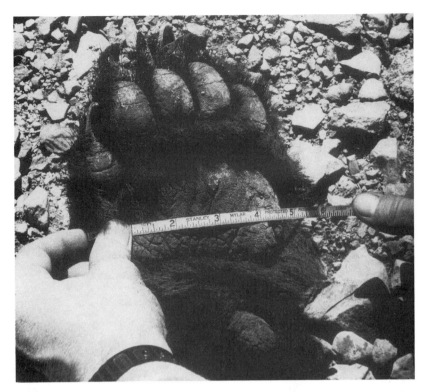

The paw on this Pope & Young black bear measures a touch more than five inches across. That's a good one!

has to be a good mix of all three to produce a boar with an exceptional skull. Some boars may be old and heavy due to an abundant food supply, but have skulls that are not book material because their genetic background does not favor large head growth.

The largest bear on record in Michigan, weightwise, is a prime example of this. The animal had a verified, dressed weight of 613 pounds. That bruin's skull scored $20^{12}/_{16}$. A bowhunter, Hawley Rhew, bagged that bear, so it easily qualified for listing among the bowhunting records, but if a gun hunter had taken the animal, it would have been too small for the book.

On the other hand, a boar with a genetic makeup that favors head growth may never become record book material if his food intake is meager, and he certainly won't if he doesn't live long enough. Black bear attain maximum skull growth by the time they are 9 or 10 years old.

The number of possibilities involving age, genetics and nutrition are numerous, but as a general rule, the heaviest black bear in a given area

Notice how large the ears appear in relation to the head on this small black bear. This is what some hunters call a "dog bear."

are the oldest and have the biggest heads. And boars average larger in size than sows. A sow weighing more than 300 pounds is bigger-than-average and basically represents the top end of the weight scale for sows. Boars attain weights upwards of 700 pounds; however, they become exceptional once they reach 400 to 500 pounds.

Judging Bears

Body, head and track size are the best guidelines available for judging a black bear's record book potential in the field. Any bruin that leaves a front footprint that measures from five to six inches or more across is definitely above average and would probably weigh a minimum of 300 pounds in the round, at least during the fall. The odds are excellent that such an animal would have a skull big enough to qualify for a Pope & Young listing. Whether or not the animal's head would have at least another three inches of bone may depend on the animal's genetic background and age.

When you're looking at a truly big bear, you'll know it! Everything about this guy says big. He'll at least qualify for Pope & Young records.

The best a hunter can do when hoping to bag a book bear is look for the biggest bear in the area being hunted and try for it. Big-bodied bruins are generally easy to distinguish from small to average animals. Their bodies are often deep from back to belly and long from head to tail. Fall bear will look thicker across the body than they will in the spring, of course. The heavy breathing of a fat bear is often audible within 20 or 30 yards, too. Their gait as they walk is slower and more swaggering than smaller animals.

The ears on the heads of small to average black bear will be prominent and snouts will have a pointed appearance. Ears will look shorter and smaller on bear with big heads, and their snouts look rounded, giving a snub-nose appearance. It takes experience to accurately judge the head and body size of black bear, and even experienced hunters make mistakes in situations where the entire animal isn't visible or only brief glimpses of animals are possible.

A good thing to do for a hunter who has seen few black bear and

A trophy is in the eye of the beholder. This guy may not make any record books, but a lot of hunters would enjoy having that beautiful pelt on the wall.

plans to hunt them is to visit a zoo that has the animals and look at them carefully. Estimate their weight and, if possible, check with the zookeeper to find out how much the animals actually weigh. Black bear are simply difficult to judge accurately. Perhaps because of the adrenalin factor which comes into play when a bear is sighted, most hunters over-estimate the weight of black bear.

Study Record Books

Bear hunters who are serious about getting their names in one of the record books should also study current record book listings to get an idea about what areas have produced the most big bear skulls. These locations can be good places to try for a book bear of your own.

Arizona, Colorado and Wisconsin, for example, lead all other states and provinces by a wide margin for the number of bear in Boone & Crockett listings through the 18th recording period. The first two have 20 listings each and Wisconsin has 19. California is next in line with 14. From there the most B&C bear from any state or province goes down to seven.

The most listings in the latest edition of the Pope & Young records are for Colorado (94), Ontario (89), Idaho (47), Maine (45) and Wisconsin (44). Also high in record book bow kills are Minnesota (36), California (31) and Michigan (20).

Although current record book listings provide valuable information, they in no way provide the total picture as far as book bear are concerned. Unlike large antlers, which are usually saved and eventually end up being measured for record book consideration, many big bear skulls have been left in the field or discarded and will never be recorded. States and provinces with the most listings probably reflect where the most bear hunting pressure is as much as where book bear are located.

The book bear producing potential of a number of Canadian provinces, I believe, is yet to be realized. Alberta, British Columbia, Manitoba and Saskatchewan all have excellent black bear populations, for example, but not many animals from those provinces are listed in the record book compared to some states with lower bear populations. New hunting areas with great record book potential are opening in the Maritime Provinces, too. A high percentage of the bear qualifying for the records that are listed for Canadian provinces were taken in the past 10 years.

Perhaps the reason more black bear are not listed from most Canadian provinces is the apparent lack of hunter interest. Many hunters from the United States who travel to these provinces, have their sights set on larger and more glamorous game such as moose, sheep, elk, caribou and

Matt Gettler (left) and his father Norm with the 22-inch black bear skull which is a Michigan state record.

grizzly bear. Many local hunters look on black bear as pests. For these reasons, black bear are largely overlooked in much of Canada. Hunters interested in a record book black bear should keep that in mind.

Any hunter who is serious about bagging a record book black bear has an excellent chance of doing so, especially with bow and arrow, not only in Canada, but in parts of the U.S. as well. To be successful in the search for an exceptional bruin, however, a hunter must be willing to pass up lesser animals and make the time to go on lengthy hunts. My best bear is one I bagged with bow and arrow in Minnesota on a fall hunt. The six-year-old boar had an 18-inch skull and is a fine Pope & Young Record Book trophy.

While guiding bowhunter Gary Lohman from Grand Rapids, Michigan, I stood next to him as he arrowed a Pope & Young bear, which was perhaps more thrilling for me than Gary at the time, because he didn't fully comprehend what he had accomplished until later.

I knew the bear was big when I saw it coming on the first evening of

Percentage Of Record Book Bear

State	B&C Bear (%)	P&Y Bear (%)
Alaska	5%	4%
Arizona	15	1
California	8	6
Colorado	12	12
Idaho	1	10
Louisiana	1	0
Maine	0	4
Massachusetts	0	*
Michigan	1	4
Minnesota	1	5
Montana	1	3
New Hampshire	0	*
New Mexico	1	2
New York	2	1
North Carolina	1	*
Oregon	1	2
Pennsylvania	4	0
Tennessee	0	*
Utah	4	1
Vermont	0	*
Virginia	1	1
Washington	3	2
West Virginia	0	*
Wisconsin	11	7
Wyoming	4	*
Province		
Alberta	6	1
British Columbia	6	2
Manitoba	1	3
New Brunswick	0	1
Newfoundland	1	*
Nova Scotia	1	0
Ontario	1	21
Quebec	1	2
Saskatchewan	4	4
Mexico	1	0

Boone & Crockett black bear skulls must have a minimum 21-inch score. Pope & Young require an 18-inch minimum. Asterisk (*) symbol indicates less than 1 percent.

the season during the last minutes of daylight. The animal reminded me of a big, round barrel with legs. Gary drew his compound bow as the big bruin approached the bait and released the arrow as soon as the animal turned angling away, making a good hit that put the boar down in about 50 yards. I'm sure the animal had a dressed weight over 400 pounds. The skull scored 18^9/$_{16}$ and is listed in *Bowhunting Big Game Records of North America*.

Trophy vs. Book Bear

The word trophy was mentioned a couple of times in the opening sentences of this chapter and appears elsewhere in this book. Before closing, I think it is important to point out that trophy and record book black bear are seldom one and the same, but they can be. Any hunter can collect a trophy black, but few score well enough to make the book.

A trophy bear is a personal thing. Each hunter sets his or her own standards for determining what is and is not a trophy. Hunters who have never bagged a black bear may consider any legal animal a trophy, especially if they only have one opportunity to hunt bear in a lifetime. To others, a trophy might be one that weighs a minimum of 200 pounds. Experienced black bear hunters might regard any bruin with a dressed weight of at least 300 pounds as a trophy.

The obvious difference between trophy and record book bruins is that the standards for record status are set by the Boone & Crockett and Pope & Young Clubs. Those standards are not flexible like they are for trophies. And that's the way it has to be to have a uniform, reliable system. Anyone who collects a black bear with a skull large enough for listing in either record book has certainly downed an exceptional representative of one of the most interesting big game species in North America.

17

Are They Dangerous?

B lack bear can be dangerous, especially those that do not fear man. However, unprovoked black bear, particularly those in areas where they are regularly hunted and have learned to fear man, are seldom dangerous. There are exceptions, of course.

Potentially dangerous bear fit in two categories. Bruins in wilderness settings have little, if any, contact with man. Because all black bear are predators, bear in those remote regions may view man as prey. The second category includes park bear. Bear that live in parks are often protected and do not learn to fear man for this reason. Many, in fact, come in contact with people on a regular basis, and associate people with food.

Black Bear Attacks

The vast majority of attacks where people have been injured or killed by black bear have occurred in remote areas or parks. At least 16 people have been killed by black bear since 1948. In one case, a single bear killed three people; in another, two people were killed by the same bruin. Thirteen different bear were involved, and all but three were in Canada, Alaska or parks.

The purpose of pointing this out is not to discourage people from venturing into parks or remote areas of Canada or Alaska. Even though black bear can be considered somewhat more dangerous in these locations than elsewhere, the odds of encountering an aggressive bruin are still slim. Over a span of 10 years, for example, there have to be thousands of times when black bear and people came in contact with one another, although in many of the cases the people probably didn't know it. Encounters that prove to be dangerous to people represent an extremely small sliver out of the overall picture. If you use good common sense when visiting or living in areas with black bear, chances are slim to none that you will ever have a problem. When you venture into unfamiliar country, check with wildlife officials first to obtain guidelines for travel in bear country.

I personally feel that some attacks by black bear are blown way out of proportion by the news media. Black bear attacks are rare enough that the media makes the most out of them when they do occur because it's a well-known fact that readers, viewers and listeners are interested in items of that sort. There has been increased reporting of bear attacks in recent years due to this interest.

Confrontations between black bear and people may also be on the increase as man continues pushing farther into remote locations, developing tracts of land that once were the home of black bear. The bruins in these cases are considered the villain when they become unwilling neighbors. Visitation rates at national parks are also on the increase, bringing millions upon millions of people into black bear habitat and in contact with bear.

If black bear weren't the easy-going, stay-out-of-man's-way animals that they most often are, there would be many more unpleasant accounts of bear attacks recorded than there are now. Anyone who willingly enters black bear habitat should accept the responsibility of trying to avoid trouble with bear as well as the risks involved, slight as they are, of being among bear. Sometimes, people increase the likelihood of a bear attack, if for no other reason than being on the black bear's turf. It seems as though black bear are often blamed for causing personal injury when the animals are only doing what is natural for them under the circumstances. We will have to accept black bear as they are rather than as we want them to be as long as we insist on invading their territory.

More often than not, black bear and people can be compatible. Hikers, campers, photographers and hunters are probably at greater risk from falls resulting in broken bones while afield than attacks from black bear, even from wounded animals. Wounded bear and those cornered by hounds are certainly potentially dangerous because the animals can be expected to try to defend themselves, that's part of the hunt. Hunters are most likely to encounter black bear that are wounded or cornered and they are usually carrying guns in preparation for what may happen.

I know of some hunters who have received minor injuries from bruins while hunting, but the hunters have always gotten the upper hand.

Black bear can look very threatening when they are encountered in the woods, but normally they will leave people alone if they are left alone.

Injured black bear will run rather than fight more often than not.

Experiences Of Researchers

Now that my opening statement has been clarified, I want to continue with that thought, re-emphasizing some of the things already mentioned. Basically, black bear do not deserve the reputation received over the years as a potential threat to human life and limb. If they were as dangerous as many people believe, most of the prominent black bear researchers in the U.S. and Canada surely would have been killed, or at least maimed, long ago, and the number of people willing to study these interesting animals would be declining rather than increasing as they are now.

These men and women handle hundreds, if not thousands, of black bear on the continent annually, and routinely work with agitated animals caught in snares and live traps. A handful of these people have received minor injuries from black bear, but nothing of major consequence. Pat Carr from Pennsylvania is one of the researchers who received minor injuries from a bear. Pat has worked with bruins in Pennsylvania and in the Great Smoky Mountains National Park.

The incident happened on Pat's first experience with a snared black bear. He was with a biologist and two game protectors when they approached a huge boar, weighing over 500 pounds, in a snare. The bear charged them when they got close, and the cable, which was kinked and weakened, snapped. The biologist jumped in the air when the cable broke and the bear went right under one of his legs. That left Pat in the bear's path and he took off running with the bear right behind him.

Pat made an abrupt change in course at one point, turning sharply to one side. Most black bear would have broken off pursuit there, continuing in the direction they were headed, but this one didn't. It turned with Pat and swatted him on the shoulder, knocking him down. The bear walked over Pat, stepping on the ground rather than on him, and left the scene.

Because Pat was wearing heavy clothes, only a couple of minor scratches resulted from being hit by the bear. However, his ribs were bruised from hitting the ground so hard. That experience heightened Pat's interest in black bear rather than souring it, because he knew only too well that bear could have easily killed him, but it didn't.

In most cases, black bear will go out of their way to avoid trouble. The bruin that hit Pat was agitated enough to instinctively strike out, but obviously wasn't the cold-blooded killer that these animals are sometimes made out to be.

Black bear researchers are living proof that the animals aren't as

Black bear become a danger when they lose their fear of humans. Improper habits around campsites can contribute to bear delinquency.

dangerous as commonly thought. These people deal with bear on a daily basis and have come to know and understand the animals better than ever before.

This knowledge and experience contradicts many long-held beliefs about black bear in general as well as their danger to people. Unfortunately, more people have read sensationalized accounts of isolated black bear attacks than routine reports written by bear biologists. That, however, is beginning to change.

Confusion With Grizzlies

There has also been confusion between black bear and grizzly bear. They are two totally different animals and seldom behave in the same way. A black bear sow is seldom as protective of her cubs, for example, as a grizzly sow with cubs. Black bear biologists routinely chase sows and cubs in an effort to tree the cubs so they can be captured and tagged. While spending a week with one biologist we chased and treed a sow with cubs on two consecutive days without experiencing any problems.

Many researchers report that sows will put on a good show, bluff charging and woofing, but most will send cubs up a tree and leave or climb a tree with them. Sows that behave in an unusually aggressive manner are either tranquilized before handling the cubs or are left alone. As forest dwellers, young black bear are often safe in trees and don't need the sow's protection, unless caught in the open or actually captured on the ground by a predator.

This does not mean that hunters can be unconcerned in the presence of a sow and cubs. Always avoid getting between a sow with cubs, or pursuing cubs. It does mean that there is no reason to panic when in the presence of a sow with cubs. Simply keep a cool head and back out of the way as quickly as possible, facing the sow if she is visible. Sows sometimes bluff charge, advancing a short distance toward an intruder, then stopping. Try not to turn and run, which can trigger an attack. Sometimes talking to an aroused bear as you back up helps keep you calm, even if it has no effect on the bear.

Boars are more aggressive than sows, and are responsible for most of the attacks on people. Records indicate boars were responsible for all fatal black bear attacks where the sex of the bruin was determined.

Fear Of The Unknown

The fact that many people tend to fear the unknown or what they don't understand applies only too well to black bear. For this reason, behavior that may be simply a warning, such as a bluff charge, or actions based on curiosity, such as a bear approaching or following a person, are often misinterpreted as aggression because the animal involved is a bear. Bear can be curious just like a white-tailed deer, but most people respond totally differently to the two. If a deer approaches a hunter, he usually gets excited and hopes the animal comes closer. Meanwhile, hunters approached by a black bear normally become scared and respond accordingly.

One summer, for instance, I was watching three black bear at a dump in northern Minnesota where a couple from Illinois were doing the same thing. All three bear were boars, which are most commonly seen at dumps, with one being an adult and the other two probably yearlings. A herring gull was caught on something among the garbage and it flipped its wings in a vain attempt to fly on two different occasions when a bear came close. On both occasions, the bear ignored the bird.

After the adult left and the two smaller bruins were on the opposite side of the garbage pile about 30 or 40 yards from the gull, I decided to free the gull. As I neared the bird, it struggled to get away as it had when

This collared black bear sow was chased into a tree with her cubs by people on foot. When alarmed, sows often send cubs up a tree, then leave the area for a while.

each bear came close. Monofilament fishing line was wrapped around one of the gull's legs, so I grabbed the line and pulled the bird toward me to hold it still while I cut the monofilament as close to its foot as possible.

Meanwhile, the guy from Illinois said, "Hey pard, one of those bear is getting close, you'd better watch out," with obvious concern in his voice.

When I looked around, one of the yearlings was watching me, but was still about 25 yards away. I could see no real reason for alarm. I figured the commotion probably aroused the bear's curiosity. I quickly cut the line and tossed the gull into the air toward the bear, expecting that to catch the animal's attention. However, at that point I noticed that the bear was looking directly at me and its gaze never shifted when the gull flew. The bear advanced toward me.

Its ears were up in a normal position and the hair on its neck was down, so I was sure the animal was still curious, but I wasn't positive of its intentions. It was getting close enough to make me uncomfortable, so I said something to it in a normal tone, but that had no effect. It kept coming.

Then I raised my voice and hollered, "Back off now," snapping my fingers at the same time. That stopped the animal, as if it understood what I said. It hesitated for a moment, then turned and walked away. The bear didn't understand the words, of course, it reacted to the volume of my voice.

By that time the guy from Illinois was hyperventilating, genuinely concerned that he was about to see a person attacked by a black bear right before his eyes. He was impressed by the simple actions on my part that it took to stop the bear, too. My interpretation of what was happening was obviously different than his, and I think I was correct in my assessment of the situation. I suspect the bear either thought I was putting out food or I was going to feed it something by hand. When it realized that this wasn't the case, it left.

Anyone can do what I did in the situation, but I don't recommend putting yourself in such a spot intentionally. I certainly didn't, having no idea that bear's curiosity would be aroused by freeing the gull. If I had known what was going to happen, I would have waited until the other two bear left before releasing the bird.

Predictable

I've read countless times that black bear aren't predictable. I strongly disagree, convinced that these animals are predictable in many cases, although I will readily admit that they aren't always predictable. The more a person watches black bear, the more they learn about the ani-

Problems start when people forget that bear are wild animals, and not lovable, cuddly cartoon characters.

mals and the better they are able to predict how the animals will respond or react under a certain set of circumstances. This is true for any form of wildlife, not just black bear.

As a photographer and hunter, I've come to realize black bear will tolerate my presence as long as I don't crowd them, and keep all of my movements slow and deliberate. I also know when to back off, either as a result of clues given me by an individual animal or when two of them get in an argument and one of them may suddenly turn and run. I've had bear run by me a few feet away, either to escape another animal or flee from an approaching motorcycle, but I try to give them plenty of room whenever possible.

How are black bear predictable? The vast majority of them will leave the area when they encounter a human. Bear that people see first usually haven't seen, heard or smelled them yet. A shout will normally take care of that. Individuals who don't want to alarm a bear can simply watch the animal until it goes out of sight. Bird hunters or deer hunters who prefer not to see any bear while scouting an area should whistle or carry a radio or bells. Carrying on a conversation with companions works, too.

Problem Animals

If a bear refuses to leave, and even comes closer, holler some more in an effort to scare the animal away while also attracting the attention of other people who may be nearby. Groups of people are more intimidating to a black bear than a lone person. At the same time you are hollering, look for a sturdy stick or branch that can serve as a club.

Black bear frequently give clues to their disposition through positioning of ears and hair, plus their actions. Bruins that have ears laid back and the hair up on the back of necks are definitely in a bad mood. Animals that snort, woof, swat the air or vegetation and advance quickly toward a person aren't happy, either. Bear that approach uncertainly with ears up could be curious, but they may also be trying to size up the prospects for a meal.

Always face a bold black bear. If it tries to circle behind you, move with it. Turning and running or climbing a tree are wasted efforts under most circumstances. These bear can outrun and outclimb anybody. Here again, don't confuse black bear with grizzly bear. A tree may provide escape from a grizzly because their claws are not adapted for climbing like those of their smaller relatives.

A number of people attacked by black bear have been pulled out of trees by bruins. At least one person who died did so as a result of injuries sustained in a fall from a tree rather than damage done by the bear. That person may have survived if he hadn't climbed a tree.

Although climbing a tree is not a good way to escape a black bear, going into the water of a river or lake may be, provided the water is deep enough. People can certainly keep their heads above water in deeper water than black bear can. Black bear are good swimmers, too, but may be reluctant to follow a person into the water or carry out an attack in that element.

When, and if, a black bear does approach and a person has the time, dropping a pack, fishing creel or other item is a good thing to do. If there's food inside it may distract the animal long enough to allow a person to escape. Once the item is dropped, back away and keep going as far as possible until reaching safety.

In situations where a bear moves in close and a club is handy, it can be used to fan the air between the bruin and the person or to beat on trees while hollering. This tactic worked for Wayne Pangborn when he met an overcurious black bear while fishing for brook trout on a stream in Michigan's Upper Peninsula. When he first encountered the bear at close range he reacted by hollering at it, which temporarily scared it off. To put some distance between himself and the bear, Pangborn crossed the stream he had been fishing only to discover the bruin was following

People fear the unknown. The more we learn about bear, the more the general public will come to respect these magnificent wild creatures.

When a black bear stands on its hind legs, it is usually because it is curious, not threatening. A black bear that walks forward with its ears laid back means business.

Despite the promotions of northern states resort owners, tourists must be made aware that dumps are not the native habitat of black bear.

him. At that point he threw his creel, containing several trout, toward the bear, which distracted the animal briefly, but it quickly turned its attention back to the fisherman. The desperate angler then grabbed pieces of wood for clubs. He used the clubs to swing at the bear and beat on trees to fend the animal off for three-quarters of a mile until he reached his car.

If a bear gets close enough to hit with a club, the end of the nose is a good target. This part of a black bear's anatomy is very sensitive.

Some black bear attacks come suddenly without warning, offering a person no opportunity to defend himself. When this happens, the recommended procedure is to assume a fetal position with bent legs protecting the stomach and hands clasped together around the back of the neck. The animal will often bite and claw its victim, but it is often best to try to play dead. Screams and struggling usually prolong the attack. An individual in this situation should wait until the bear is gone before attempting to get up. If a bruin is still in sight when movement resumes, it may renew the attack.

Although passive response is recommended when under immediate attack by black bear—and most people who have done this survived—others have survived by fighting, either using a knife or their fists. A lot depends on the victim's size, strength, inclination and circumstances. Some who tried to fight off a black bear apparently made the wrong choice, having been killed for their efforts. However, they may have been, anyway.

Avoid Contact

The best way to handle confrontations with black bear is to avoid them in the first place. Most bruins favor this approach as well when it comes to dealing with people. When camping in bear country all food and sweet smelling items such as toothpaste and perfumes should be kept at least 60 feet from a tent.

Avoid cooking inside a tent in bear country because odors will linger, especially if things are spilled. Also keep clothes that contain odors, such as fish, blood from game or food stains, outside the tent.

There is evidence that bear may be attracted to human menstrual odors, so women who are in bear country during their menstrual cycles should be extra careful about disposal of tampons and pads. A study using black bear in Ontario found that the animals were attracted to used tampons.

While I maintain that black bear are generally not dangerous, there are exceptions, and outdoor enthusiasts in black bear habitat should be mindful of this, doing what they can to avoid confrontations with bear. Black bear are certainly capable of being dangerous, using their speed and strength to catch and kill or injure people, if they choose to. Fortunately for us, black bear seldom react that way toward humans. They should be respected for the way they are, not feared.

18

Management

W here black bear have little contact with man, the animals usually manage quite well on their own. However, where man and bear routinely interact, which today is the case throughout much of the animal's range, they sometimes need help to maintain healthy populations.

But as wonderful as it is to see bear and know they exist, an equally important facet of black bear management is keeping their numbers at a low enough level so that they don't create too many problems for people. In effect, people management is also an essential part of managing black bear because man's activities play a key role in the survival of bear, and our actions can normally be more easily controlled than those of bruins.

One of the most important management tools for maintaining existing, healthy black bear populations is hunting. Where healthy bear populations exist, but hunting isn't permitted, such as in national parks, different management strategies have to be used. In areas where bear numbers are low and unstable, total protection of the animals and their habitat is required to ensure survival and population expansion. Managers can even use methods to speed up black bear population increases and reintroduce animals to suitable habitat that isn't already occupied.

A Difficult Task

Black bear management isn't easy. The nature of the animals and the attitudes of some people toward them don't lend themselves to compromise. However, professional wildlife managers in most areas have been doing a good job and will be able to do even better in the future as more information about the animals is gathered, and as their constituents develop a better understanding of black bear and their habitat.

In regard to hunting black bear, there have been changes in regulations governing the activity in some states and provinces during recent years and more can be expected in the future. Some changes will be more restrictive than they are now and others will liberalize black bear hunting opportunities.

Hunting Regulations

Black bear hunting regulations are geared toward providing a maximum amount of recreational opportunity for hunters while, at the same time, ensuring the harvest of only surplus bear. Surplus animals are those that aren't necessary for reproduction to keep the population at optimum levels. Boars are the most expendable members of the population, so where black bear numbers are at or near stable levels, hunting regulations may be geared toward maximizing the harvest of boars and minimizing the harvest of sows. Where bear populations are high and the animals are underharvested, regulations don't have to be as restrictive.

Mature sows are the most important segment of black bear populations because it takes them a number of years to reach the age of fertility. As discussed earlier, that's from three to seven years of age. Once they mature, sows generally produce cubs on an every-other-year basis, and sometimes less frequently. The harvest of too many mature sows will reduce production, perhaps resulting in a decline of the population. Since boars are polygamous, the removal of some of them won't significantly affect future reproduction.

One of the biggest problems managers have in setting hunting regulations for black bear is that optimum populations and harvest levels are nebulous factors that can be difficult to pinpoint. The only reliable method of estimating black bear populations at the present time is capturing and marking a segment of the population. This has been done in a number of states and provinces and is continuing in some of them. Since this process is expensive and time consuming, it is not used on a wide scale. On top of that, bear productivity and hunter harvest often varies from year-to-year in the same area.

Consequently, hunting regulations are sometimes changed as bear populations increase or decline in response to hunting pressure and environmental factors. In most cases today, hunting regulations are more restrictive than they have to be to reduce the chances that too many black

This tagged bear has been recaptured in a snare. Information on its movement and growth will help determine future hunting regulations in the area.

bear will be bagged by hunters. This is better than being too liberal, as was the case years ago in some areas when lack of information and/or concern led to overharvests of black bear.

Such was the case in the northern regions of Michigan's Lower Peninsula and in Pennsylvania. Bear were totally protected once a decline was identified. The animals responded well to protection, enabling their numbers to rebuild to huntable levels and annual hunting seasons are now held in both areas.

In Pennsylvania, for example, the bear population doubled after two years of protection, and that state now has the second largest number of black bear in all of the eastern U.S., estimated at 7,500. Maine has more bruins, with an estimated 18,000 roaming the state.

There were a record 1,614 black bear tagged by hunters in Pennsylvania during a recent season and biologists there say that is the minimum harvest needed to keep the population stable. They would like to see hunters collect at least 2,000 bruins during future hunts to reduce damage and nuisance complaints. Pennsylvania's bear harvest was achieved during only three days of hunting. Plans are underway to change bear hunting in this state to benefit both the animals and hunters. At the present time, 100,000 bear permits are issued that are good anywhere where bruins can be hunted in the state.

The Pennsylvania season can be extended to one full week if the state is broken down into management units, with permit quotas established for each unit. Pennsylvania game managers report that this would distribute hunting pressure more evenly and result in a higher number of permits for units with the most bear. This would put hunters where their chances of success are best, and would result in the harvest of bruins from locations where they should be thinned to reduce nuisance complaints, while building healthy populations in other areas.

The number of hunters who could participate in Minnesota's bear hunt has been limited by permit for various management units since 1982, and the system appears to be working well. Permits are issued early enough in the year to enable some permit holders to fill their tag with a nuisance bear before the regular season opens, if they choose. This program of handling nuisance bear was begun on an experimental basis during 1984, and it remains to be seen how effective it will be.

Besides limiting the number of hunters, black bear harvests are regulated by seasons, bag limits and hunting methods. When managers want to protect sows, seasons can be set early enough or late enough so that most of the bear that are active during the hunt are boars, with most sows in dens. Where black bear are abundant and lightly hunted such as parts of Alaska, bag limits may be liberal, allowing hunters to take two or more bear a year. In most areas, though, bag limits are one bear a year per hunter. Bag limits sometimes protect sows with cubs and their cubs, too. Some hunting methods are outlawed or restricted because they result in too high a harvest of sows as well as for other reasons. What bear hunting methods are traditionally acceptable often plays a role in which ones are legal.

Sows with cubs and their cubs are almost uniformly protected during spring hunts, as they should be. There is some variability and disagreement on the protection of sows with cubs, and especially cubs, during fall hunts, though. In some states it is legal to shoot sows with cubs during fall hunts, but not cubs, and in other states any bear, including cubs, are legal. Still other states, most frequently in the western U.S., protect sows with cubs and their cubs during fall and spring seasons. Part of the reason for this is that sows in the West aren't as productive, on the average, as they are in the Midwest and East. States where sows with cubs can be taken by hunters during the fall do not protect adult sows because cubs can usually take care of themselves by then.

Cub Laws Of Questionable Value

A basic flaw with regulations that protect cubs during the fall is that in some cases it is impossible for hunters in the field to distinguish cubs from yearlings because there is an overlap in size. Male cubs, for example, will sometimes be bigger than yearling sows, and sometimes even look as big as adult sows.

Size is the only feature hunters can go by to tell cubs from older animals. In some cases, the difference in size is obvious, but in others it isn't. Where cubs are protected, the best rule of thumb is not to shoot if you sight a small bear that you think may be a cub. However, I know hunters who shot cubs, convinced they were legal bear. The only way to determine if a black bear is a cub or a yearling once it's down is to look at the teeth. Cubs will have milk teeth in place of canines. Bear that have canine teeth are at least a year old.

Bear hunters who use poor judgement and mistakenly shoot cubs where these animals are protected, automatically become violators through little fault of their own.

Once the hunter realizes his mistake he has three options. He can walk away from the carcass and let it go to waste, salvage the meat and risk getting caught, or turn himself in and face the possibility of being fined.

Black bear hunters shouldn't have to face these alternatives. In my opinion, cub laws are not only biologically unsound, they are wasteful. In Michigan, where cubs are protected, I've found the rotting remains of

Some bear managers are questioning the validity of laws which protect cubs from hunting. Actually, they may be the most expendable part of the population.

small yearlings, which were legal bear, but were abandoned because the hunter who shot them looked at their size and assumed they were cubs.

Two biological considerations commonly affect the opportunities hunters will have to pursue black bear. They are the high natural mortality among black bear as cubs, and the survival of cubs to the age of reproductive maturity. Where cubs are legal, hunters who bag them are taking the most expendable part of the population (boars average larger than sows and are most likely to be shot). Some tags filled with cubs, which are actually almost a year old by late fall, would otherwise have been used on older, more productive animals.

Even where cubs are legal, only the larger ones weighing 70 to 100 pounds are usually taken by hunters, and that's the size of many white-tailed deer bagged by hunters every fall. Most bear hunters aren't going to knowingly shoot small cubs weighing 50 pounds or less. The average fall weight of cubs in Pennsylvania, where cubs are legal, is 82 pounds for females and 97 pounds for males. Female cubs ranged in weight from 34 and 110 pounds and males from 65 to 126 pounds. In Virginia, West Virginia, North Carolina and Tennessee, cubs averaged between 75 and 100 pounds.

The best reason of all for the ineffectiveness and waste of cub laws is that, according to available information, the rate of harvest of cubs is basically the same in states where they are protected as those where they aren't. In southern New York, for example, juvenile black bear were protected until 1978. Cubs made up an average of seven percent of the bear harvest from that region from 1970 through 1975. When cubs were legal there during 1978 and 1979, cubs made up seven percent and 5.4 percent of the harvest respectively.

Sanctuaries

As a means of providing further protection for black bear besides hunting regulations, some states have established sanctuaries for them where no hunting is permitted. The animals themselves that are in sanctuaries are not only protected, so is their habitat, which is perhaps more important. Without large tracts of suitable habitat, there will be no black bear. This has been proven in states where black bear are unhunted, having been protected for years. As the animals' available habitat shrinks, so do their numbers. Clearing of land for farming and development has totally eliminated black bear from some areas without a sportsman firing a single shot.

A few states with designated black bear sanctuaries are North Carolina, West Virginia and Tennessee. Although not created specifically for black bear, national and provincial parks also serve as refuges for the animals. The same thing can be said for large tracts of bear habitat with few roads, limiting access to hunters even though hunting may be permitted. Without easy access, black bear hunting will be minimal. The bear populations in these "sanctuaries" serve as a reservoir for supplying surrounding habitat. In most cases, the overflow from refuges consists of juvenile boars.

Park Management

Although black bear are protected in most national and provincial parks, this doesn't mean that bear living there and people visiting there don't have to be managed. They certainly do, for the benefit of both. Most management actions in regard to bear, and regulations established for visitors revolve around reducing the animals' access to food from people. All available park information points to the fact that the bears' association of "unnatural" foods with humans leads to property damage and injuries to park visitors, plus the eventual extermination, or at least

Bear nuisance problems can be reduced by eliminating the animals' access to dumpsters and other human-supplied food sources.

relocation, of bear responsible for repeated offenses.

Access to food at dumps and from trash containers was eliminated at most parks long ago by park personnel through closure of dumps and by erecting bear-proof fences around those that remain in use. Dumpsters and garbage cans were also bear-proofed, leaving sources of food that visitors bring with them as the only "unnatural" food normally available to black bear. Regulations have been established making park visitors responsible for seeing that black bear do not obtain food from them. Persons who feed bear or who don't store food properly are subject to fines.

Despite repeated warnings against feeding black bear in parks, some people continue to do it, causing problems for other visitors, if not themselves, and the bear they feed. One must assume that people who insist on feeding bear in park settings don't fully understand the real purpose of national parks. The objective of most parks that contain black bear is to maintain natural populations of the animals that are able to survive on their own without any dependence on man to supplement natural diets.

As Jane Tate and Dr. Michael Pelton from the University of Tennessee put it in a paper on Human-Bear Interactions in Great Smoky Mountains National Park, "National Parks are not zoos without bars; they are sanctuaries where animals can have a natural existence and not be placed on display."

People who feed bear in parks are breaking the law in addition to circumventing the purpose of these natural areas. The actions of black bear seen along park roads and in campgrounds are also totally misunderstood by persons who insist on feeding the animals. Conditioned bruins may come seeking food from humans. To obtain food, black bear may tolerate close association with people, until the food is secured. People who interpret the acceptance of food by bear as a sign of tameness or "friendship" simply don't understand wild animals. Individuals who try to get too close to or even pet bear as a result of how they view the animals usually get a big surprise.

The horror stories about people feeding bear in parks are absolutely amazing and usually reflect the victim's total ignorance of wild animals. As unbelievable as it may seem, one visitor to the Smokies was observed putting a baby on the back of a bear. Fortunately, the bruin did not react in an antagonistic manner and the child wasn't hurt. Had that baby been hurt, or even killed, though, the bear probably would have been held responsible and destroyed.

Other people have put their hand inside the mouths of black bear to feed them. Still more have smeared honey on hands and faces, then allowed bear to lick it off. The fact that more people haven't been hurt by black bear when feeding, crowding or touching them reflects the amount of restraint these animals often exhibit. Even when irritated about the proximity or actions of humans, black bear usually give ample warning before actually biting or striking a person.

Because many black bear accustomed to human food prefer not to have to put up with the presence of people, they often resort to stealing what goodies they find improperly stored. Coolers, tents, backpacks and cars have all been damaged to get at human food. Park visitors who leave food accessible to bear are as responsible for getting the animals in trouble as are those who intentionally feed them.

Avoid Bear Confrontations

Some rules and safeguards have been established at major parks with black bear in an effort to reduce accessibility of food from visitors to the animals. They are also good, common-sense measures for hunters and other nature enthusiasts outside of park boundaries. Campers should not leave food in tents or in the open such as on picnic tables. This includes containers in which foods were stored, cooking utensils and table scraps. All garbage should be deposited in containers designed for this purpose.

When at campgrounds accessible by road, food should be stored in vehicle trunks. In situations where a trunk is not available, food and food containers should be covered and stored out of sight. Some black bear learn to recognize food and coolers that are visible in vehicles, and sometimes break in to get at them. Windows that are left partway open make it easy for bear to get inside the car.

At walk-in campsites, food should be suspended in a bag or pack about 10 feet off the ground and several feet below a limb and away from a tree trunk, where the container will be out of reach of a bear from all directions. Food containers can be suspended with a rope over a limb that extends at least five feet away from a tree trunk. If no suitable limb is available, a second rope can be tied between two trees and a rope holding the food can be hung over that. Cables have been provided to suspend food in Yosemite National Park in California and metal poles for the same purpose have been installed at backcountry campgrounds in the Smokies. Moth balls put in food containers can help mask the odor of edibles.

Personnel at popular parks have become increasingly intolerant of people feeding bear and of bear stealing food, often resulting in damage to equipment and vehicles. People who don't follow the rules are being ticketed, and offending bear are being captured and transferred to remote areas. Park personnel mark and monitor bear activities closely and black bear that are repeat offenders are often eliminated from the

Wild black bear should remain wild. In large parks, management styles have changed to prevent the problems associated with freeloading bruins and over-generous tourists.

population. This type of aggressive management has resulted in the restoration of natural populations of black bear to Yellowstone National Park. The animals aren't as visible as they used to be, but injuries to park visitors and damage to visitors' personal property have been reduced tremendously.

Elimination of human-related foods from the diets of black bear in the parks is definitely desirable. However, the cooperation of all park visitors is necessary to make it possible. Campers and hikers who are confronted by an aggressive animal or lose food to one, should report it to park personnel as soon as possible. Visitors who feed bear should also be reported. After all, their actions may, in some cases, be as good as signing a death warrant for the animals they contact. Parks cannot be the places they are intended to be with this type of interference.

Nuisance Complaints

Nuisance complaints about black bear outside of parks can be as much of a headache for wildlife managers as inside. In many cases, improper handling and disposal of garbage or the presence of a source of food accessible to bear are responsible for complaints. Bruins are attracted to residences by dog food left outside as well as some livestock feed, plus items such as bread put on the ground or in feeders for birds and fruit trees. Once the attractant is removed, if that is possible, bear usually wander off.

If the animals persist, they are sometimes captured and relocated. In situations where that isn't possible or practical, permits are sometimes issued to complainants to shoot the animals. In the western U.S., Fish & Wildlife Service personnel frequently dispose of black bear that kill livestock or damage crops. State and provincial wildlife personnel deal with these problems in some cases, too. In Michigan, for example, conservation officers handle most, if not all, black bear nuisance complaints.

Disposal of nuisance bear is the most common practice in states and provinces where the animals are relatively abundant and are not highly regarded as game animals. Where the opposite is true, efforts are at least made to trap and transfer bruins. In some states, property owners are also reimbursed for the value of bee hives, livestock and other damage incurred by black bear.

Every year across the black bear's range some of the animals, often dispersing yearlings, wander into cities and towns while traveling cross country or looking for an easy meal. When daylight comes, they often end up in a tree. The presence of either dogs or people will force surprised or disoriented black bear to seek refuge in a tree. In some cases these bear aren't actually nuisance animals, but they are often treated as such. Many of them end up dead, either intentionally when gunned down by police officers under the guise of protecting the citizens, or accidentally when tranquilized and allowed to fall to the ground. Injuries usually result from such a fall.

There are better ways to handle treed bear in an urban setting under those circumstances. Gary Alt demonstrated one of them while I was with him in Pennsylvania during June. Alt received a call one afternoon about a bear up a tree at Lucerne Burrough near Wilkes-Barre. The animal was originally thought to be a cub, but was later estimated to weigh 150 pounds.

Once the situation and directions were clear, Alt and his assistants loaded necessary equipment and headed for the scene. The plan was to tranquilize the bear and either catch it in a net or lower it to the ground to prevent any injury to the animal. On the way there, assistants Pat Carr and Janice Gruttadauria prepared two darts with enough drug to put a

Bear Biologist Gary Alt darts a nuisance bear inside city limits. Calls like this are becoming more and more frequent.

Volunteers and game department personnel stretch a net under a tree to prevent a tranquilized bear from hurting itself in a fall from the tree.

200-pound bear to sleep. They wanted to be on the safe side in case the weight estimate was off, as they often are. The drug used by this crew is safe, and does not kill an animal even if the dosage is larger than necessary. Extra drug simply keeps bear asleep longer. Two darts were prepared on the chance Alt's first shot with a dart gun missed.

As expected, a crowd of people were gathered around the treed bear. The bruin was in a small tree not far off the ground. Alt put a dart in the animal's rump while Carr got the net out and recruited volunteers from the crowd to stretch it tight under the bear, on the chance the bruin fell out from the tree.

When dealing with a treed bear, biologists wait until the animal starts getting "drunk" from the drug, then climb the tree. Alt uses climbing spurs where necessary. The bear biologist carries a heavy rope and set of cuffs with him when climbing a tree to reach a drugged bear. Cuffs consist of four lengths of stout rope with loops at the end of each to put over a bruin's feet. The cuffs are connected by a heavy metal ring

A bear is always a curiosity. Gary Alt carries a tranquilized bear to his vehicle so that it can be released far from town and out of harm's way.

through which a rope is passed to lower an animal to the ground.

The rope is thrown over a limb and one end is held by the ground crew, which often includes more volunteers, and the other end is attached to cuffs. When the time is right, which is shortly before a bear loses control and falls, the biologist slips the cuffs over its feet. Then the ground crew gently lowers the bear to the ground. That's exactly how the episode at Lucerne Burrough went. The net, although unnecessary in that case, was an extra margin for error in case Alt didn't get the cuffs in place on time.

The bear proved to be a 91-pound female. Besides weighing the animal, the crew put ear tags in place, removed a tooth for aging (although they were sure it was a yearling) and took a blood sample, while the crowd watched. Children touched it.

Whenever possible, biologists turn these episodes into educational experiences for onlookers, creating a positive attitude toward black bear. Once the bear was processed, it was transported miles from the city and released.

Although the procedure this crew uses is the best for tranquilizing treed bear, a sturdy net is all that is really necessary to ensure the safety of a darted animal. A net will break the bruin's fall, eliminating the potential for injury.

Bear treed in residential areas will also come down on their own, if given the chance. Once threatening influences are gone—people and dogs—black bear will usually descend trees and head for the nearest cover. They will sometimes wait until after dark to do so.

A sow and two cubs that climbed a tree in a yard in Iron Mountain, Michigan, were wisely allowed to climb down by themselves. They waited until after midnight to leave their perch and were followed out of town by a pair of police cars.

Black bear that end up in urban settings are out of their element, and for this reason the situation poses a greater danger to the animals than people in the area. As valuable big game animals that are often misunderstood, bruins deserve the best treatment possible in the best condition possible. Anything short of the methods mentioned here fails to accomplish this goal.

Orphaned Cubs

Orphaned cubs represent another potential problem that biologists have learned to deal with to maximize the number of bear in the wild. The sows of young cubs are sometimes killed or chased away from dens and don't return. There was a time that orphaned cubs were destined to live the rest of their lives in a zoo. Now they are just as likely to be

Research on denned bear provides information on the animals and is of interest to the medical community searching for a cure to arthritis.

adopted by another sow who already has cubs in the wild.

Biologists explain that sows will readily adopt orphans when the adult sows are still in dens. The orphans are simply placed in dens with their new mothers and the cubs they already have. A sow will even come out of a den to get an orphan, perhaps thinking it's one of her own. For this to be possible, of course, the location of a den containing a sow and cubs must be known.

Getting sows to adopt cubs after they leave the den is a more difficult proposition, biologists report. By then, sows distinguish their own cubs from others by smell. When encountered, foreign cubs are often killed and sometimes eaten. Apparently, this is what happens to orphaned cubs that are not yet weaned. If they aren't killed by adult bear, other predators get them.

Cubs orphaned after they leave dens may go to the first bear they see, whether it's a boar or sow. I observed an example of this while at the home of Ed and Mary Lepuski in Pennsylvania. They maintain a state-approved live trap there for the capture of bear. Every time a bear is caught, a biologist processes the animal.

The day before I met the Lepuskis, on June 18, a radio-collared sow with three cubs had abandoned two of them in the Lepuski's yard during a thundershower. The pair of cubs climbed a tree and refused to come down, even after the sow climbed the tree to get them. The sow ended up leaving with only one of her cubs.

On the 20th, a bear was in the live trap there and it was assumed it was the sow returning for her two cubs, which spent most of their time in trees. However, when we arrived, we found out it was an unmarked boar that was probably $2^{1}/_{2}$ years old. A biologist processed the boar and left it in the shade to recover.

Meanwhile, the abandoned cubs saw the drugged boar and went to it, apparently not recognizing the fact that it wasn't their sow, although we thought they should. Rather than backing off when they reached the boar, they excitedly climbed all over him as though they thought they found their lost parent. In a matter of seconds the boar raised its head and started to grab one of the cubs in its mouth.

"He's going to kill 'em," the biologist shouted, recognizing what was about to happen.

He then hollered at the boar and raced toward it, scaring all three of them. The cubs ran off, climbing trees again. The biologist reacted just in time to save those cubs. In the wild, orphaned cubs are probably killed like those two almost were.

The boar, which was starting to regain his senses, was chased into the woods to prevent the same thing from happening again. Before the evening was over, one of the two abandoned cubs was reunited with its sow.

So how do bear biologists get sows to adopt orphan cub after they leave the den? Gary Alt found "a two-dollar answer to that million-dollar question." He discovered that Vicks Vapor Rub will temporarily block a sow's sense of smell. So the substance is rubbed all over the body of the cub that is ready for adoption, or it is put in an adopting mother's nose. This is accomplished by either trapping and tranquilizing the sow or treeing the sow and her cubs and sending the greased orphan up to join them.

Alt routinely trees radio-collared sows with young cubs by homing in on the signal from their collars. I was with him when he did it twice. The sow we treed had four cubs of her own and three orphans she adopted. Since Alt always has a number of sows with cubs collared, introducing orphans to foster mothers isn't very difficult. The same thing can be done in other states and provinces where sows with cubs are collared.

Transplants

In areas where bear numbers are low, the best management involves total protection of the animals and their habitat. Protection of the habitat, where possible, is often more important than the animals. A lost bear or two can be replaced by reproduction or transplants. Lost habitat is difficult if not impossible to replace.

Uninhabited black bear habitat will sometimes be naturally reoccupied by bruins, provided a population of the animals exists within a reasonable distance and there aren't barriers to prevent this from happening. Spring dispersal of yearling boars sometimes brings them into locations of this type. Without sows, however, permanent populations aren't likely to be established. Biologists have been successful in transplanting mature sows into new habitat.

Breeding populations of black bear have been re-established in southwest Pennsylvania through introduction of sows. Initially, pregnant sows were released in their new homes during summer months. This proved unacceptable because they wandered miles from release sites, sometimes being killed by cars. Winter relocation of sows, shortly before they were expected to have cubs, yielded better results.

When there is snow on the ground, sows usually go less than a mile before settling into a den or building a nest. During winters without snow, sows have been kept in porta-dens (wooden crates) to prevent them from wandering too far, and where they give birth to cubs. When spring arrives, the man-made dens are opened to allow the occupants to become familiar with their new home.

Large-scale transplants have resulted in the reintroduction and increase of black bear in portions of two states—Arkansas and Louisiana. The best results were obtained in Arkansas. Bruins were transplanted, 254 of them, from Minnesota and Manitoba between 1959 and 1967. They were released at three sites in northern and western Arkansas in the Ozark and Ouachita National Forests.

An estimated 2,000 black bear now roam Arkansas, a considerable increase over the 40 to 50 estimated in the state during the 1950s. Limited hunting seasons have been held there since 1980.

Louisiana obtained 161 bear from Minnesota from 1964 through 1967. The transplants there also resulted in an increase in the population, but recent information isn't available as to how much. The state's bear population was estimated at 350 during 1977. Bear hunting was resumed in Louisiana during 1974, but there has been little interest in hunting them. One reason for this is most of the habitat occupied by bruins is either privately owned or leased by private clubs, limiting public access.

Trapping Bear For Management Purposes

Live-trapping black bear is an essential part of many management and research programs. There are a number of devices used to capture bruins without harming them. Portable culvert traps and Aldrich foot snares are two of the most commonly used. Nets are appropriate under some circumstances for catching bear, too. Capture guns, which shoot drug-filled darts, are also employed on occasion to immobilize bruins.

Culvert Traps. Bear biologist Al Erickson is credited with the development of culvert traps during the early 1950s. He was working in Michigan at the time.

Culvert traps resemble large barrels resting horizontally on wheels, and that's basically what they are. Some are made from 55 gallon drums. However, these large-scale live traps are often made of corrugated steel piping of the type used for culverts. Typically, they measure three feet in diameter and six feet in length. The ends are fitted with heavy steel covers, one of which is a sliding door. The end with the door has a wooden frame extending above the barrel for holding the door when the trap is set. The covers are ventilated to promote the flow of fresh air.

Horizontal or oval peep holes are cut in sides of barrel traps to enable trappers to see what they've caught. These same holes are used to put jab sticks through when bears are injected with drugs to sedate them. Some culvert traps also have small doors in back covers that can be opened to examine drugged bruins or as access to the inside of the trap in case of emergency.

Trigger mechanisms are toward the back of these traps to ensure bear are all of the way in before tripping the door. The door falls when bruins grab food attached to triggers, which usually consist of wires or cables.

Mounted on wheels, these traps can be towed to sites frequented by black bear and quickly set. Live traps are often used to catch nuisance animals frequenting areas also used by people, such as campgrounds, picnic areas, farms and rural homesites.

Once a black bear is captured, the trap and its passenger are simply towed away and released in a remote location where the chances of the animal getting in trouble again are reduced. The largely mysterious homing ability of bruins enable many of them to return to the location where they were caught. The experience of being caught and relocated improves the behavior of lots of bear, though. Even animals that return to the general area where they were trapped don't necessarily repeat the habits that made them a problem.

Although effective for catching some black bear in selected areas, the usefulness of culvert traps for catching, marking, managing and studying the animals is limited. The size and weight of the traps limits the locations where they can be set. They must be near roads where they

Game departments sometimes employ culvert traps like this to catch nuisance bear and relocate them to wilderness surroundings.

can be positioned with a vehicle or pushed a short distance into place. And if they have to be towed long distances, a lot of time is invested in the possibility of catching one animal. Culvert traps don't come cheap, either, and they take up a lot of space, which limits the number available to managers.

Snares. Aldrich foot snares are much more versatile for catching black bear, and they have proved to be extremely valuable for managing the animals. Snares basically consist of lengths of cable and a spring-operated trigger mechanism. They are much cheaper than culvert traps, hardly take up any space and can be set practically anywhere. A number of them can be set in a reasonable amount of time, increasing the chances of catching bruins.

These snares are named for the man who invented them—Jack Aldrich from Castle Rock, Washington. The devices were probably developed during the late 1950s, but were widely used by 1960. Snares were originally used by trappers to control black bear causing timber damage in Washington, but their most important purpose now is in bear research. Aldrich foot snares are also the only legal means of catching black bear in the one state and the Canadian provinces where trapping bear is still legal.

Snares replaced the heavier, more expensive and more dangerous leghold traps once used to trap black bear. The large, steel bear traps are no longer legal to use. Unlike critters unfortunate enough to be caught in one of those giant leghold traps, non-target animals, including people, caught in snares can be released with no harm. A person who happens to stumble into a bear snare, which isn't likely because their locations are usually clearly marked with signs, can remove the cable with no problem.

The main purpose of signs marking the location of snares is so people don't stumble into a snared bear. Outdoor enthusiasts who encounter snared bears should stay clear and inform local wildlife officials. Although bear snares are routinely checked on a daily basis, usually early in the morning, animals can be caught in snares after they've been checked. In Washington, where large numbers of snares were often set by individual trappers to catch as many bear as possible, the devices were eventually equipped with transmitters that were activated when a bear was caught.

Aldrich snares consist of two pieces of $^3/_{16}$-inch cable. One piece of cable is normally anchored to a solid tree, although in some cases a heavy drag is used, and the other piece consists of the loop that is thrown over a bear's foot by a spring when it steps on the trigger. The loop is tightened and locked around a bear's foot or leg when the animal at-

Snares are most often used to live trap bear for research in wilderness areas where the chances of the general public running across the sets are slim.

tempts to run or walk away. The two pieces of cable are connected by heavy-duty swivels.

When snares are anchored to trees, animals that are caught remain there. In situations where snares are attached to movable logs as drags, bear pull the drag with them until it gets caught in brush and they can go no farther. It is not a good idea to use drags with snares in areas frequented by human visitors because bruins move away from warning signs marking sets. Another problem with drags is that black bear sometimes pull them up trees where the drags can get caught in branches and animals may end up hanging by a leg if they fall, jump or try to climb down.

Snares are set by digging a hole for the spring-operated trigger, setting the trigger, covering the trigger with small twigs, then moss or leaves, setting the snare loop over the trigger and covering that.

Once the snare is set, the spring is covered and sticks are placed on either side of the covered loop to direct a bear's foot into the snare. When a bear puts its foot down on what it thinks is solid ground, its weight usually breaks twigs and the trigger throws the loop up.

Snares are most often set along trails or in cubbies. When trail sets are made, obstacles are frequently placed on both sides of the trail next to the snare to decrease the chances of a bear walking around it. Food is sometimes placed on both sides of a snare along a trail, but not always. Cubbies are small enclosures composed of natural materials with food placed in the back of them and snares hidden at the entrances where bear that are attracted to the food are most likely to step.

Snared black bear must be tranquilized for handling. Both jab sticks and dart guns are used for this purpose. After processing, bear that are to be relocated are placed in a vehicle or live trap for the trip. A second injection is sometimes given to bruins that will be transported long distances to make sure they don't wake up too soon. Helicopters are occasionally employed to relocate black bear in remote country.

After being caught in a snare or culvert trap one or more times, some black bear become trap shy and it can be difficult, sometimes impossible, to recatch them with these devices. Culvert traps are easily identified and avoided. Experienced bears also learn to recognize snare sets. Some smart bruins even learn how to avoid getting caught in snares if they step on them. Biologists report that clever bruins that step in snares simply stop as soon as the cable is on their foot and shake their leg until the cable drops off.

Darting. Dart guns are sometimes useful for capturing trap-shy black bear. These gas-operated rifles provide an immediate means of securing animals during chance encounters, such as when they are treed in town or in the process of making a nuisance of themselves. In addition to the treed bruin I watched Gary Alt dart, I witnessed the recapture of a radio-collared sow with a well-placed shot from the capture gun. The transmitter in the sow's collar was dead, so Alt wanted to put a new collar on her, but she avoided traps.

He was processing another bear in the development where the sow was frequently seen when a neighbor reported the sow was in their yard at that moment. Alt quickly loaded the rifle and rushed over. The sow was in the yard upon their arrival, but walked off a short distance when he got out of the car with the rifle. A little coaxing from the home owner brought her back though, and the biologist put a dart in the bear's neck as she stood up on her hind legs to sniff a container hanging on a clothes line.

The collared sow had a cub in a tree when she was darted, but the cub dropped to the ground and both of them ran off with the biologist right

Unless properly managed and conditioned to humans, bear will become downright brazen about raiding whatever food supplies they can find.

behind them. He kept them in sight until the sow laid down, then he hollered for the rest of us. Due to the safe drugs now in use for immobilizing black bear, no damage is done if a darted bear is not located. They simply wake up after their unplanned nap and go on their way.

A darted sow generally won't go far if her cubs are in a tree and stay there. However, if they are on the ground, or a lone animal is involved, the darted animal sometimes runs off. When this happens the shooter has to keep the bear in sight until the drug takes effect, which can be a challenge.

The effective range of capture guns is not far. Maximum range is 20 to 30 yards, with closer shots preferred. Biologists and control officers have to be able to get close to black bear for dart guns to be effective.

After being caught once, some bears avoid all methods of recapture, including dart guns. A mature female that developed a habit of raiding garbage cans and coolers at Tahquamenon Falls State Park in Michigan's Upper Peninsula fits in this category. The sow, which had a lame front foot, and her cub were caught in a culvert trap during July at the Lower Falls Campground. Bear biologist El Harger processed them, then released them 60 miles away.

The following year the sow was back. Her injured foot gave away her identity. All attempts at trapping her failed. She even ignored food containing immobilizing drugs. Harger made a number of attempts at darting the sow, but he couldn't get close enough to her, although anyone else could get within 10 feet of the animal. The sow not only remembered her experience with the trap and drugs, she apparently recognized who was responsible.

That bear never was recaptured. However, her insistence on stealing food in the campground led to her demise. After hunting season opened, she was shot nearby. Her ear tags confirmed that she had been the animal trapped at the campground the previous year.

Nets. Rocket nets aren't as widely used for catching black bear as traps, snares and dart guns, but they are occasionally put into service. When I interviewed Gary Alt he said he had caught 20 bear using this device. Rocket nets are usually employed at locations that have been baited to attract bruins, or where they are already being fed. When the animals are in position, rockets are fired, carrying a net over them. Once netted, bear are drugged and processed.

When dealing with denned bear, nets are stretched across den entrances and the bruins are caught as they exit, then immobilized. In situations where a sow and yearlings occupy the same den, the entrance is blocked until the first bear out is processed, then the others are netted one after another.

Steel traps like these, used to catch black bear for many years, are now little more than desirable collector's items.

Leghold Traps. Although leghold traps are not generally used to catch black bear anymore, they are on occasion. Michigan Department of Natural Resources Wildlife Biologist John Ozoga used size $4^1/_2$ traps, which are basically designed for catching wolves, to catch three small black bear that gained access to a square-mile enclosure used for white-tailed deer research. Two of the three bear killed fawns. Ozoga made a cubby and set the traps at the entrance.

Traps of this size are not suitable for black bear weighing 200 pounds or more, according to Ozoga. They will simply pull their foot out. These traps will hold smaller animals without serious injury. Before foot snares were developed, bear biologist Al Erickson used the same size traps to catch bruins in Michigan.

Black bear occasionally end up in leghold traps intended for coyotes and bobcats. These animals can be safely released in most cases. Michigan trapper Jerry Weigold has had a lot of experience in this regard. The procedure he usually follows to release a bear from a trap is to lasso the bruin's head with a strong nylon rope and tie the rope tightly around a tree when the bear is at the end of the trap chain. Secured by the head and a foot, an animal is held stationary while the trap spring is depressed, releasing the bear's foot.

Weigold said he normally cuts a strong stick with which to open the trap while standing behind a tree, if one is available. There's usually so much tension on the trap, he says, it doesn't take much pressure to open it enough for the bear's foot to slip out. Once their foot is free, bear easily slip out of the noose around their head. Weigold has released a lot of bear in this fashion and none of them have attempted to attack when released. Instead, they run off. When small cubs are involved, a strong forked stick can be used to hold the animal's head down until released.

Trappers who don't want to release a black bear from a trap themselves should contact a wildlife biologist, conservation officer or game warden for assistance. Black bear that are trapped accidentally should not be shot! They can be released safely without harm to the bear or trapper.

Former coyote trapper Bill Niemi almost shot an adult bruin in one of his traps when it resisted his initial efforts to release it, but is glad he didn't. The trap was attached to a drag and the bear pulled the drag about 100 yards into thick cover where it hung up. Bill's brother, Arnie, was with him when he located the trapped bruin.

The trapper chopped some brush out of the way with an axe, giving him room to lasso the bear's head. Arnie then wrapped the rope around a tree and held it. Before Bill could release the bear, though, the animal started flopping around and got its free front foot under the noose around its neck, stretching it enough to pull free. Arnie talked Bill out of shooting the bear at that point so he decided to try something else.

He got behind the bear and started stroking the animal with his axe. The bear didn't seem to mind the attention, so Bill went closer and scratched behind its ears with his hands. The bear didn't mind that either. With the bruin calmed down, the two men used the axe and a stout stick to depress the trap springs while standing in front of the bear. The bear simply sat there the entire time, not even taking its foot out of the trap once it was open. Bill eventually reached down and removed the bear's paw from the trap. Even then, the bear hung around for a while before slowly walking off a short distance and finally running away.

Marking Bear For Management

If the primary purpose of catching bear is to mark rather than relocate them, the animals are often released where caught after being processed. For tranquilizing trapped bruins, a syringe is fitted on the end of a jab stick, a metal pole about six feet long, and the shot is administered in muscle tissue when the animal is in a favorable position. It usually takes seven to 10 minutes for a bear to become immobilized after an injection.

After a bear is sedated, it is dragged from the trap for processing. When black bear are marked, numbered tags are usually attached to ears. Colored streamers are sometimes attached to ears, too, for easy identification of certain animals. A number is also tattooed on the inside of an

Sound black bear management depends on support from hunters and non-hunters alike. We've got to work together for the bear's benefit.

upper lip of some tagged bear as a precaution against loss of ear tags. In cases where that happens, tattooed animals can still be identified.

If the movements of a particular bear are to be monitored, a radio collar is fitted around the animal's neck. As the most important members of black bear populations, mature sows are collared more often than boars to study their denning habits and productivity, among other things. The smaller necks of sows are also easier to properly fit with collars, although the movements of boars have been monitored, too. Transmitters inside most radio collars are good for at least a year.

Poaching

At any rate, it has been proven that relocating black bear is a means of re-establishing populations of the animals. Despite the advances in managing black bear, there is at least one problem managers have not yet been able to solve, and they will need the help of all outdoor enthusiasts to do so.

The problem is widespread poaching of black bear. Illegal bear harvests appear to be highest in western states such as California, Washington, Idaho and Oregon. However, the problem has also been identified in other parts of the country.

There's a large, illegal black market for the gall bladders, paws and meat of black bear. These items are favored by some Orientals for medicinal purposes and as food. Poachers only interested in monetary gain take bear where and whenever they can regardless of regulations. Some bear populations are facing a large-scale decline as a result of poaching. Legitimate hunters will be penalized through reduced hunting opportunities.

Anyone seeing or hearing about illegal black bear hunting activity should contact the appropriate authorities. Most states have toll-free telephone numbers for reporting game violations, and callers can remain anonymous, if they wish. Uniform regulations making it illegal to sell bear parts will go a long way to help solve the problem; the practice is now illegal in some places, but legal in others.

19

The Future

Ahead lies a bright future for black bear in North America and those who hunt them. However, the picture is clouded with uncertainty about what role politics and anti-hunter/animal rights groups will play in the effective management of black bear. Bear hunters themselves will have to become more unified, informed and active in bear management and educating the public about bear hunting to counteract the threat anti-hunters pose.

Groups that oppose bear hunting rate as the number one threat for the future. They were responsible for the closure of bear hunting in California in 1989 and also had a hand in the banning of bear hunting in Wisconsin during 1985. Wisconsin hunters have since rallied and reopened the bear season, but there's no telling where the anti's will strike next.

Conflicts among bear hunting factions is another threat to the future of bear hunting that is linked to the success anti-hunters have in getting their way. Bickering among hunters strengthens the position of groups who hope to ban bear hunting and weakens the stance of hunters. Bear hunters themselves initially played into the hands of anti-hunters in bringing about the Wisconsin closure by being disorganized, poorly informed and greedy. The same thing may happen in other states if changes aren't made soon.

Other threats to the future of bear and bear hunting are habitat loss and poaching brought on by the high price tag put on bear parts such as gall bladders and paws in the Oriental marketplace.

Management By Professional Wildlife Biologists

In spite of these threats to bear hunting, the future of the animals and the recreational activity they support will remain bright as long as their management stays under the control of trained wildlife biologists who know how to protect the resource by using hunting as an effective management tool. The role hunting plays in managing black bear is the same as with other big game species—it helps maintain healthy populations that are in balance with available habitat. Annual bear harvests prevent bruins from becoming too numerous and causing conflicts.

In situations where there's room for expansion of bear populations, biologists should have the ability to vary regulations to limit hunter numbers, hunting techniques or seasons in an effort to control the harvest. Permit hunts are proving to be the best way to manage black bear in many states and many expect this trend to continue.

Hunters' Role In Effective Bear Management

Closures on bear hunting like those that took place in California and Wisconsin are not in the best interest of the resource and were politically rather than biologically motivated. The sale of hunting licenses is responsible for a significant portion of the funding game departments receive. Those funds not only pay for time employees spend establishing hunting seasons and regulations, they also pay for the time employees spend on bear research and handling nuisance complaints, as well as helping to protect and maintain bear habitat.

The closure of bear seasons effectively reduces or eliminates money necessary for the long term protection of bruins. Elimination of legal bear hunting increases the opportunity for illegal harvest of the animals as well as increasing the chances that bear responsible for damage to crops, bee hives and other property will be killed rather than live-trapped and moved. In other words, the closing of hunting seasons does not protect bears.

Politics And Closures

Despite the fact that bear hunting closures do not benefit the species, politics make them possible. A judge that was either elected to the post or appointed by a politician, handed down the ruling closing bear hunting in California. Anti-hunters stumbled into a judge who was sympathetic to their cause. Hunters should become more politically active to remove that judge from the bench and to have a voice in the selection of future judges as well as state legislators. The fate of all types of hunting can be affected by politicians at any level. It is far better that decisions affecting hunting be made by representatives who understand or support

The future of black bear and black bear hunting, to a large degree, will depend on dedicated professional biologists and hunters who support their efforts.

the activity than those who either oppose or don't understand hunting.

The role politics played in the ban on bear hunting in Wisconsin for one year was different than in California. Due to concern about bear harvests that were considered too high, state wildlife biologists wanted to limit hunter numbers under a permit system which would enable managers to better control annual bear harvests. However, the Department of Natural Resources (DNR) needed legislative approval before the necessary changes in regulations could be made. The DNR didn't get enough support from hunters. In fact, some hunters opposed the plan and contacted their representatives. Legislators were understandably confused about the division among hunters and they also heard from anti-hunters who wanted bear totally protected.

As a result, there was no bear hunting in Wisconsin during the 1985 season. Fortunately, most hunters did rally in support of the DNR in time for the necessary changes to be made the following year. Those who opposed the plan didn't fully grasp the potential repercussions of their actions until they found themselves with no hunting season at all. They quickly realized a permit hunt was better than no hunt. In the long run, both bear and bear hunters have benefited from Wisconsin's management program.

Hunters obviously could have helped prevent the one year moratorium on bear hunting by lending the necessary support to the DNR. They can help prevent the same thing from happening in the future, not only in Wisconsin, but in all states and provinces that have bear seasons, by doing whatever it takes to make sure game managers have the authority they need to manage black bear without the intervention of politicians. The most effective way to become involved in making helpful changes is to join and become active in state and national organizations that support the interests of hunters and proper wildlife management.

Educated Hunters

Hunters should also become as informed as possible about bear management and the real, rather than imagined, impact changes in regulations will have on both them and the resource. Far too often, hunters consider their interests over those of the resource, and this short-sightedness ends up negatively affecting hunting in the end, as it did in Wisconsin. The same thing almost happened in Michigan when that state went to a permit hunt.

Through 1989, an unlimited number of resident bear licenses were available in Michigan. A permit hunt to limit hunter numbers through a lottery system was approved in 1990. The reason for the change was to better control bear harvests. Hunter numbers had been steadily increasing along with the harvest and the change was considered necessary to prevent an overharvest. Instead of being concerned about the future of bear, some hunters could only think that their ability to obtain a bear license every year, as they had in the past, would be reduced. Some hunters supported shortened seasons or kill quotas over limiting hunter numbers.

Shortened Seasons

These individuals ignored information the state DNR had gathered during previous experimental hunts before adopting a permit system. Michigan managers tested shortened seasons and kill quotas and neither proved as desirable as a permit system. In one area where the DNR wanted to reduce the bear kill, for example, they shortened the season by a full month and put no limits on hunter numbers. Despite the drastic reduction in hunting time, hunters in that area bagged two more bruins than they had the year before. The shorter season intensified hunting effort and harvest. Hunters who may have passed up small to average-size bears during a longer hunt, shot the first legal bear they saw.

Another disadvantage of shortening seasons is that it becomes difficult, if not impossible, to regain seasons that have been lost, even if bear numbers rebound.

Harvest Quotas

Harvest quotas were tested on another area in combination with a permit system that limited participation to 30 hunters. A minimum harvest quota of 12 bear and a maximum harvest of 20 bear was set. The seven-day Michigan hunt would close at the end of the day on which bear number 12 was registered or at the end of the seven-day hunt. All hunters were required to register animals they bagged by 11:00 a.m. on the day after harvesting the bruin.

The hunt only lasted three days. Ten bear were taken on opening day, two on the second day and one on the third for a total of thirteen. Hunt participants with unfilled tags at the end of the third day were obviously disappointed. Use of a harvest quota cut their hunt short. Hunters have a more satisfying experience when beginning and ending dates of a hunt are set in advance. They can then plan the amount of time to spend in the field accordingly.

In addition, harvest quotas emphasize the harvest over hunter recreation and selectivity by encouraging hunters to shoot the first legal animal possible before the season closes. This unnecessarily intensifies competition among hunters. There are other problems associated with controlling bear harvests by quotas, especially on a statewide basis. As the harvest approaches the quota, some hunters might be less inclined to register animals, not wanting to be responsible for ending the season. Getting the word to all hunters, some of them camped in remote locations, that the season has ended could pose a problem, too. Also, accurately tallying all of the bear registered on a timely basis across the state would be difficult.

Permit Hunts

Another seven-day hunt with 30 participants was tried on the same area the following year without a harvest quota. The Michigan hunt ended after seven days with 15 bear harvested for a 50 percent rate of success. The rate of satisfaction in that hunt was much higher than the one in which a harvest quota was used.

In reality, permit hunts for black bear benefit both bear and hunters. By limiting hunter numbers to control bear harvests, bear numbers often increase. Hunters who draw permits usually enjoy a quality hunt and have an excellent chance of filling their tag. Many states that have permit hunts for bear have a preference system as part of it, meaning an applicant's chances of drawing a permit increases each year he or she applies.

Minnesota is a perfect example of the benefits of a permit hunt for black bear. This state was one of the first to go to this type of management system, starting it in 1982. Bear numbers have steadily increased since then and the number of bear permits issued annually has also increased. A milestone was reached in 1989 when more bear were taken by hunters in Minnesota than before the permit system started. A record 1,907 bruins were registered compared to 1,660 during 1981—the last year an unlimited number of bear licenses were available.

Another advantage of permit bear hunts is that they are easy to defend in court against lawsuits brought by anti-hunters, such as the one in California.

Hunter Conflicts

In addition to supporting sound bear management practices, hunters can help themselves by ending nonproductive squabbles. Controversies among hunters over how black bear should be hunted are generally self-serving and do more harm than good. Hunters who criticize a hunting technique without facts to support their position open the door for anti-hunters to outlaw that method as well as the one they may favor. In other words, the practice is self-destructive.

In states where both hunting with hounds and baiting are legal, the two factions are sometimes at odds, which is unfortunate. Disagree-

Minnesota bear harvests have exceeded previous levels since the state went to a permit system for their fall hunting season.

ments of this type ultimately hurt all hunters. All bear hunters are hunters regardless of the methods used, as long as they are legal. More can be accomplished by working together than as separate entities.

What happened in Wisconsin will, once again, serve as an example of what I mean. Back in 1973 a bill was introduced in the state legislature to outlaw the use of bait for bear hunting. Houndsmen supported the bill, but those who preferred to stand hunt obviously didn't. Eventually, an amendment was tacked onto the bill to outlaw all bear hunting in Wisconsin, and the legislation was passed by both bodies of state government.

Fortunately for all bear hunters in the state, the governor vetoed the bill. However, the result was that both baiters and dog hunters ended up with less than what they had before the controversy started. This is an example that all bear hunters in North America should pay particular attention to because there is a valuable lesson to be learned from it.

Hunters who prefer one method over another are always poor judges

As land is posted, it becomes more difficult for houndsmen to find places to enjoy their style of bear hunting.

of what should or should not be permitted or what is right and wrong because they have a vested interest. Final determinations of what hunting methods are legal for black bear and when they should be employed, should be left to wildlife biologists, because their chief concern and responsibility is the resource. Input from all hunters should be sought and should play a role in the decision-making process, of course, but the ultimate decision rests with managers, and hunters should be able to live with those decisions, as long as they are based upon pertinent facts.

Respecting One Another

Beyond that, bait hunters should respect the rights of hunters using hounds and vice versa. Black bear feeding on a bait do not belong to hunters maintaining the bait until the animal is bagged. The same is true for bruins being chased by hounds. That animal is not the property of hunters who own the hounds until one of them tags it.

However, as an ethical consideration, houndsmen should try to refrain from running bear they know are visiting someone else's bait, although I know it is impossible for dog hunters to know where all baits in a given area might be. By the same token, the ethical thing for bait hunters to do is not interfere in hunts with hounds. If a bear is seen ahead of hounds or treed, it shouldn't be shot.

Bait hunters and dog hunters must work together to see that hunting opportunities remain available for all.

There's nothing wrong with watching a treed bear and waiting for the hunters to arrive. In some situations the hunter, as the first person to the tree, may be given the option of shooting the bear, but don't count on it. Hunters who become part of a hunt with hounds by accident should play the role of observer.

What if the dog handlers don't show up at the tree after an hour? Hunters who find themselves in such a situation will have to decide what to do based on the circumstances. Frankly, I don't think I would shoot the bear in such a situation for a number of reasons. First and foremost would be concern for the dogs' safety. The welfare of hounds treeing a black bear becomes the hunter's responsibility as soon as he pulls the trigger.

As mentioned in the chapters on dogging bear, hounds should be tied away from a tree before a treed bear is shot. If this can't be done, a bear that comes out of a tree alive can kill or seriously injure one or more dogs. A dead bear can crush a hound it falls on. I wouldn't want to be responsible for the injury of someone else's dog, and hunters finding a treed bruin would be best off to wait for the hounds' owners.

Also worth considering is that it can sometimes take more than an hour for hunters to reach a treed bear, depending on how far it is from a road and if the hunters are following on foot. Dog handlers may be min-

Bowhunters must work with rifle hunters to achieve compromise that will allow maximum time afield for everyone.

utes away from the tree after an hour, and shooting the bear would deprive them of a sight many houndsmen live for—their hounds at the base of a tree with a bear in it. Do not shoot a treed bruin if you aren't a member of the hunting party. Hunters who leave a treed bear when houndsmen have not yet arrived may be able to locate the dogs' owners on nearby roads and let them know where their hounds are. Such an ethical and thoughtful gesture is sure to win the other hunters' friendship and appreciation.

Hunters who do decide to shoot a treed black bear after an hour and the dog handlers eventually arrive, should offer the carcass to them. The dogs are responsible for the harvest, regardless of who pulled the trigger, and the houndsmen are indirectly responsible for the hunting ability of their hounds through training.

Bear dogs that are lost in country where baits are located will sometimes end up at baits because they will be hungry after a long chase. Bait hunters should try to catch the hound to find out who its owner is from the collar. Once caught, hunters should take the dog with them until the owner can be contacted. Another option is to tie the dog under an evergreen tree where the dog has shelter from rain and room to lie down, until the owner is notified and can pick up the hound.

Some bear dogs are shy of strangers and may avoid them. However, these hounds can sometimes be coaxed close enough with food to read their collars. If this doesn't prove possible, the dog's owner may be lo-

Rifle hunters must recognize the efficiency of their chosen hunting tool and compensate by being more selective about the bear they take.

cated on nearby logging roads and can be informed about the animal's whereabouts.

Bear hunters who find someone else's bait while looking for a place to put their bait, should move to another spot. It is unethical to hunt at a bait established and maintained by another hunter without his permission.

"Do unto others as you would have others do unto you." The golden rule applies to black bear hunting as well as everyday life. It sometimes helps to put situations of the type mentioned above in proper perspective by trying to put yourself in the other hunter's position. There are always two sides to every issue.

Poaching/Selling Bear Parts

The illegal harvest of black bear certainly poses more of a threat to the future of bear and bear hunting than any legal hunting techniques, but how much of a threat poaching poses is often unknown. Poaching may be perceived to be a bigger problem than it really is due to illegal trafficking in bear parts such as gall bladders. In some states and provinces it is illegal for hunters to sell parts of bear they've legally taken and in other states it's legal. Sting operations may turn up large numbers of bear galls that were illegally sold, but were legally harvested.

What is known is that where it is illegal to sell bear parts, a black market develops and the prices paid for these parts increases. The higher the price paid for bear parts, the more incentive there is for poaching. On the black market in California, for example, a black bear gall bladder may bring as much as $1,000. In the state of New York, however, where it is legal for a hunter to sell the gall bladder from a bruin he tags, $40 is the most he can expect to obtain for the part and $25 is closer to an average price paid.

Laws making it illegal to sell the parts of black bear taken legally were established as a means of protecting the animals from commercial exploitation, but it appears as though they are having the opposite effect. The market for bear parts is still alive and well and probably will remain that way into the future. A more effective way to reduce poaching of black bear across North America may be to legalize the sale of parts of bear taken by hunters everywhere. If nothing else, that move would reduce the average price paid for galls and other bear parts rather than elevate them as has been happening.

An estimated 42,000 black bear are legally shot in North America annually. Those bruins would go a long way toward satisfying the demand for bear parts and would probably help save the lives of bear that might otherwise be poached. Since prohibiting the sale of bear parts in some areas seems to have had limited effectiveness, going the other way might be a better solution and would provide uniformity of regulations. An alternative would be to go to the other extreme and ban the sale of bear parts everywhere, but that would certainly elevate the value of bear parts as well as the risk of poaching more than ever before.

Don't get me wrong. I'm not advocating that hunters who shoot bear sell gall bladders from the animals where the practice is illegal. I'm simply bringing up an issue for consideration that may help reduce poaching. I follow all game laws and unequivocally advocate every bear hunter do the same. I've never sold a gall bladder myself; however, when hunting in states or provinces where galls can be legally sold, I've frequently given these parts from bear I've shot to my guide or host.

Report Poachers

If hunters are to protect the future of bear hunting, they also must do their part to report any violations they witness or learn about to the proper authorities. All hunters should be the eyes and ears of game wardens and conservation officers. Violators are not only stealing from you and me, they give all hunters a black eye. Toll-free phone numbers are available for reporting game law violations in most states and provinces, and the caller can remain anonymous. Use them when necessary.

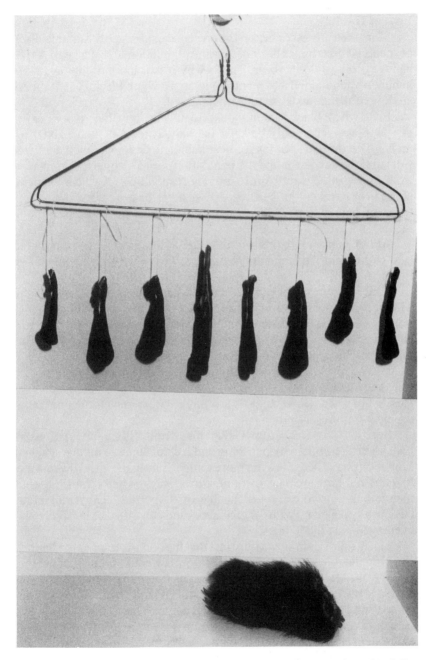

Bear parts, including hanging gall bladders and the bear paw pictured, are big dollar items in the illegal markets. This trade puts pressure on future black bear populations.

Loss of Habitat

More than any other factor, the presence or absence of suitable black bear habitat determines the location and population of black bear. As the habitat goes, so do the bear. That's why it is important that available habitat be maintained and managed in areas where black bear numbers are low, if the animals are to be maintained.

Even where black bear numbers are now healthy, the vigor of existing populations can only be kept that way as long as their habitat remains. The shrinkage or loss of bear habitat to development usually results in the loss of bear and the population shrinks. In letters I received from biologists across North America responding to a questionnaire about bear numbers in their respective states or provinces, the importance of habitat for healthy black bear populations was a common theme.

Al LeCount in Arizona wrote, "Habitat loss is the biggest threat to bear populations and if habitat is not saved, we can forget about having bear to hunt."

Cathy Carter, Associate Curator of Mammalogy at the Mississippi Museum of Natural History wrote, "The last reported breeding population was in Issaquena County in 1976, when five bear, including two cubs, were present in a 4,300-acre wooded tract surrounded by agricultural land. This tract has since been cleared and converted to agricultural usage. The black bear is officially listed as a threatened species in the state and receives protection under the non-game and Endangered Species Act of 1974. However, this law has no provisions for habitat management nor preservation."

Reggie Thackston from Oklahoma wrote, "Bear populations in Oklahoma are limited by poaching and lack of suitable habitat. Habitat limitations have become even more critical during the past 10 years due to industrial forest management practices. Rugged and remote areas of mature oak-pine forest, once capable of supporting bear populations, have been opened up with logging roads and converted extensively into even-aged pine plantations."

Thackston's comments illustrate that the composition of the habitat, meaning the types of trees present, is as important as the size of habitat. Eugene Widder in Alabama made similar statements: "Alabama does have a black bear population, although it is relatively small when compared to more northern states such as Michigan. This is mainly due to the lack of favorable habitat types. Alabama's forestry practices have created extensive pure pine stands with a scarcity of mature hardwood and mixed pine-hardwood types."

Even though the future outlook for black bear in North America is

With everyone doing their part, the future of the black bear in North America is bright indeed. They can be a trophy game animal for a long time to come.

generally good, there are some trouble spots where habitat quality and size is and has been declining. If unchecked, the situation will worsen as will the status of black bear in these areas. It's not a matter of these bear being intolerant of development. As mentioned earlier, the animals are adaptable to some human encroachment, such as housing developments, and, in fact, may be more healthy and productive in association with humans than are those in wilderness settings.

However, problems result when large-scale habitat changes are made, especially where environmentally critical and sensitive habitats such as swamps and bogs are involved. These areas are important to black bear as well as to many other forms of wildlife, plus they have an impact on flood control and clean water supplies.

We know that black bear can adapt to people, but can people adapt to bear? In areas where they can't, the bear will suffer. As Gary Alt wisely said, "It isn't what the bear do that get them in trouble so much as what people think that they might do. People are afraid of bear, basically. It's one of the biggest problems we have. That's cost the bear a lot over the years. If we can do any justice to bear, it would be to try and convince the people not to fear bear, but to respect them as you would any large mammals."

The future of black bear and black bear hunters could and should be bright. I know the animals will do their part. It's up to people of all types who interact with them to do theirs. A readjustment of attitudes will go a long way toward making sure the future is as bright as possible.

Black bear are not the fearsome critters they are often made out to be and can become acceptable neighbors, if they are allowed to be. Black bear are challenging and exciting to hunt, regardless of how they are hunted, and should be hunted where their populations warrant, to both control their numbers and to promote the wisest use of the resource. Where conflicts between hunters are possible, mutual respect and ethical practices will increase their compatibility.

Index